A History of Asian American Theatre

In 1965, the first Asian American theatre company, the East West Players, was founded by a group of actors who wanted to find better opportunities in the acting industry. Forty years later, Asian American theatre is one of the fastest growing theatre sectors with over thirty active theatre companies and numerous award-winning artists such as Frank Chin, Jessica Hagedorn, Ping Chong, David Henry Hwang, Philip Kan Gotanda, Velina Hasu Houston, and B. D. Wong. Based on over seventy interviews, the book surveys the history of Asian American theatre from 1965 to 2005 with focus on actors, playwrights, companies, audiences, and communities. Emphasizing historical contexts, Esther Kim Lee examines how issues of cultural nationalism, interculturalism, and identity politics affect a racially defined theatre. Addressing issues ranging from actors' activism to Asian diaspora, the book documents how Asian American theatre has become an indispensable part of American culture.

ESTHER KIM LEE is Assistant Professor in the Department of Theatre at University of Illinois, Urbana-Champaign. Her work has appeared in *Modern Drama* and the *Journal of Asian American Studies*.

The American theatre and its literature are attracting, after long neglect, the crucial attention of historians, theoreticians, and critics of the arts. Long a field for isolated research yet too frequently marginalized in the academy, the American theatre has always been a sensitive gauge of social pressures and public issues. Investigations into its myriad of shapes and manifestations are relevant to students of drama, theatre, literature, cultural experience, and political development.

The primary intent of this series is to set up a forum of important and original scholarship in and criticism of American theatre and drama in a cultural and social context. Inclusive by design, the series accommodates leading work in areas ranging from the study of drama as literature to theatre histories, theoretical explorations, production histories, and readings of more popular or para-theatrical forms. While maintaining a specific emphasis on theatre in the United States, the series welcomes work grounded broadly in cultural studies and narratives with interdisciplinary reach. Cambridge Studies in American Theatre and Drama thus provides a crossroads where historical, theoretical, literary, and biographical approaches meet and combine, promoting imaginative research in theatre and drama from a variety of new perspectives.

A History of Asian American Theatre

ESTHER KIM LEE

CAMBRIDGE
UNIVERSITY PRESS

CAMBRIDGE UNIVERSITY PRESS

Cambridge, New York, Melbourne, Madrid, Cape Town, Singapore, São Paulo

CAMBRIDGE UNIVERSITY PRESS

The Edinburgh Building, Cambridge CB2 2RU, UK

Published in the United States of America by Cambridge University Press, New York

www.cambridge.org

Information on this title: www.cambridge.org/9780521850513

First published 2006

Printed in the United Kingdom at the University Press, Cambridge

A catalogue record for this publication is available from the British Library

ISBN-13 978-0-521-85051-3 hardback
ISBN-10 0-521-85051-7 hardback

6.ft '07

To Bert O. States
who taught me to dream in color

Contents

Illustrations

Acknowledgements

I could not have completed this book without the support of numerous individuals. I first thank Albert for sharing his perspective on this project and in life. He and our families, with their unwavering patience and love, offered their time and service, which I could never pay back fully. To my mentor Thomas Postlewait, I owe immense gratitude for guiding me intellectually and for encouraging me to find my voice as a theatre historian. Other professors at the Ohio State University, including Alan Woods, Esther Beth Sullivan and Lesley Ferris, opened my mind to what is possible in the scholarship of American theatre. This project is a revision of my dissertation, which I wrote with the financial assistance of the Five College Dissertation Fellowship. During my tenure as a fellow at Hampshire College, I had the privilege to meet and work with Lorna Peterson, Carol Angus, Ynez Wilkins, Ellen Donkin, Mitzi Sawada, Roberta Uno, and many others, all of whom made my stay in the Pioneer Valley productive and enjoyable.

At University of Illinois, Urbana-Champaign, the faculty and staff in the Department of Theatre and the Asian American Studies Program have been selfless with their encouragement. In the Department of Theatre, I thank Robert Graves for his responses to earlier drafts of this book and for believing in the project to the fullest. I thank George Yu, Kent Ono, and Sharon Lee for their generous support and for advocating the need to include performing arts in the curriculum of Asian American studies. The Faculty Summer Research Awards in Asian American Studies were especially vital to the completion of this project. The Research Board at University of Illinois, Urbana-Champaign was instrumental in this project: the Humanities Release Time gave me time to write, and the Arnold O. Beckman Research Award allowed me to travel and purchase equipment essential to my research. The award also supported my research assistant, Clara Mee-Young Shim, whose work always exceeded my expectations.

The scholarship of Asian American theatre is a small but growing field, and I am truly honored to be part of an excellent group of colleagues and friends. Josephine Lee has not only been a role model, but her suggestions on earlier drafts of this book were invaluable. The conversations I have had with Dan Bacalzo, Lucy Burns, Yuko Kurahashi, Daphne Lei, SanSan Kwan, Sean Metzger, Emily Roxworthy, Karen Shimakawa, Priya Srinivasan, and Yutian Wong have informed this project. I have also benefited greatly from the writings of Terry Hong, whose vast knowledge of Asian American theatre has guided me. Richard Kim helped me gain access to interviewees, and I thank him for acting as my informal agent during the research process. The staff at the following libraries and archives were tremendously resourceful: The California Ethnic and Multicultural Archives at the University of California, Santa Barbara; Arts Library Special Collections at the University of California, Los Angeles; The Billy Rose Theatre Collection at the New York Public Library for Performing Arts; Tamiment Library and Robert F. Wagner Labor Archives at New York University.

I wish to thank Don Wilmeth and Victoria Cooper for recognizing that Asian American theatre should be included in American theatre history. Along with their advice, the guidance of Rebecca Jones of the Cambridge University Press consistently improved this project, and a number of friends gave me the confidence and strength to finish it. The intelligence, kindness, and sense of humor of Valleri Robinson Hohman, Barbara Kim, Moon-Kie Jung, and Cynthia Oliver have sustained me throughout my career. I also thank my students at the Ohio State University, Hampshire College, University of Southern California, and the University of Illinois, Urbana-Champaign for their insightful comments, many of which I have borrowed for this project.

Finally, I would like to acknowledge all of the Asian American artists who helped me with this project. Without their participation, this book could not have been written. I give special thanks to Harold Byun, Joanna Chan, Tisa Chang, Ping Chong, Frank Chin, Tim Dang, Alvin Eng, Philip Kan Gotanda, Eric Hayashi, Velina Hasu Houston, David Henry Hwang, Mia Katigbak, Bea Kiyohara, Dan Kwong, Corky Lee, Mako, Soon-Tek Oh, David Oyama, Ralph B. Peña, Wayland Quintero, Sung Rno, Rick Shiomi, Roger Tang, Marilyn Tokuda, Denise Uyehara, and Cynthia Kiki Wallis. I apologize in advance for any inaccuracies in this book and request the continued patience, generosity, and indulgence of all interviewees. They are my inspiration, and this is their story.

Select chronology of Asian American theatre: 1965–2005

1965   East West Players (Los Angeles) is founded by Mako, Rae Creevey, James Hong, June K. Lu, Guy Lee, Pat Li, Yet Lock, Soon-Tek Oh, and Beulah Quo.

1966   East West Players produces *Rashomon*, a play based on a short story by Japanese writer Akutagawa Ryunosuke and adapted by Fay and Michael Kanin.

1968   East West Players receives a $38,500 grant from the Ford Foundation. The first playwriting competition is held at the East West Players, and Henry Woon's *Now You See, Now You Don't* wins the first prize.

   Oriental Actors of America, an activist group formed by actors in New York City.

1970   Ellen Stewart supports the establishment of La MaMa Chinatown led by Ching Yeh.

1971   Kumu Kahua (Original Stage) founded in Honolulu, Hawaii by a group of University of Hawaii students and their professor, Dennis Carroll.

   Frank Chin's *Chickencoop Chinaman* and Momoko Iko's *Gold Watch* receive the first prize in the East West Players' playwriting competition.

1972   East West Players relocates to a permanent performing space (99 seat theatre) on 4424 Santa Monica Boulevard in Los Angeles' Silverlake area.

   Frank Chin's *Chickencoop Chinaman* premieres at the America Place Theatre in New York City.

1973   Asian American Theater Workshop (San Francisco), led by Frank Chin, is established as part of the American Conservatory Theater (ACT) in San Francisco.

Asian Multi Media Center (Seattle) begins as an acting group and receives a $14,500 grant from Washington State Arts Commission.

Chinese Theater Group is formed as a workshop in La MaMa Experimental Theater Club in New York City under the direction of Tisa Chang.

Sining Bayan (meaning Filipino People's Performing Arts) founded as a subgroup within the Filipino American political group, the Katipunan ng mga Demokratikong Pilipino/Union of the Democratic Pilipinos (KDP).

1974   Theatrical Ensemble of Asians (Seattle) is formed by a group of students from the University of Washington and produces its first play, a staged adaptation of Carlos Bulosan's writings.

Frank Chin's *The Year of the Dragon* premieres at the American Place Theatre in New York City.

1975   Theatrical Ensemble of Asians moves out of the University of Washington campus and becomes affiliated with Asian Multi Media Center. It is renamed as Asian Exclusion Act (Seattle) with Garrett Hongo as the artistic director.

Pacific Overtures, a musical by Stephen Sondheim, opens on Broadway with all-Asian American cast.

1977   Pan Asian Repertory Theatre (New York City) is founded by Tisa Chang, Ernest Abuba, Lu Yu, and Hsueh-tung Chen.

Frank Chin resigns as artistic director and leaves the Asian American Theater Workshop.

The East West Players produces Wakako Yamuchi's *And the Soul Shall Dance.*

1978   Asian Multi Media Center in Seattle loses its funding and closes. Garret Hongo leaves Asian Exclusion Act, and Bea Kiyohara becomes the artistic director.

Great Leap (Los Angeles, CA) is founded by Nobuko Miyamoto.

Winston Tong performs "Three Solo Pieces" at La MaMa Experimental Theater Club.

Soon-Tek Oh founds Korean American Theatre Ensemble in Los Angeles.

1979   Philip Kan Gotanda's musical, *The Avocado Kid*, premieres at the East West Players.

Roberta Uno founds Third World Theater (later renamed New WORLD Theater).

1980   Wakako Yamauchi's *The Music Lessons* and David Henry Hwang's *FOB* premiere at the Public Theater in New York City.

1981   Asian Exclusion Act is renamed Northwest Asian American Theater Company.

   Philip Kan Gotanda's *Bullet Headed Birds* opens at Pan Asian Repertory Theatre.

   Cold Tofu, a comedy group, is founded by Denice Kumagai, Marilyn Tokuda, Judy Momii, and Irma Escamilla.

1982   R. A. Shiomi's *Yellow Fever* opens at Pan Asian Repertory Theatre.

1983   Japan America Theater (Los Angeles) has a grand opening with the performance of kabuki from the National Theater of Japan.

1984   Asian American Theater Company loses its ninety-nine seat theatre due to financial troubles.

1987   Northwest Asian American Theater Company opens its permanent performing space, Theater Off Jackson, with the world premiere of *Miss Minidoka* 1943 written by Gary Iwamoto.

   Velina Hasu Houston's *Tea* premieres at the Manhattan Theater Club in New York City.

1988   National Asian American Theatre Company in New York founded by Richard Eng (Executive Director) and Mia Katigbak (Artistic Director).

   hereandnow (college touring company based in Los Angeles) is founded

   David Henry Hwang's *M. Butterfly* debuts at the Eugene O'Neil Theater on March 20 with John Lithgow and B. D. Wong starring, runs 777 performances, and wins a Tony Award for best play.

1989   Angel Island Theater Company (Chicago) founded by eight local Asian American community leaders and theatre artists.

   Ma-Yi Theater (New York) founded as a Filipino American theatre.

   Mako resigns from East West Players. Nobu McCarthy becomes the new artistic director.

   Asian American Theater Company secures a permanent performing space with a 135-seat main stage in the Asian American Theater Center.

   Teatro ng Tanan (San Francisco) is founded.

1990   The controversy over the casting of the musical *Miss Saigon* begins.

   Asian American Repertory Theater (Stockton, CA) founded.

   Kumu Kahua attends Edinburgh International Festival, Washington DC, and the Los Angeles Festival of the Arts. Becomes the first group to tour with plays that had been written wholly, or in part, by the people of Hawaiian ancestry.

1991   Asia On Stage (Boston, MA) founded as a part of Chinese Culture Institute, a membership organization.

1992   Theater Mu (Minneapolis and St. Paul) founded by Rick Shiomi, Dong-il Lee, Diane Espaldon, and Martha Johnson.

1993   Eric Hayashi, a twenty-year veteran with Asian American Theater Company resigns, and Pamela Wu becomes the executive director.
        Tim Dang becomes the artistic director of East West Players. Club O'Noodles, a Vietnamese American troupe, is founded in Los Angeles.

1994   18 Mighty Mountain Warriors (San Francisco) founded.
        Community Asian Theater of the Sierra (Nevada City, CA) founded.
        InterACT (Sacramento) founded.
        QBD Ink (Washington, DC) founded.

1995   Asian Pacific Theater Project (Sacramento, CA) is founded.
        Asian American Repertory Theatre (San Diego, CA) is founded.
        Lodestone Theatre (Los Angeles) is founded.
        Slant (New York City) is founded.

1998   East West Players moves to a 240-seat theatre space in downtown Los Angeles.

1999   Asian Stories in America (Washington, DC) founded.

2000   SALAAM! (South Asian League of Artists in America) and Disha Theater, a "South Asian diaspora theatre," founded in New York City.
        Mango Tribe Productions (Chicago) is founded.

2002   David Henry Hwang's version of the musical, *Flower Drum Song*, opens on Broadway.

2003   Due East (Chicago) is founded.
        Shunya (Houston), an Indian-American theatre company, is founded.

2005   Mark Taper Forum's Asian Theatre Workshop (Los Angeles) closes.

Introduction: The links and locations of Asian American theatre

> Linking is particularly important in cultural history, because culture is a web of many strands; none is spun by itself, nor is any cut off at a fixed date like wars and regimes.
>
> Jacques Barzun[1]

THE SINGLE EVENT THAT PUT ASIAN AMERICAN THEATRE ON the national and international cultural map was the Broadway production of David Henry Hwang's *M. Butterfly*, which won the Tony Award for best play in 1988. Hwang was widely publicized as the first Asian American playwright to be produced on Broadway, but very few knew the history that brought Hwang to the Great White Way. Most did not know that Asian American theatre debuted in New York City for the first time in 1972 with works by Frank Chin and Ping Chong, or that Hwang interned at the East West Players in Los Angeles during his college years. *M. Butterfly* quickly became canonized in drama anthologies, but Asian American theatre history, in its richness and complexity, rarely found its audience. Indeed, Asian Americans were "strangers from a different shore," as the historian Ronald Takaki famously put it, not only in immigration history but also in American theatre history.[2] This book places these strangers center stage and offers their history from 1965 to the early years of the twenty-first century. The year 1965 appropriately marks the beginning of "Asian American theatre," as stipulated in this book, because the first Asian American theatre company, the East West Players, was founded that year

---

[1] Jacques Barzun, *From Dawn to Decadence: 500 Years of Western Cultural Life* (New York: Harper Collins Publisher, 2000), ix.
[2] Ronald Takaki, *Strangers from a Different Shore: A History of Asian Americans*, rev. edn. (Boston: Back Bay Books, 1998).

and the concept of "Asian America" emerged in the consciousness of artists, activists, intellectuals, and community leaders around the country in the second half of the 1960s. And the new millennium, as I will show, marks the start of a new era for Asian American theatre.

After Hwang's success on Broadway, a number of anthologies of Asian American plays began to appear, and editors such as Misha Berson, Roberta Uno, Velina Hasu Houston, and Brian Nelson, provided invaluable examinations of Asian American theatre in their introductions and editorial notes.[3] Of course, plays by individual authors such as Frank Chin had been published in the 1980s, and *Kumu Kahua Plays*, a collection of plays produced by Kumu Kahua (the first Asian American theatre company in Hawaii), had been in print since 1983.[4] But it was in the 1990s that a noticeable number of Asian American plays received publication and mainstream reception. Also in the 1990s, scholarly works by Josephine Lee, James Moy, Dorinne Kondo, and others provided historical, theoretical, and literary studies of Asian American theatre. Their scholarship explored various issues, themes, and developments while rooting their research in both Asian American Studies and Theatre Studies. More recently, Alvin Eng's anthology of New York City Asian American performances, Yuko Kurahashi's study of the East West Players, and Karen Shimakawa's theoretical examination of abjection and embodiment have added to this growing field.

As indispensable as their scholarships have been, however, many questions have remained unanswered and many historical details unmentioned. As a scholar trained in theatre history and historiography, I wanted to know about the most basic facts of Asian American theatre; about causes and effects, the progress, and stasis, of its history; and about how the history should be researched and told. Accordingly, this project began with a simple query about who participated in Asian American theatre, what they did together, what happened, and in what chronology. Such a survey of Asian American theatre seemed long overdue.

At the beginning of this project, I vastly underestimated the scope of the topic and overestimated my ability to document it. I naïvely planned

---

[3] Misha Berson, *Between Worlds* (New York: Theatre Communications Group, 1990); Roberta Uno, *Unbroken Thread* (Amherst: University of Massachusetts Press, 1993); Velina Hasu Houston, *Politics of Life* (Philadelphia: Temple University Press, 1993) and *But Still, Like Air, I'll Rise* (Philadelphia: Temple University Press, 1997); and Brian Nelson, *Asian American Drama* (New York: Applause, 1997).

[4] Dennis Carroll, *Kumu Kahua Plays* (Honolulu: University of Hawaii Press, 1983).

on talking to a dozen Asian American theatre artists and reading all available scripts – and actually worried about not having enough material for a book-length project. Moreover, without any background in ethnography or journalism, I decided to use interviews as the primary mode of research. I was driven by my ambition for research and knowledge, but I did not know where to start or who to contact for interviews. But fortune was on my side: in the spring of 1999, I heard about the first conference on Asian American theatre in Seattle at the Northwest Asian American Theater Company where major Asian American theater artists and producers were to gather to discuss the state of their profession. Without any hesitation, I jumped on the plane and registered for the conference. At first, I did not know anyone at the conference, but by the end of it, I had a handful of interview audiotapes and dozens of contacts for future interviews.

As I gained more access to my research subjects (i.e. Asian American theatre artists who graciously agreed to talk to me), I realized that the Asian American theatre community is a huge web of links that are profoundly personal, professional, chronological, geographical, spatial, racial, ethnic, gendered, generational, and multicultural. Because of theatre's inherently collaborative nature, each artist's career was linked to numerous others. It was imperative that the most "truthful" survey of Asian American theatre include and represent all of those links in the fairest way. Thus, my worries of not having enough material were soon replaced with the bigger concern of how I could best document the constantly growing community without excluding any important strands. Moreover, every interviewee had a different perspective of the past and often contradicted what others said, making a "truthful" history challenging. Everyone's memory was both unreliable and trustworthy. The result is a *Rashomon*-like history, in which everyone tells a different version of an event.[5] It is fitting, then, that *Rashomon* was the first production presented

---

[5] The stage version of *Rashomon* adapted by Fay and Michael Kanin is based on a film by Japanese director Akira Kurosawa. The story is about a court trial of a double-crime of rape and murder. In ancient Japan, a bandit sees a woman who is passing through the woods with her husband. The bandit becomes sexually infatuated with the woman and decides to rape her. He takes the husband to the bush, ties him up, and rapes the woman. Later, the husband is found dead with a stab wound to the chest. A woodcutter witnesses this and is later called to testify during the trial, along with the wife, the bandit, and a medium who speaks for the dead husband. The story is told by the woodcutter who, after the trial, stops at the Rashomon gate to avoid rain. The woodcutter tells his listeners about how each witness told the judge his or her own distinct version of the story. The versions contradicted one another although each witness sincerely believed in his or her testimony.

by the East West Players in 1965. *Rashomon* serves as a metaphor for Asian American theatre history, and the different versions bring about a rich history full of contradictions and short-circuited links.

Charlotte Canning expresses similar concerns and observation in her study of feminist theatre that was also based on interviews. According to Canning, many of the interviewees, like mine, told her, "You'll have to get other parts of the story from other people."[6] But she also notes that in the process of research, the interviewer inevitably becomes "part of the story": "Concomitant with the narrative created by the interviewee, the interviewer's own interpretation plays a vital role in the construction of the oral history."[7] In other words, I'm like the woodcutter in *Rashomon* who ultimately narrates his version of the story to whoever is willing to listen to him, and variant versions of Asian American theatre history are interpreted by my assumptions and expectations.

Moreover, archival materials (such as original program notes, meeting minutes, newspaper clippings, photographs, letters, manifestos, and objects) are as, if not more, prone to interpretation. As Thomas Postlewait describes, "a gap thus exists between the event and our knowledge of it," and archival materials are "traces, footprints in the sand."[8] Indeed, theatre history is an attempt to reconstruct an aspect of our cultural past with the "traces" and "footprints" of what is already ephemeral to begin with: rehearsals, performances, audience responses, meetings, protests, documentations, and many other elements that, together, form the "event" of theatre.

Because there is no explicit consensus on what Asian American theatre history is or should be, I find it necessary to stipulate what I mean by Asian American theatre. I have tried my best to be as inclusive as possible and believe that the history should be about anyone who has worked in Asian American theatre. This question, however, begs further questions of who are Asian Americans and how we define theatre. For instance, is a Peking opera performer from China who immigrates to the United States an "Asian American theatre artist" from the day he sets foot in the country? And does he have to give up Peking opera and perform in naturalistic American dramas? Such questions of labels and boundaries

[6] Charlotte Canning, *Feminist Theaters in the U.S.A.: Staging Women's Experience* (New York: Routledge, 1996), 20.
[7] Ibid., 19.
[8] Thomas Postlewait, "Historiography and the Theatrical Event: A Primer with Twelve Cruxes," *Theatre Journal* 43 (1991), 160.

are endless, and the struggles to define Asian American theatre are part of the history. In this book, I have focused on the locations of production (both artistic and cultural) as the primary stipulation of Asian American theatre. In other words, I have looked to, and always come back to, Asian American theatre companies, rehearsal and performance spaces, meeting and protest locations, and geographical areas. Whoever is associated with such spaces (artists, producers, audiences, or critics) is part of Asian American theatre history. For instance, I consider the actor John Lone – a trained Peking opera performer who immigrated to the United States – part of Asian American theatre history, not because he is an Asian performer in America but because he was once a major member of the East West Players, an Asian American theatre company. Such locations are linked to each other and collectively create a national space from which Asian American theatre has emerged.

In terms of national geography, the term "Asian America" applies to all fifty states in the United States, and this book certainly attempts to capture the regional diversities. However, Hawaii presents a unique challenge for the discourse of Asian American theatre. For example, plays written by students of the University of Hawaii in the first half of the twentieth century are considered by some, as Roberta Uno has suggested, the first Asian American plays written for the stage.[9] And throughout the second half of the twentieth century, Asian Americans from Hawaii, such as the actor Randall Duk Kim, have made an indisputable contribution to Asian American theatre. I discuss some of these artists in the following chapters, but I have not included Hawaii as a geographical space in my study. My primary reason stems from a debate within Asian American Studies: some in Asian American Studies argue that Pacific Island Studies should be included and that the term "Asian America" should be replaced with "Asian Pacific America." Others (including scholars of Pacific Island Studies) argue against the inclusion for a number of reasons. The debate continues, and thus I have chosen to focus on Asian American theatre on the mainland. In my view, the inclusion of Hawaii would necessitate a shift in the paradigm of Asian American theatre history, and the nature of this shift would hinge on whether Asian American theatre is considered as part of the larger Asian diaspora theatre.

Indeed, as Josephine Lee points out, the inclusion of Hawaii in Asian American theatre history would "illuminate the fault lines" in how we, as

---

[9] See Roberta Uno's introduction to *Unbroken Thread*.

theatre historians, have imagined Asian American culture.[10] For this book, however, I've been more interested in how Asian American theatre artists I have interviewed have imagined their theatre. I have observed that in their minds the inclusion of Hawaii was not as important as their desire for acceptance in American theatre. In other words, they emphasized "American" in Asian American theatre and wanted to write and perform like other American theatre artists. That is why they founded theatre companies modeled after American regional theatres and presented their shows using American naturalistic sets. Future studies of Asian American theatre should include Hawaii and even Asian diaspora theatre, but the purpose of this book is to provide an introduction to the who, what, where, how, and why of Asian American theatre as told by the artists and as interpreted by me.

Accordingly, I have focused on four major cities – Los Angeles, San Francisco, New York City, and Seattle – as the key locations of Asian American theatre. The research is based on over seventy interviews and archival findings in and around those cities.[11] There are, however, scores of artists I did not get to interview, and the oral histories documented in the interviews I have conducted are so vast that only a fraction is incorporated in this study. Telling all of the stories and histories would require a multi-volume book with details that can only be captured with an encyclopedic approach. Thus, this book is by no means a comprehensive history of Asian American theatre. Rather, it is intended to be an introduction and an invitation to the scholarship of Asian American theatre history. What I provide is a sketch that reveals the essentials links and locations of the history. I have broadly and perhaps swiftly suggested the major trajectories of Asian American theatre while slowing down at certain points in order to provide specific examples and case studies. I have no doubt that a fuller picture of Asian American theatre will soon emerge with the growing participation of scholars in the field. As I envision this optimistic future, I also anticipate more Asian Americans appearing on stages, not as strangers but as indisputable citizens and artists of America.

---

[10] Josephine Lee, "Asian Americans in Progress: College Plays 1937–1955," in Josephine Lee, Imogene L. Lim and Yuko Matsukawa, (eds.), *Re/Collecting Early Asian America: Essays in Cultural History* (Philadelphia: Temple University Press), 308.

[11] As I discuss in chapter 8, a growing number of Asian American theatre companies emerged in the 1990s in other cities, including San Diego, Boston, Washington, DC, and Minneapolis, and most of these newer companies were modeled after the earlier companies in the four major cities.

I

Asian American theatre before 1965

THE TERM "ASIAN AMERICAN" DID NOT EXIST BEFORE 1965, AND neither did "Asian American theatre." But theatrical activities by Asian immigrants and their descendents have been around as long as they have lived in the United States, and Asians and Asianness have appeared on mainstream American stages at least since the eighteenth century. Historian Yuji Ichioka coined the term "Asian American" in the second half of the 1960s as he and others of the Asian American Movement rejected "oriental" as racist and imperialistic.[1] The classification of the "oriental" and the pseudo-scientific "Mongolian" race had made no distinction between those living in the United States and those abroad. The conflation had been used by the US government to justify systematic and consistent denial of Asians' basic rights as immigrants and citizens. It did not matter that Asians had lived in the Americas long before the thirteen colonies declared their independence from Britain.[2] What did matter was that "orientals" and "Mongolians" were among other "inferior races" such as "Negroes," "Indians," and "Mexicans" that were disenfranchised and excluded from the national imagination of the ideal new country.

---

[1] See Yuji Ichioka, Yasuo Sakata, Nobuya Tsuchida, and Eri Yasuhara, *A Buried Past: An Annotated Bibliography of the Japanese American Research Project* (Berkeley: University of California Press, 1974). For studies on the Asian American Movement, see William Wei, *The Asian American Movement* (Philadelphia: Temple University Press, 1993) and Steven G. Louie and Glenn K. Omatsu, eds., *Asian Americans: The Movement and the Moment* (Los Angeles: University of California, Los Angeles, Asian American Studies, 2002).

[2] In the sixteenth century, many Filipino sailors who worked on Spanish ships during the Spanish galleon trade between Manila and Mexico jumped ship and sought freedom on the coast of Louisiana. And Mexico City had a thriving Chinatown as early as the seventeenth century. See Helen Zia, *Asian American Dreams: The Emergence of an American People* (New York: Farrar, Straus and Giroux, 2001), 23–25.

From the beginning of American history, the imagined Asianness that appeared on theatre stages often had little to do with the realities of Asia or Asian immigrant communities in the United States. As Erika Fischer-Lichte articulates, theatre is a "communal institution, representing and establishing relationships which fulfill social functions."[3] The first relationship American theatre established with Asia and Asianness was founded on exoticism and voyeurism. James S. Moy points out that the first appearance of Chineseness (and by extension Asianness) in American theatre occurred in the production of Voltaire's *Orphan of China* (1755), which was adapted into English by Arthur Murphy and appeared at Philadelphia's Southwark Theater on January 16, 1767.[4] According to Moy, the production was "vaguely 'oriental'" and far from authentic. All Chinese characters were played by white actors in yellowface makeup and wore Middle Eastern looking costumes. As Moy notes: "Indeed, the notion of Chineseness under the sign of the exotic became familiar to the American spectator long before sightings of the actual Chinese."[5] The European American impression of Asia was similar to that of Europeans, who viewed the civilizations of China, India, and the Arab world as wealthy, culturally sophisticated, and exotic, yet past its glory and in decline. Americans, especially those who emulated the European aristocratic class, were fascinated with the products from the East, such as porcelain, spices, tea, and art. But as John Kuo Wei Tchen remarks, "ardent nationalists proclaimed Europeanized America the next great occidental civilization."[6]

As Americans increasingly sought their new national identity in the context of older world civilizations, their curiosity for the "oriental" exotic grew. Museums and circus performances featured the "oriental" as well as other racialized groups for both anthropological education and freakish entertainment. In 1834, for instance, a "Chinese Lady" named Afong Moy

---

[3] Erika Fischer-Lichte, *The Show and the Gaze of Theatre: A European Perspective* (Iowa City: University of Iowa Press, 1997), 26.

[4] James Moy, *Marginal Sights: Staging Chinese in America* (Iowa City: University of Iowa Press, 1993), 9.

[5] According to John Kuo Wei Tchen *The Orphan of China* was produced in New York City before, during, and after the Revolution, and the productions signified the "cultural values" of the period. It "simultaneously allowed for a critique of the British monarchy, gaining the legitimacy of Chinese civilizational precedent for American values, while also reconnecting U. S. cultural perspectives to an Anglo-Saxon cultural tradition." See John Kuo Wei Tchen, *New York Before Chinatown: Orientalism and the Shaping of American Culture: 1776–1882* (Baltimore: The Johns Hopkins University Press, 1999), 19–22.

[6] Ibid., xvi.

was put on display for public viewing at the American Museum in New York City. This actual person "performed" her Chineseness along with magicians, glassblowers, "Canadian dwarfs," and other spectacles for the next three years at several locations. As James Moy notes, her "simple foreignness" was "deemed sufficient novelty to warrant her display."[7] Other exotic displays and "performances" from Asia followed throughout the nineteenth century, including the most famous, the "Siamese twins" Chang and Eng.

The audiences of such entertainment were mostly on the East Coast in the first half of the nineteenth century, but on October 18, 1852, the first real Chinese theatrical performance was presented on stage at the American Theater on Sansome Street in San Francisco by the Tong Hook Tong Dramatic Company, a forty-two member Cantonese opera troupe from Guangdong Province. When gold was discovered at Sutter's Mill in 1848, the Chinese population in California did not exceed one hundred, but by 1850 about 25,000 were residing in the state. Just as Chinese miners were lured to leave their homeland by the promises of gold and quick fortune, Chinese opera performers expected to make their fortunes entertaining their compatriots.[8] As the performers had hoped, the performances were successful in San Francisco, where thousands of Chinese men paid up to $6 per seat to see entertainment from their homeland. Wherever there were sizable populations of Chinese immigrants, permanent theatre buildings and companies emerged. For instance, the first Chinese theatre opened in San Francisco on December 23, 1852, with a seating capacity of 1,400, and in Portland, Oregon, three Chinese theatre companies were operating by the 1890s.[9]

Encouraged by the success in San Francisco, the acting manager of the Tong Hook Tong Dramatic Company signed a lucrative contract with a promoter from New York City. Chinese themes had always been popular with the European American audience in New York City, as they had been in Europe since the eighteenth century. For instance, popular plays such

[7] James Moy, *Marginal Sights*, 12.
[8] John Kuo Wei Tchen, *New York Before Chinatown*, 86.
[9] See Thomas Postlewait, "The Hieroglyphic Stage: American Theatre and Society, Post-Civil War to 1945," in *The Cambridge History of American Theatre, Volume Two: 1870–1945*, edited by Don B. Wilmeth and Christopher Bigsby, 3 vols. (Cambridge: Cambridge University Press, 1999), 139. Also see "Pear Garden in the West – America's Chinese Theater, 1853–1983" by The New York Chinatown History Project in Patricia Haseltine, *East and Southeast Asian Material Culture in North America: Collections, Historical Sites, and Festivals* (New York: Greenwood Press, 1989), 48.

as *The Yankees in China* (1839), *Irishman in China* (1842), *The Cockney in China* (1848), and *China, or Tricks Upon Travelers* (1841) had entertained New Yorkers with comedic images of Chinese characters (although they were played by white actors in yellowface). So, when the acting manager was presented with a contract that promised large sums of money and support from powerful investors such as P. T. Barnum, the future seemed too good to be true for the Tong Hook Tong Dramatic Company.

When the company arrived in New York, they realized that the contract was, indeed, too good to be true. All promises were broken, and Barnum denied any involvement. To salvage what they could, the company performed on May 20 at the Niblo's Garden, but the performances were vastly misunderstood by the New York critics and audiences, who did not know what to make of the real Chinese theatre. They had only seen Western versions of Chinese performance with Western staging techniques and white actors in yellowface, so even the most basic elements of the Cantonese opera performance confused them. Subsequent performances utterly failed, and the company made no profit while expenses grew.

In assessing the failure of the Tong Hook Tong Dramatic Company, John Kuo Wei Tchen concludes that "faux Chinese" representations had several advantages over the real thing: "As exemplified by the failure of the Tong Hook Tong opera troupe, authentic Chinese culture was too strange for New Yorkers' tastes. The sensibility of the Chinese opera was quite different from European American traditions."[10] The bottom line was that "faux Chinese" or "simulated Chinese" were more profitable for theatre producers and investors in New York City. Unfortunately, this tradition would continue throughout the nineteenth and the twentieth centuries in American theatre. Caricatures of Asians continued to appear on stages, and white actors in yellowface were seen as more "real" than real Asians. "Oriental" exoticism always had more box-office appeal than the actual Asians and Asian immigrants in the United States.

The fate of the Tong Hook Tong performers in the 1850s foreshadowed what would happen to Chinese laborers in the second half of the nineteenth century. Between 1850 and the 1930s, almost one million Asians from China, Japan, Korea, the Philippines, and India came to the United States, while approximately thirty-five million came from Europe and Russia during the same period.[11] At first, America welcomed Asian

---

[10] John Kuo Wei Tchen, *New York Before Chinatown*, 123.
[11] Most Asian immigrants were young men who came to work on the sugarcane plantations in Hawaii and in the goldmines in California. Many Chinese men from Canton in South China

participation in the US workforce. However, as competition for jobs grew, Asian workers faced unimaginable hardships and disappointments, including taxes targeted specifically at them and fierce and often lethal rivalry with workers from European countries. Numerous Chinese men were murdered and cheated, but US laws rarely protected them.[12] When Chinese miners lost their jobs, they turned to the Central Pacific Railroad, which was desperate for workers. About 12,000 Chinese worked to build the most difficult part of the transcontinental railroad in the Rocky Mountains. However, once the transcontinental railroad was completed in 1869, Chinese men were fired and not included in the celebrations. In fact, they were not allowed to ride on the railroad they built and had to walk back to San Francisco. Such mistreatment was only the beginning of a long history of an anti-Chinese movement that galvanized the West in the 1870s and 1880s, a period of a devastating economic recession. A series of Chinese exclusion laws were passed in order to get rid of all Chinese (and "Mongolian") people and solve what the government called the "Chinese question."[13] However, many Chinese men and women chose to stay and attempt to gain American citizenship, with all the associated rights that this conferred, as did Irish, Italian, and Eastern European immigrants. They challenged the exclusion laws at every chance and fought for their rights in numerous court battles and demonstrations. Many fled California, which had the harshest exclusionary laws, and

---

left their villages to escape war and poverty with dreams of striking it rich in "Gold Mountain," a name they used for America. In contrast Chinese women were forbidden by the government from traveling abroad. For a study on early Chinese immigration, see K. Scott Wong and Sucheng Chan, eds., *Claiming America: Constructing Chinese American Identities During the Exclusion Era* (Philadelphia: Temple University Press, 1998).

[12] For instance, *People v. Hall* in 1854 forbade Chinese from testifying in court even in cases of self-defense. And, after the Civil War, when African American men gained the right to vote, Chinese were denied citizenship because they were neither black nor white.

[13] The first of many anti-Chinese laws appeared in California as early as 1858, barring entry of Chinese and "Mongolians" in order to control the number of Chinese immigrants and to make sure that they did not settle in the United States once their contracts expired. The Page Law of 1875 barred entry of "Chinese, Japanese, and 'Mongolian' prostitutes, felons, and contract laborers," and in 1882, the Chinese Exclusionary Law suspended immigration of laborers for ten years. These laws, among other things, prohibited Chinese women from immigrating in order to prevent permanent immigration of families. By 1890, the Chinese population in the United States had a ratio of twenty-nine men to one woman, and Chinatowns were virtually synonymous with "bachelor society." In 1892, the law was renewed for another ten years and required all Chinese to register, and in 1902, in addition to another ten-year renewal of the law, police in major cities raided Chinatowns and arrested those who allegedly had not registered. And in 1924, the Immigration Act closed the door to virtually all Asians.

scattered to major cities on the East Coast. A number of them adopted Anglo-American last names and married Irish-American women. Moreover, they made their intention to stay in America clear by building schools, churches, temples, community organizations, and theatres.

During this period, popular representations of Asians and Asianness in mainstream theatre began to reflect the anti-Asian sentiments. Stereotypical characters, both male and female, repeatedly appeared on American stages and made a lasting impression on the public imagination. In Henry Grimm's play, *The Chinese Must Go* (1879),[14] for instance, two diametrically opposite Asian male stereotypes appear: the first is the childish Chinaman speaking pidgin English (and who is often drunk, high on opium, and chases white women), and the second is the intelligent "evil genius" Chinaman who speaks perfect English and has the ability to negotiate with white Americans. The latter threatens to take over California and plots to ruin the lives of white Americans while the former corrupts innocent white children and women with his immoral and ignorant acts. As Robert G. Lee notes, these images were "frequently contradictory, often to the point of appearing mutually exclusive," but they were also powerful.[15] Variations of these types appeared in other mainstream theatre shows such as *Ah Sin!* (1877) by Mark Twain and Bret Harte.[16]

Female stereotypes were not any better: the images were either the innocent self-sacrificing lotus blossom or the much feared dragon lady. These images began to receive increasing visibility and popularity with the emergence of orientalist romantic melodramas at the turn of the

[14] The play was probably performed for anti-coolie clubs in San Francisco when anti-Chinese sentiment was at its peak. See Dave Williams, *The Chinese Other: 1850–1925: An Anthology of Plays* (Lanham: University Press of America, Inc., 1997), 57.

[15] Robert G. Lee, *Orientals: Asian Americans in Popular Culture* (Philadelphia: Temple University Press, 1999), xi.

[16] Other plays include Joaquin Miller's *The Danites in the Sierras* (1877), Clay M. Greene's *The Chinese Question* (1877), Bartley Campbell's *My Partner* (1879), Charles E. Blaney and J. J. McCloskey's *Across the Pacific* (1900), Owen Davis's *Chinatown Charlie* (1906), Menyhert Lengyel's *Typhoon* (1912), David Belasco's *Son-Daughter* (1919), *His Chinese Wife* (1920), *Lady of the Lamp* (1920), *Poppy God* (1921), Forrest Halsey and Clara Beranger's *Out of Seven Seas* (1923), and John Willard's *The Green Beetle* (1924). This list was provided by Sung Hee Choi in her conference paper, "Performing the Other: Asian American Actors on Broadway in the 1950s," presented at the American Society for Theatre Research Annual Meeting, November, 1998, Washington, DC. Also see the recent publication of Krystyn R. Moon, *Yellowface: Creating the Chinese in American Popular Music and Performance, 1850s–1920s* (New Brunswick, NJ: Rutgers University Press, 2005). Moon's book details the involvement of Chinese American performers in American popular culture during the time when anti-Chinese sentiment was at its peak.

century – *The Darling of the Gods* (1902) and *Madame Butterfly* (1900) by David Belasco and *The Yellow Jacket* (1912) by J. Harry Benrimo and George C. Hazelton. These plays were usually set in Asian countries and featured clearly distinguishable heroes and villains involved in exotic adventures and mystical events. The popularity of these plays had much to do with the innovations in theatrical staging, in which smoke, water, fire, and other dramatic effects attracted audiences. But the main attraction was the presentation of the distant land with an imperialistic perspective. Often, female Asian characters embodied imperial presumptions about "Asianness." They were submissive (as the West wanted to see Asia) or powerful, evil, and threatening (as representative of the Yellow Peril).

The orientalist melodramas on American stages could not have been farther from the realities of Asian American experiences. For instance, at the same time that Japanese characters like Cio Cio San in *Madame Butterfly* displayed orientalist exoticism on the stages of American main-stream theatre, Japanese Americans were experiencing something entirely different in their theatres. In 1909, Nippon Kan (Japanese Hall) Theater was built at the heart of the Japanese American community in Seattle, Washington, for Japanese immigrants and their children to enjoy a variety of entertainments. The theatre was the primary venue for actors and musicians from Japan, as well as Kabuki performances, movies, concerts, judo and kendo competitions, and even community meetings. During the same period, Sadakichi Hartman, arguably the first Asian American play-wright, wrote plays titled *Christ* (1893), *Buddha* (1897), and *Confucius* (1923). Hartman was Eurasian with a German father and a Japanese mother. He grew up in Germany and the USA, later becoming an art critic, journalist, theatre artist, writer, and "intellectual Bohemian." Although his plays do not address Asian American issues, they are rare American symbolist plays with intercultural themes.[17]

The discrepancy between the popular representation of Asians on mainstream stages and the actual experiences of Asians in America widens further in the 1920s. The passing of the Immigration Act in 1924 prohib-ited virtually all Asians from immigration and excluded Asians already in the country from citizenship. The Chinese Exclusion Acts had effectively stopped Chinese immigration, so the actual intention of the Immigration Act was to cease Japanese immigration, which had grown exponentially

---

[17] See Jane C. Weaver, ed., *Sadakichi Hartmann: Critical Modernist: Collected Art Writings, Vol. 1*, 3 vols. (Berkeley: University of California Press, 1991).

since the turn of the century.[18] Before the Act was passed, many "oriental" shows in mainstream theatre featured Asians as "alien residents" living in the United States. Some were portrayed as foreigners unable to assimilate (often comically), while others assimilated too well and thus seemed threatening. After 1924, such "alien residents" appeared less on stage, and Asians in Asia began to dominate American theatre and, increasingly, film. Plays such as *Shanghai Gesture* (1928), *Sakura* (1928), *The Good Earth* (1932), *If This Be Treason* (1935), and *A Woman of Destiny* (1936) portrayed Asians living in various "oriental" settings far from America and Asian America. It was as if the Immigration Act of 1924 erased Asian Americans from the national domestic imagination.

During this period, individual Asian Americans began to participate in American theatre on and off stage. Their activities never led to a collective Asian American theatre, and all of them experienced severe discrimination, which often hampered the artists' careers. The first known appearance of an Asian American actor in mainstream theatre occurred in the production of George M. Cohan's *Get Rich Quick Wallingford* in 1912, in which Yoshin Sakurai, a first-generation Japanese American, played a valet.[19] All major characters in theatre and film were played by white actors, and Asian American actors had no choice but to take minor roles. The first Asian actors to play major roles in theatre and receive national and international recognition were Sessue Hayakawa (1890–1973) and Anna May Wong (1905–1961).[20]

Sessue Hayakawa began his career in theatre and film unexpectedly when he was on vacation in Los Angeles and attended a performance in The Japanese Playhouse, a community theatre in Little Tokyo. He had just received a bachelor's degree in political science from the University of Chicago and was on his way to Japan, where he was born and raised.

[18] The Immigration Act of 1924 was worded to bar immigration of those "forbidden to be a U.S. citizen." The only groups barred from citizenship were Chinese, Japanese, and other Asians. The Act did not affect immigrants from European countries.

[19] It is said that Sakurai was not a professional actor, but instead, he was a valet in real life for the star actor, who offered him the part to play himself in the production. Tooru Kanazawa, "Issei on Broadway," *Scene* 5.10 (Feb 1954), 15–17.

[20] The Korean American actor Philip Ahn (1905–1978) was a renowned character actor in film and television from the 1930s to the 1970s, but unlike Hayakawa and Wong, Ahn did not work in live theatre. Ahn's father was the famous Korean nationalist Chang Ho Ahn, a revered figure who stood against the colonial Japanese rule in the early twentieth century. For a biography on Ahn, see Philip Ahn Cuddy, "Philip Ahn: Born in America," The Philip Ahn Admiration Society, www.philipahn.com/pacessay.html; "Philip Ahn Dies, Portrayed Oriental Actors on TV, Film," *Washington Post* March 3, 1978, C4.

According to his autobiography, *Zen Showed Me the Way* (1960), Hayakawa disliked the Japanese Playhouse performance so much that he went up to Toyo Fujita, the man running the theatre, and presented a harsh criticism. Fujita challenged him to do a better job, and Hayakawa accepted. He directed and acted in the company's next play *Hototogisu*, and eventually played in many others, becoming something of a celebrity in Little Tokyo. However, Hayakwa wanted wider acceptance and went on to direct and act in the company's first English-speaking production, *The Typhoon* by Walker Whiteside. The production was unprecedented in many ways. Hayakawa sought out Japanese American actors because he wanted to cast Japanese characters with Japanese actors who could speak English fluently. He had seen a production of *The Typhoon* in Chicago with all white actors and felt that it was "artificial" and not "authentic." To everyone's surprise (including Hayakawa's), he found enough Japanese American actors in the Los Angeles area. As Hayakawa intended, the production attracted many mainstream audience members who were curious about an all-Japanese cast playing English-speaking roles.

Thomas H. Ince, one of the most powerful directors of silent films, attended the performance of *The Typhoon* and noticed Hayakawa's acting talent. Ince offered him a role in a film, and Hayakawa's career took off. He quickly became one of the highest paid actors, rivaling Douglas Fairbanks and Charlie Chaplin. However, the growth of his popularity and success coincided with the increasing anti-Asian sentiments during the 1920s. He attempted to transcend discrimination by hosting lavish parties and mingling with the rich and famous of Hollywood, but in 1922 he surprised everyone by suddenly returning to Japan. He later revealed that the decision was the result of a quarrel he had had with a head of a motion picture company who called him a "chink" and other "unpardonable insults."[21] After staying in Japan for about a month, he returned to the United States and went to New York City, bypassing Hollywood. He had a successful career on Broadway as a star actor, but he consistently experienced racism. Like other minority actors of the period, he was more accepted and admired in European countries, especially England and France.

Anna May Wong also enjoyed international fame throughout her career, which spanned more than three decades. Unlike Hayakawa, who was born in Japan, Wong was a third-generation Asian American born

---

[21] Sessue Hayakawa, *Zen Showed Me the Way* (Indianapolis: The Bobbs-Merrill Company, Inc., 1960), pp. 90–91.

in Los Angeles. Her "American Chinese" identity often baffled mainstream critics and audiences, but to Asian Americans, she was clearly the
star of their community. The mainstream preferred to see her as "oriental,"
and she was always typecast as an exotic slave girl or treacherous dragon
lady and often died on screen and stage (the death of an "oriental"
character was the most common resolution of a dramatic conflict). By
1928, she had appeared in over twenty silent films and perfected the fearful
yet desirable Asian female archetype. Despite her talent, beauty, and
success, she was not protected from racism. She was repeatedly denied
nonstereotypical roles and watched leading roles go to less experienced
white actresses in yellowface makeup. After losing the leading role to
Myrna Loy in *The Crimson City* (1928), Wong left the USA for Europe.
She told interviewers in London that she grew tired of dying in films:
"Pathetic dying seemed to be the best thing I did."[22]

Wong entered the world of theatre in 1929 in London, where she
starred in *The Circle of Chalk*, a Chinese play, with Laurence Olivier.
The role was not stereotypical, but Londoners had difficulty accepting
Wong as Chinese because she had a Californian accent.[23] Ironically, she was
too American for them. She returned to the United States and continued
her career in theatre by debuting on Broadway in Edgar Wallace's *On
the Spot* (1931). Her stardom remained unquestioned when she returned
to film in 1931, but nothing had changed in terms of racial discrimination.

Other Asian Americans attempted to pursue careers in American
theatre and film, but most did not find mainstream success. The case of
Peter Hyun, for instance, illustrates how racial discrimination directly
affected and even halted an Asian American's career in theatre. Hyun
was born and raised in Korea and arrived in Hawaii at the age of seven-
teen. He was the first in his family to attend college, but in 1930, at the
beginning of his junior year at DePauw University in Indiana, he left
his educational opportunities to pursue a career as a theatre director in
New York City. He began as a stage manager and received training from
Eva LeGallienne at the Civic Repertory Theater and founded the Studio
Players in Cambridge, Massachusetts, with other members of the Civic

---

[22] Choi, "Performing the Other," 137. For biographical studies on Anna May Wong, see Anthony
B. Chan, *Perpetually Cool: The Many Lives of Anna May Wong, 1905–1961* (Lanham, MD:
Scarecrow, 2003) and Graham Russell Gao Hodges, *Anna May Wong: From Laundryman's
Daughter to Hollywood Legend* (New York: Palgrave Macmillan, 2005).
[23] When Wong visited China later in her career, she was criticized – much to her surprise – for
portraying a negative image of Chinese people. She was seen as "too American" to be Chinese.

Repertory Theater. As a young, ambitious director in Cambridge, he directed Ibsen's *When We Dead Awaken* and Chekhov's *Uncle Vanya*, both of which reflected his passion for experimental theatre. However, as he writes in his autobiography, he faced incessant racism in theatre and constantly questioned his career choice: "Would I always be a stranger in the American theatre?" and "Would I always have to face and battle the insufferable racial slurs?"[24]

But Peter Hyun did not lose his passion for theatre and continued to make a name for himself as a director. Hyun joined the New York Federal Theater Project,[25] where he was assigned as a director of the Children's Theatre. Within a few years, Hyun became the director of *Revolt of the Beavers*, one of the most controversial plays of the Federal Theater Project.[26] While the production was one of Hyun's best works, it also ended his career in theatre. According to Hyun, he was involved with the production from the very beginning. He cast the actors, directed them in developing the stylized acting that characterized the play, and collaborated with other artists in choreography and dance. The rehearsals went well, and Hyun felt the production to be "the ultimate synthesis of all my work in the theatre."[27] When Philip Barber, the director of the Federal Theater Project, told Hyun that the show would be produced on Broadway, he shared his surprise and excitement with the cast and crew. However, he found out in the next few days that the cast refused to go to Broadway

---

[24] Peter Hyun, *In the New World: The Making of a Korean American* (Honolulu: University of Hawaii Press, 1995), 119.

[25] The Federal Theater Project (FTP) was established in 1935 as part of the Works Progress Administration supported by President Franklin Delano Roosevelt. Until 1939, the FTP functioned entirely as part of the federal government and was intended to provide employment to theatre professionals during the Great Depression. The productions ranged from full-length plays to musical revues and puppetry. It also supported a number of ethnic theatres and provided unprecedented opportunities to African American theatre artists. The FTP was the first and (so far) the last government supported theatre in the United States.

[26] The National Archive describes *Revolt of the Beavers* as a children's play that "stirred political passions from the moment it premiered." It describes: "In the play, two small children are transported to 'Beaverland,' where society is run by a cruel beaver chief. The Chief forces the other beavers to work endlessly on the 'busy wheel,' turning bark into food and clothing, then hoards everything for himself and his friends. With the help of the children, a beaver named Oakleaf organizes his brethren, overthrows The Chief, and establishes a society where everything is shared. The show played to packed houses during its brief New York City run, but its message drew fire. Theater critic Brooks Atkinson labeled it "Marxism à la Mother Goose." See National Archives and Records Administration, "A New Deal for the Arts," www.archives. gov/exhibit_ hall/new_deal_for_the_arts/activist_arts2.html.

[27] Hyun, *In the New World*, 154.

with Hyun as the director. They wanted a "name director," but to Hyun, the message was clear: they did not want a "Chinaman" as their director. The cast enlisted Elia Kazan of the Group Theater as their new director. Although he found some consolation in finding his name as a co-director in the program of the Broadway production, the damage had been done, and he left the world of theatre in 1938.[28]

Peter Hyun never returned to theatre, but other Asian Americans who were rejected by the mainstream theatre sought opportunities in alternative theatrical venues. In the 1930s, the number of US born Asian Americans was at its highest, and the community's taste for theatrical entertainment changed to reflect the generational shift. In San Francisco's Chinatown, for example, traditional Chinese opera theatres began to lose audiences to popular nightclubs that were more "all-American" than Asian. After the end of the Prohibition in 1933, nightclubs became the hottest spots in all parts of the country, including Chinatowns. The first nightclubs in San Francisco's Chinatown opened in 1936, and they included Chinese Penthouse, Club Shanghai, Dragon's Lair, Kubla Khan, and Lion's Den. Although some in the community rejected them as low-class burlesque shows, the nightclub performances generated much needed tourism and profit for the community. They also provided rare opportunities for Asian American performers. Forbidden City in San Francisco was the most infamous of them all.[29] Founded in the late 1930s by Charlie

---

[28] Hyun later found out that Kazan had given up and Lewis Leverett, another member of the Group Theater, directed the play. Hsiu-chen Lin Classon writes in an unpublished article that some of Hyun's recollections are inconsistent with the archival findings about the production of *The Revolt of the Beavers*. Classon provides a thorough examination of the contradictory facts, especially of the ones surrounding the question of who indeed deserved to be named as the director. Classon concludes: "What exactly happened during the long rehearsal process for *The Revolt of the Beavers* would probably remain unclear. But in Peter Hyun's mind, his ambition and passion for theatre was defeated by racial intolerance after his experience with *The Revolt of the Beavers*." Hsiu-chen Lin Classon, "Looking for Peter Hyun: A Korean American Director in New York in the 1930s," Unpublished paper, 19.

[29] See Lorraine Dong and Arthur Dong, "Chinese American Nightclubs: A Brief History," an introductory pamphlet included in the Collector's Edition of *Forbidden City U.S.A.* (1989) in DVD format. The video is an award-winning documentary film by Arthur Dong and features interviews with surviving performers of Forbidden City. For published studies, see: Lorraine Dong, "The Forbidden City Legacy and Its Chinese American Woman," in *Chinese America: History and Perspectives* (San Francisco: Chinese Historical Society of America, 1992), 126–148; Anthony W. Lee, "The Forbidden City," in *Picturing Chinatown: Art and Orientalism in San Francisco* (Berkeley: University of California Press, 2001), 237–285; Susan Waggoner, *Nightclub Nights: Art, Legend, and Style, 1920–1960* (New York: Rizzoli, 2001); and Judy Yung, *Unbound Feet: A Social History of Chinese Women in San Francisco* (Berkeley: University of California Press, 1995).

Low, Forbidden City was a restaurant and nightclub that featured singing, dancing, chorus lines, magicians, and other forms of entertainment.
As William Wei describes it, Forbidden City was the "Asian American
counterpart to the Cotton Club" that featured "rebels" challenging "segregated show business, with its stereotypes of Chinese as speaking only
pidgin English, having bowed legs and no rhythm."[30] It was a Chinatown
version of the "Cole Porter and Sophie Tucker, dancing tap, ballroom, and
soft-shoe, parodying Western musicals in cowboy outfits, and kicking it
up in chorus."[31]

Forbidden City marketed its shows to white audiences who found
the Chinese versions of popular entertainment novel and worth a trip to
San Francisco's Chinatown. Although the performers were multiethnic
(many were Japanese, Korean, and Filipino Americans), they were called
"Chinese Frank Sinatra," "Chinese Bing Crosby," "Chinese Ginger
Rogers," and "Chinese Sophie Tucker." And shows with titles such as
"Chinatown Fantasy" unabashedly capitalized on exoticism and orientalist
stereotypes. With catch phrases like "Come along with me please! I'll
show you how to have fun in Chinese" and "It's true what they say about
Chinese girls," Forbidden City enticed the public's imagination and played
to their assumptions about Asians, and especially about Asian women.
Moreover, female performers baring their legs – and sometimes everything else – attracted thousands of US soldiers who passed through San
Francisco during World War II. Often, many audience members who had
never seen Asians in their towns got their first impressions of "orientals"
upon watching the performances at such nightclubs.

The attack on Pearl Harbor by Japanese bombers in 1941 changed the
fate of Japanese American performers literally overnight. They were
forced, along with more than 120,000 Japanese Americans, to relocate to
internment camps designated by the Department of Justice. Justified as
a "military necessity," the mass relocation affected Japanese immigrants
and their children who were US citizens. All activities in the internment
camps centered on questions of loyalty and civil rights, and theatre was
no exception. Robert Cooperman, in his study of internment camp theatre, notes that theatrical productions at the camps were "primarily [. . .]
Western plays" with two significant purposes: (1) "a means to combat the
tedium of the internment camp experience"; and (2) to participate in the

---

[30] Wei, *The Asian American Movement*, 57.
[31] Yung, *Unbound Feet*, 202.

camp administration's education policies of speeding up "the assimilation of Japanese Americans into the dominant pattern of American life."[32] Internment camp theatre has been dismissed and even forgotten mainly because of its controversial emphasis on assimilation and accommodation, but it nevertheless produced a generation of Japanese Americans who would go on to have careers in theatre, film, and television. The late Yukio Shimoda (from Tule Lake camp) performed on Broadway in the 1950s and later supported Asian American theatre companies (for example, by acting in the East West Player's productions). Another case was that of the late Jack Soo (from Topaz camp), who changed his original name from Goro Suzuki after the war because he could not find employment in theatre with a Japanese last name.

The decade of the 1950s was kinder to Japanese Americans and other "oriental" actors, as Asia became less of a threat to the United States for reasons that included Japan's defeat. Broadway productions reflected this growing sympathy but also renewed colonialist curiosity for Asian characters. Indeed, the indisputable theatrical fad of the 1950s was the "oriental" shows featuring likeable Asian characters: *The King and I* (the longest running show in 1951), *The Teahouse of the August Moon* (the longest-running show in 1953), *The World of Suzie Wong* (the second longest running play in 1958), and *A Majority of One* (the second longest running play in 1959). While major roles continually went to white actors in yellow-face makeup, "oriental" actors of the 1950s had unprecedented opportunities to appear on Broadway. However, in all of these "oriental" shows Asian characters were foreigners while actors playing the roles were mostly US born.

In 1958, "oriental" actors finally got the chance to play major Asian American roles in Rogers and Hammerstein's musical *Flower Drum Song*. The musical was based on a novel by Chin Yang (C.Y.) Lee, a graduate of the Yale Drama School and addressed generational and cultural issues between the older Chinese immigrants and the US-born Chinese Americans. Set in San Francisco's Chinatown, the musical presented an idyllic community of Chinese Americans who celebrated the merging of American and Chinese elements in their culture. The story of *Flower Drum Song* features a Chinese American son of a conservative father

---

[32] Robert Cooperman, "The Americanization of Americans: The Phenomenon of Nisei Internment Camp Theater," in *Re/Collecting Early Asian America: Essays in Cultural History*, edited by Josephine Lee, Imogen L. Lim and Yuko Matsukawa (Philadelphia: Temple University Press), 326–328.

who wants his son to marry a "picture bride" from China. He wants his son to respect the Chinese tradition, but the son is more attracted to a stripper (who is Americanized and aggressive, unlike the shy picture bride) in a Chinatown nightclub. After much commotion, the sons chooses the picture bride, and the story ends happily for everyone.[33]

The musical presented a historic opportunity to Asian American actors, but it also perpetuated theatrical conventions that were too familiar. For one, in the Broadway version, the two leading female roles were played by Asian American actresses, Miyoshi Umeki and Pat Suzuki. But the central male character, the nightclub owner, Sammy Fong, was played by Larry Blyden, a Jewish American actor from Texas. (In the film version, the role was played by Jack Soo.) Such selective authenticity had been long accepted as the norm in American theatre. Another accepted convention was the conflation of different "oriental" ethnicities. For example, Miyoshi Umeki (who played the picture bride) was conspicuously Japanese in mannerism and speech, but she played a quintessentially Chinese lady. The mainstream audiences, however, did not seem to notice. Umeki fulfilled their expectations of a "real" Asian woman, one who is coy, feminine, and polite. In fact, Miyoshi Umeki and Pat Suzuki were on the cover of the *Time* magazine. The cover story describes Umeki and Suzuki as "the embodiment of the ancient, universal Chinese principles of Yang and Yin – the opposite of active and passive, sun and shadow, fire and water."[34]

Overall, ethnic and cultural specificities of Asian or Asian American actors did not matter as long as they "looked" oriental and satisfied social preconceptions and stereotypes. Indeed, the majority of the cast, in both the Broadway and film versions, were not Chinese American. While Asian American actors resisted most conventions (especially the practice of yellowface), they voluntarily participated in the categorization of "oriental" actors. They accepted the conflation of specific ethnicities for the purpose of gaining advantage in employment and popularity. In the 1930s,

---

[33] The musical production (both the stage version and the film version) of *Flower Drum Song* has received criticism for portraying Asian Americans as model minorities as envisioned by the mainstream Anglo-Americans. C. Y. Lee's original story, without singing and dancing, provides a more realistic view of the Chinatown immigrant community. Many Asian American theatre artists I interviewed expressed the view that *Flower Drum Song* inspired them to pursue careers in theatre and that it remains a "guilty pleasure" to watch the film version on video. In 2001, David Henry Hwang adapted the musical with an altered storyline while using the same music. The musical opened at the Mark Taper Forum and, in 2002, received a Broadway premiere at the Virginia Theatre.

[34] "Broadway: The Girls on Grant Avenue," *Time* (December 22, 1958), 43.

all of the performers at Forbidden City in San Francisco marketed themselves as "Chinese" when in fact many were Japanese, Korean, and Filipino Americans. It was for the same reason that Jack Soo changed his last name. Accordingly, the group of "oriental" actors in the 1950s dealt with racism in the industry by making a savvy compromise. With the label "oriental" actors, Asian American actors of all ethnic backgrounds found the artistic solidarity and political empowerment that became the foundation of Asian American theatre in the 1960s and 1970s.

2

Actors in the 1960s and 1970s

That's all there was, Bradley. That's all there was! But you don't think
I wouldn't have wanted to play a better role than that bucktoothed, grovel-
ing waiter? I would have killed for a better role where I could have played an
honest-to-god human being with real emotions. I would have killed for it.
You seem to assume "Asian Americans" always existed. That there were
always roles for you. You didn't exist back then buster. Back then there was
no Asian American consciousness, no Asian American actor, and no Asian
American theaters. Just a handful of "orientals" who for some god forsaken
reason wanted to perform. Act. And we did. At church bazaars, community
talent night, and on the Chop Suey Circuit playing Chinatowns and Little
Tokyos around the country as hoofers, jugglers, acrobats, strippers – anything we could for anyone who would watch. You, you with that holier than
thou look, trying to make me feel ashamed. You wouldn't be here if it
weren't for all the crap we had to put up with. We built something. We built
the mountain, as small as it may be, that you stand on so proudly looking
down at me.

Vincent in Yankee Dawg You Die by Philip Kan Gotanda[1]

As philip kan gotanda's character reminds us, "just a
handful of orientals" who wanted to act built the "mountain" that became
the foundation for Asian American theatre. Before there were Asian
American playwrights, directors, or theatre companies, there were "oriental" actors, and what they did during the 1960s and 1970s began a movement that became the institution of Asian American theatre. During the
1960s, the "oriental" actors faced a devastating prospect: the orientalist
fad of the 1950s had disappeared, and the war in Vietnam complicated
the representation of Asians on stage and screen. Virtually overnight,

---

[1] Philip Kan Gotanda, *Yankee Dawg You Die* (New York: Dramatist Play Services, Inc., 1991), 25–26.

"oriental" actors found themselves unemployed in large numbers.[2] They realized that a show like *Flower Drum Song* was a rarity on Broadway and that they could not depend on mainstream theatre, film, and television for their livelihood or artistic fulfillment. As Frank Ching describes in his *New York Times* article, they were determined to "fight for jobs and image."[3] The actors were keenly aware of the power of images in dramatic media and how those images directly affected their employment opportunities. They knew they were caught in a vicious cycle of typecasting and never received serious consideration for nonstereotypical roles because they lacked experience.

The first and toughest fight the actors faced was the perception of what was considered the "real" Asian in theatre, film, and television. On stage and screen, a "real" Asian was any number of popular stereotypes: a houseboy, butler, gardener, Japanese soldier in World War II, Kung Fu master, Charlie Chan's son, geisha, or dragon lady. "Real" Asians were also white actors in yellowface makeup. Every Asian American actor has an anecdote about being told by producers and directors that they were not "real" as "orientals" or Asians (i.e. that they were "too Asian" or "not Asian enough"). For example, when actor Makato Iwamatsu (Mako) auditioned in the early 1960s for the role of the Bandit in the television version of *Rashomon* to be filmed live in New York City, he believed he had a good chance. Although he had experienced consistent rejection in previous auditions because of his Asian look, Mako thought he was at an advantage with his Japanese background (he was born in Kobe, Japan in 1933) and solid acting training at the Pasadena Playhouse (which he attended on his GI Bill with Dustin Hoffman as a classmate). Thus, he could not believe his ears when the casting director of *Rashomon* told him, "You gave a great reading, but as a real Japanese, you'd be too conspicuous. All of the other actors are white made up to look Japanese."[4]

Seen as "too Asian" or "not Asian enough," actors such as Mako were caught in the complex web of racism, perception, representation, employment, and the inherently paradoxical nature of theatre (which, after all, is an illusion of reality). After over a hundred years of reinforcement, "oriental" stereotypes and white actors in yellowface were solidly cast as

---

[2] There were exceptions. For example, Sab Shimono appeared in the 1966 production of *Mame*, as the Japanese houseboy Ito.

[3] Frank Ching, "Asian American Actors Fight for Jobs and Image," *New York Times*, June 3, 1973, 65.

[4] Irvin Paik, "The East West Players: The First Ten Years are the Hardest," *Bridge: An Asian American Perspective* 5.2 (1977), 14.

the "real" and "authentic" archetypes in the minds of producers, directors, and audiences. This perception has not disappeared from American culture entirely, and Asian American actors are still asked to act more "ethnic" or speak with an accent for the sake of recreating a convincing "reality" for white Americans. However, it was in the 1960s and 1970s that Asian American actors decided to respond and take charge of their careers. The actors began by forming coalitions with three primary goals: (1) to protest "oriental" stereotypes; (2) to increase awareness of Asian American actors' wide-ranging talents; and (3) to demand that they be allowed to play all roles, both Asian and non-Asian.

The actors joined together to create a collective force in order to better market themselves, but there were notable exceptions. Randall Duk Kim, for instance, led a unique career path, refusing to align himself with other Asian American actors. A classically trained actor, Kim debuted as Malcolm in *Macbeth* at the age of eighteen in his native home Hawaii and continued to perform in plays by Molière, Chekhov, Brecht, O'Neill, and other European and American writers. He is a distinguished Shakespearean actor, having played title roles in Shakespeare's *Pericles* at the New York Shakespeare Festival in 1974 and *Hamlet* at the Guthrie Theater in 1978. He also co-founded the American Players Theater, in Spring Green, Wisconsin.[5] Although he appeared in Frank Chin's *Chickencoop Chinaman* in 1972 in New York City, Kim did not participate in the political and artistic coalition formed by other Asian American actors.

The actors' activism broadly coincided with the Asian American Movement (which emerged in the late 1960s) and implemented the spirit of the civil rights movement by joining forces for equal rights for all members of society. What brought Asian American actors together, as Sung Hee Choi points out, was "not a common political or aesthetic belief but their *personal* experiences – the shared treatment and frustration they experienced in the theatre and film industry."[6] Actors of wide-ranging background (by ethnicity or acting experience) came together because of the shared experiences of being treated as "oriental" actors. The actors' activism resembled the civil rights and later women's rights movements, which emphasized the transformation of personal issues into political activism through coalitions. Moreover, as a group, the actors identified themselves racially (Asian) rather than ethnically (Chinese, Japanese, etc.),

---

[5] See Mary Z. Maher, "Randall Duk Kim: Sir, a Whole History," *Modern Hamlet and Their Soliloquies* (Iowa City: Iowa University Press, 1992), 153–174. Also see www.randalldukkim.com

[6] Sung Hee Choi, *Performing the Other: Asians on the New York Stage Before 1970* (PhD dissertation: University of Maryland, 1999), 212. Original emphasis

as did other minority groups in the 1960s for group rights and recognition.[7] Actors turned their personal frustrations into artistic and political activism and agreed to "fight for jobs and image" together.

During the 1960s and 1970s, several Asian American actors' coalitions were formed. Many disappeared as quickly as they appeared, but two groups made their mark in history with different purposes and results: the East West Players (Los Angeles) and the Oriental Actors of America (New York City). The East West Players (EWP) began as an "oriental" actors' group that wanted to showcase their talents to Hollywood producers, but thirty years later, it had become an Asian American regional theatre company, the only one of its kind in the country.[8] The Oriental Actors of America (OAA) focused mainly on political activism and networking among its members and eventually succeeded in educating the New York City theatre community. Partly because of OAA's activism, Stephen Sondheim's *Pacific Overtures* in 1976 featured an all-Asian American cast (even for non-Asian roles), the first Broadway show to do so.

The beginning of the East West Players

In the early 1960s, Hollywood actors James Hong and Beulah Quo knew the problems of "oriental actors" better than anyone. "I'm tired of doing the 'ching chong Chinaman' bit," Hong told Quo while they were driving to a theatre in Anaheim, California, where both were appearing in the play *The World of Suzie Wong*. Quo replied, "The opportunities are so scarce for us that we will never realize our full potential."[9] Quo had participated in an acting workshop for Asian actors taught by David Alexander, who repeatedly urged Quo and other participants to form an Asian American group. Hong had presented successful productions of Chinese Medicine shows in Chinatown in Los Angeles, and he was looking for another opportunity to make his acting career more meaningful. Thus, the two, and a few others, began discussing the possibility of forming a group for Asian American actors. The purpose was to create a venue for demonstrating their acting abilities to Hollywood producers

---

[7] See Yen Le Espiritu, *Asian American Panethnicity* (Philadelphia: Temple University Press, 1992), for a study on the formation of "reactive solidarities" and self-identification in racial and panethnic terms.

[8] By regional theatre, I am referring to the Equity level theatres that have more than ninety-nine seats.

[9] Paik, "The East West Players," 14.

and non-Asian audiences and for improving their image as actors. This exposure, they thought, would bring them better roles.

Hong began to inquire about other actors who could participate in the group, and with the help of El Huang (who had been a leading dancer in *Flower Drum Song*), identified several people, including Mako, Pat Li, Guy Lee, Rae Creevey, Irvin Paik, George Takei, and Soon-Tek Oh.[10] After being turned down for the role in *Rashomon* in New York, Mako had appeared in an Off-Broadway production of *A Majority of One* and had toured with the show nationally. When Hong called him, Mako responded positively to the idea of forming an Asian American theatre group because, he said, he "wanted to disprove the myth that Chinese and Japanese actors could never work together."[11] The members decided to produce *Rashomon*, which was not only a popular play at the time, but also represented the spirit of what the actors wanted to do: "the fusion of Eastern and Western cultures."[12] Jade Hong, James Hong's sister, came up with the name "East West Players" for the group.

Although the EWP was fortunate in finding a performance space at Bovard Auditorium at the University of Southern California (USC) with the help of its Asian Studies Program, the actors nevertheless faced various stylistic differences. Once the rehearsals started and the cast was selected, the "Hollywood group" of actors expressed dissatisfaction with Roma Satterfield, the director brought in by Mako. Her style of directing was foreign to film actors. Satterfield stepped down, and Norman Gerard was hired to replace her. Things did not improve much with Gerard. According to Rae Creevey (who had served as the lighting designer for James Hong's variety shows and was a co-founder of the EWP), many actors had difficulty memorizing lines and following Gerard's "wild directorial theatrics."[13] The production, nevertheless, was presented once as planned at USC on April 3, 1965 and received encouraging reviews from the critics.

However, the tension between film actors and stage actors escalated, and some actors left the group. Personnel changes were made, and at the request of Mako, Beulah Quo became the producer. George Takei also left the group in order to join the cast of "Star Trek" as one of very few Asian characters on television in the 1960s. Soon-Tek Oh replaced him

[10] Yuko Kurahashi, *Asian American Culture on Stage: The History of the East West Players* (New York: Garland Publishing, Inc., 1999), 16.
[11] Paik, "The East West Players," 14.
[12] Kurahashi, *Asian American Culture*, 21.
[13] Paik, "The East West Players," 14.

in the role of the Husband in *Rashomon*. After other cast changes, the group presented nine additional performances at the University of Judaism Theater in Hollywood. Again, the reviews were positive, especially of Mako's performance in the role of the Bandit. The members decided to pursue a commercial venue and in July 1965 moved the production to the Warner Playhouse, where it ran for six more weeks (four performances per week). Unfortunately, the run was cut short when the Watts riot erupted in Los Angeles. A few months later, performances continued at the Los Angeles County Museum as part of the exhibit of National Treasures from Japan.

While most actors thought of the group as a steppingstone towards better jobs in film and television (hoping for a break like George Takei's), Mako insisted on rigorous acting training. He strongly believed that quality acting was the best weapon against "oriental" stereotypes and wanted to shape the EWP into a repertory theatre with a "solid foundation in workshop":

> By this time I already sensed that the average level of acting ability was very low or sub-par for Asian American actors in general. So I said "let's get [a] workshop going." A lot of people didn't really care for it. I guess they're too lazy to study because being a TV or movie actor, you know the lines, have some idea about the character you're working with and you can get by. But I chose acting as my profession, my career, and I just didn't want to waste the momentum that we had started.[14]

Although some actors objected because they wanted a more experienced acting teacher, Mako taught the first acting classes at the EWP. Mako had received his training from some of the best acting teachers in Los Angeles and New York City and professed to understand "Stanislavsky's method as taught by Lee Strasberg," through the teaching of Nora Chilton, and maintained: "My reason for teaching was to share what she had opened up for me."[15] As the acting teacher, Mako's prominence and leadership at the EWP began to increase.

In fact, Mako's role as the leader of the group became even more obvious when he received a nomination for Best Supporting Actor Award by the Academy of Motion Picture Arts and Sciences for his role in the film *The Sand Pebbles* (1966). Robert Wise, the producer of the film, saw the EWP production of *Rashomon* and "discovered" Mako, James Hong, and Beaulah Quo for the film. Ironically, Mako (who had insisted on

---

[14] Ibid.
[15] Ibid. 16.

theatre acting training) became the "star" Asian American film actor and eventually the first artistic director of the EWP. The publicity created around Mako and the EWP brought administrative organization within the company and support from financial sources and the community. As I discuss in Chapter 3, Mako led the EWP for the next two decades, during which the company continued to serve Asian American actors by showcasing their performances. But also during his tenure, the EWP became the premier Asian American theatre company in a more encompassing way by consistently supporting original plays and developing local audiences.

Oriental Actors of America, New York City

The decade of the 1960s was difficult for Asian American actors in New York City. Unlike African American actors who made advancements on Broadway in shows like Lorraine Hansberry's *Raisin in the Sun* (1959), Asian American actors were virtually invisible on New York City stages. Moreover, the practice of blackface performance had disappeared for good, but white actors in yellowface makeup continued to play Asian parts without giving it a second thought. Experienced Asian American actors knew they deserved better, and they had to do something about it. On March 3, 1968, a group of such actors made two announcements: (1) the formation of an organization called "Oriental Actors of America" whose purpose was to protest yellowface practices and to promote "greater use of Oriental talents"; and (2) the intention to picket the opening of *Here's Where I Belong* (a Broadway musical adaptation of *East of Eden* by John Steinbeck) at the Billy Rose Theater.[16] The organization, according to co-chairman Alvin Lum, objected to the white actor playing the role of a Chinese servant character. The picketing received a short mentioning in *Variety*, which concluded that "on the basis of the show, [OAA] had a point."[17] Receiving poor reviews, the musical closed after one performance,

---

[16] I give special thanks to my research assistant, Clara Mee-Young Shim, for researching articles and clippings on Oriental Actors of America. There never was any major reporting on the organization, and all announcements were briefly and randomly mentioned in various newspapers. This required careful (and eye-straining) screening of dozens of back issues in microfilm format. The announcement of the OAA's formation appeared in the March 4, 1968 issue of *The Reporter* magazine.

[17] "Here's Where I Belong," *Variety* (March 6, 1968), 73. The entire passage reads: "Incidentally, members of an organization called Oriental Actors of America picketed the theatre before the premiere to protest the employment of an Occidental in an Oriental role. On the basis of the show, they had a point."

Figure 1. The 1968 picketing of *Here's Where I Belong* at the Billy Rose Theater by the Oriental Actors of America. One of the posters read "Oriental-American Actors Demand an Open Door Policy in the American Theatre."

so OAA did not have to continue the picketing. However, the organization was formed, and the members kept a lookout for other practices of yellowface on Broadway.

They didn't have to look very far or wait long. On May 22, 1968, OAA issued a press release through their representative, Milton Rubin Associates, stating their plan to picket the opening of *The King and I* at New York City Center the following day. The demonstration was organized by OAA and supported by the Ethnic Minority Committee of the Actors' Equity Association, the Joint Equality Committee of the American Federation of Television and Radio Artists and the Screen Actors' Guild, and others. According to the press release, OAA's main complaint was that out of nine Asian parts in the musical, eight were cast with Caucasian actors. Even the understudy roles, with one exception were given to non-Asians. They also protested the stereotypes in the musical. In addition to the picketing (which was to continue throughout the show's run), OAA filed formal protests to Mayor John Lindsay, the City Council, and the city and state commissions on human rights. They emphasized that the City Center was a civic project paid for with the tax money of all New Yorkers, including Asians. The press release also stated that the creators of the show (Jean Dalrymple, director of City Center, Richard Rodgers, composer of *King and I*, John Fearnley, director, and Jonathan Anderson, musical director) responded to OAA's complaints with "lame excuses about 'pre-casting.'"[18] Alvin Lum cited that "the unemployment rate among our members is the highest in the show business" because producers and casting directors do not think of Asian Americans in parts that have "nothing to do with skin color" despite the fact that they are found in "every walk of life as professionals, doctors, teachers, art directors, scientists, reporters, and bankers." They expressed their complaints with signs that read: "Open Door Policy in the American theater"; "'A Puzzlement' – Why Doesn't Richard Rodgers Cast Orientals in Oriental Roles?"; "Down With Token Integration of Oriental-American Actors in the American Theater"; "If Caucasians Are Given Oriental Roles, Why Doesn't It Work Both Ways"; "Mr. Rodgers: Save On Yellow Greasepaint and Black Wigs – Hire Orientals"; "Mr. Rodgers: 'Something Wonderful' Would be Ending Bias Toward Oriental-American Actors"; "N. Y. City Center Should Not be a Center of Discrimination."

The members of Oriental Actors of America and actors of other racial backgrounds continued to picket, but their demands were not heard. Performances went on with yellowface, but they didn't give up. In August of 1970, OAA resurfaced to protest the casting decisions at the Repertory Theater of Lincoln Center. This time, the members made sure the issue did not go away when the show ended; they began a battle that would last three years by turning to the city and state's human rights commissions. It began when the repertory held its audition for *Lovely Ladies, Kind Gentleman*, a musical adaptation of *Teahouse of August Moon*. The musical called for at least forty-five Okinawan characters, including the lead role, Sakini. Asian American actors noticed that they were not given the chance to audition for the main roles, and non-Asian actors freely auditioned for the minor Asian roles.

As soon as the actors noticed discrimination and racism, they voiced their complaint to the repertory and repeatedly requested open auditions for the main roles. But, they were repeatedly denied. Several talented

---

[18] Oriental Actors of America, "Press Release" (May 22, 1968), 1. All quotes in this paragraph are from this press release. The press release is archived in the clipping file under the heading "Oriental Actors of America" at the New York Public Library for the Performing Arts.

Asian American actors, including Jack Soo, James Shigeta, and Mako, wanted to audition for the role of Sakini, but they were not even given the chance. The repertory announced the final casting decision: the role of Sakini would be played by the white actor Kenneth Nelson and only twelve out of forty-five Asian roles went to Asian American actors, making yellowface inevitable. In response to the decision, OAA members decided to protest what they considered "unfair employment practices of the new production," even though they were not necessarily against the content of the show.[19] They picketed the office of Herman Levin, the artistic director of the Repertory Theater, for failing to audition a single Asian American actor for a lead role and for "tokenism in casting other roles."[20]

The musical was to tour nationally to Philadelphia, Los Angeles, and San Francisco before opening in New York City in December 1970. Accordingly, OAA decided to coordinate a national protest with the help of other minority actors' organizations such as the Brotherhood of Artists and the East West Players. About 127 professional actors of Asian descent joined the New York City based group. The protests followed wherever the musical opened in the country. For instance, on August 19, 1970, the Philadelphia premiere was marred by OAA's protest outside of the Shubert Theater. Benjamin Lin, who organized the protest, describes the evening as a typical "lazy calm" summer evening "shattered by gongs, cymbals, and low, rhythmic drum beating":

> In front of the theater, a Chinese lion began prancing up and down the sidewalk. Passers-by looked upon the spectacle with amusement and curiosity and probably thought everything was as it should be. After all, the show . . . had an Oriental setting. It would only be fitting to mark the grand opening with an air of Oriental festivity. However, they were soon surprised to see a group of Orientals marching around in a circle, carrying placards such as "Asian American Actors Want Equal Opportunity," "Herman Levin Unfair to Oriental Actors," "Orientals for Oriental Roles," "Tokenism Is Not Equality," and "End Adhesive Tape Orientals." And, in accord with established custom at all demonstrations, flyers were passed out to all receptive hands.[21]

[19] Benjamin Lin, "Adhesive Tape Orientals: The Use of Tape by White Actors to Portray Asians is Odious," *Bridge: An Asian American Perspective* 2.3 (1973), 7. This distinction is repeated in the Miss Saigon protest. See Chapter 7.
[20] "Asian Actors Angry Over Musical Roles," *New York Times*, August 7, 1970, 28.
[21] Lin, "Adhesive Tape Orientals," 7.

For the first time in the history of Philadelphia, Asian Americans were out in the street protesting injustice, but the crowd was not large. Lin solicited support from other theatre groups, Asian organizations in Philadelphia, and various civil-rights groups, but only twenty people showed up to protest on the opening night. Ten OAA members from New York joined the protest. However, even with the small number, the protest caused quite a stir, attracting local radio and television reporters and the police. According to Lin, things got a bit heated as curtain time drew near: "There was consternation and anger on people's faces and a number of them heaped verbal abuse on us. One man was on the verge of striking one of our pickets after a particularly hot exchange. Many who paid $7 to $10 to see a show about the Orient paradoxically avoided us like the plague and stubbornly refused our leaflets."[22] While some showed sympathy and support (including a black actress who joined the picketing), most audience members were either upset by, or apathetic towards, the protest.

The following day, the protest was featured on front-pages of the *Evening Bulletin* and *Philadelphia Tribune*. Levin responded to the protesters through the press by denying that "he had refused to audition Oriental actors for the Sakini role," which was in direct contradiction to the affidavits filed by Mako, Soo, and Shigeta stating otherwise.[23] He argued that the protesters were "racially-minded in seeking Oriental roles for Orientals" and charged them of "reverse racism."[24] Although it was rumored that Levin might ultimately audition Mako, Soo, and Shigeta, the show went on with Nelson in yellowface. Toward the end of the show's run, the Philadelphia protest lost much of its steam, and the members decided to forego picketing. Instead, they released a letter to the press and sought less militant options.

The Philadelphia protest ended quietly, but when the show went to Los Angeles (for eight weeks) and then to San Francisco (for seven weeks), the picketing by Asian American actors resumed. The show came back to New York City on December 28, 1970. The New York City production included Asian American actors Tisa Chang, Sab Shimono, Lori Chinn, Sachi Shimizu, and Alvin Lum, some of who were members of OAA. These actors had the difficult job of protesting yellowface in the show while acting along side fake Asian characters played by white actors. Incidentally, another Lincoln Center production featuring yellowface had come and

---

[22] Ibid, 9.
[23] Ibid.
[24] Ibid.

gone while the musical was on its national tour. Bertold Brecht's *Good Woman of Setzuan* opened on November 5, 1970, and closed on December 15, 1970, angering the members of OAA, who believed that their protest against the Lincoln Center and the tour of *Lovely Ladies, Kind Gentleman* had absolutely no effect. Although Brecht's play does not profess to be an authentic story about Asians but tells an allegorical story using a mythical province called "Setzuan," the casting of non-Asians in roles with Chinese names upset Asian American actors who were already sensitive about yellowface at Lincoln Center. Realizing that their protest was falling on deaf ears, the members of OAA decided to file a formal complaint with the Actors' Equity Association and New York State Division on Human Rights.

In January 1972, yet another production by the Repertory Theater of Lincoln Center opened with white actors playing Asian parts. Again, the Asian American actors protested against the play on the opening night. This time, the play was set in Japan in the 1700s; most of the characters were Japanese, and all of them were played by white or black actors. Written by British playwright Edward Bond, the play *Narrow Road to Deep North* was based on a Matsuo Basho poem, "The Records of a Weather-Exposed Skeleton," which is about the rise and fall of a dictator. Similar to *The Good Woman of Setzuan, Narrow Road to Deep North* combined an Orientalized background with what Clive Barnes calls "Brechtian simplicity."[25] In other words, the Japanese setting allowed the director to create a kind of solemnity and distance to tell a moralist story. The reviews for the production were severely negative. *Variety* advised its readers not to return for the second act, and Clive Barnes found it "distressingly tedious."[26] Barnes was most disturbed by the acting. He found the actors playing the principal Japanese characters miscast but did not mention cross-racial casting as a contributing factor.

New York City reviewers, including Clive Barnes, did not mention the protest by Asian American actors on the opening night of *Narrow Road*, but it would have been impossible for them to not have noticed the crowd and noise. It would have also been impossible to ignore the emerging Asian American theatre artists such as Ping Chong and Frank Chin, both of who would debut their first works in New York City in 1972. Moreover, the increasing discussions of racial equality in the country began to affect the mainstream theatre community. Taking advantage of the changing

---

[25] Clive Barnes, "Stage: Narrow Road," *New York Times,* January 7, 1972, 27.
[26] Ibid.

momentum, the members of OAA made sure their complaint would be heard and real changes would take place.

Represented by Alvin Lum, Sab Shimono, Calvin Jung, Lori Chinn, Katie San, and Irene Sun, the OAA accused the Repertory Theater of Lincoln Center of discrimination in a complaint filed with the New York State Division of Human Rights. They contended that the shows, *The Good Woman of Setzuan, Lovely Ladies, Kind Gentlemen,* and *Narrow Road to Deep North,* had "Oriental themes and characters, which required preferential casting of Oriental actors."[27] The case became "Sab Shimono et al vs. the Repertory Theater of Lincoln Center," and the first hearing took place on September 7, 1972. Without much publicity, the Asian American actors lost the case, and they immediately decided to appeal and send the case to the New York State Human Rights Appeal Board.

Almost a year later, the actors felt vindicated when in early June 1973 the Appeal Board reversed the earlier ruling and found the Repertory Theater of Lincoln Center guilty of discrimination. It was a unanimous decision by the four-member board. It stated that the Repertory Theater of Lincoln Center "systematically failed or refused to give equal opportunity" to Asian American actors, "particularly as evidenced by the regular awarding of Oriental parts to non-Oriental actors."[28] According to Frank Ching, who wrote an article about the ruling for *The New York Times,* Albert S. Pacetta, a member of the appeals board expressed that the decision took in "not just Lincoln Center but the theater industry – films, legitimate theater and the entertainment industry."[29] Pacetta cited examples of how the exclusion of Asians from theatre signified not only job discrimination but also the reinforcement of negative stereotypes. With this ruling, Pacetta hoped to put "enough pressure" on the theatre community to "give due consideration to Oriental actors, particularly, but not exclusively, for Oriental parts."[30] The appeal board's ruling was indeed a victory for the Oriental Actors of America. Five years after its foundation and after numerous pickets, the voice of its members was finally heard.

However, the ruling was not without a catch. The appeal board ordered the State Division of Human Rights to hold a public hearing to "establish facts in the case."[31] The Repertory Theater of Lincoln Center at the time

---

[27] Margarita Rosa, "Asian Actors Lost in a '73 *Miss Saigon* Case," *New York Times,* September 28, 1990, 26.
[28] Ching, "Asian American Actors," 65.
[29] Ibid.
[30] Ibid.
[31] Rosa, "Asian Actors," 26.

was in the process of closing for good, but it received support from some powerful figures in the New York theatre community. For example, Clive Barnes of *The New York Times* testified as an "expert witness" that "while the plays had Oriental settings . . . they were not Oriental plays, but universal parables, and did not require preference for Oriental actors."[32] Julian Olf, another "expert witness" stated "a director should be free to interpret, cast and present a play according to his own artistic concept."[33] Although Asian Americans argued their side and cited years of discrimination by Lincoln Center, they did not have much support from mainstream theatre. Finally, Commissioner Werner Kramarsky of the Division ruled that the Repertory Theater of Lincoln Center was "exercising legitimate artistic judgment, and [was] not motivated by considerations of race or national origin" in casting for the plays and, finally, dismissed the case citing "insufficient evidence to prove discrimination."[34]

Pacific Overtures

The efforts of the Oriental Actors of America did not go totally unrecognized, and in 1976, Asian American actors finally got their break on Broadway. Harold Prince, a successful and influential Broadway director, decided to cast the new Stephen Sondheim musical, *Pacific Overtures*, with Asian American actors in all roles, including white characters. (And he made the distinction between Asian and Asian American actors, maintaining that his cast be comprised of Americans of Asian descent.) *Pacific Overtures* tells the story of the opening of Japan to the West, from the arrival of Commodore Matthew Perry of the US Navy in Tokyo Bay in 1853 to the modernized Japan of 1975. The Prince-Sondheim concept was intellectual, radical, and risky. It featured Kabuki styles of acting and choreography, Japanese pentatonic scales in the music, and English-speaking Asian American actors (mostly male) without much Broadway experience. Prince and Sondheim did not want to create another *Madame Butterfly* or *The King and I*, which they thought were Western treatments of Eastern subjects. According to Sondheim, *Pacific Overtures* had to capture the conflict between East and West: "it's a musical as if written by a Japanese playwright who has been to New York, seen a couple of musicals and who primarily brought his own cultural background into

---

[32] Ibid.
[33] Ibid.
[34] Ibid.

force."[35] Prince and Sondheim did not pretend to be experts on Japan or attempt to represent the most realistic story about Japan; they experimented freely with contradictory styles and concepts.

When it came to casting, Harold Prince faced the challenge of finding Asian American actors to fill all sixty-one parts. Because he wanted to keep the Kabuki tradition of males playing female parts, he sought mostly male Asian American actors who could sing, dance, and act. Asian American actresses had been seen on Broadway in shows like *Flower Drum Song* and *The World of Suzie Wong*, but no show had demanded male actors in large numbers or featured them in principal roles. When the musical opened in January 1976 with nineteen actors playing all parts, every established Asian American actor had been auditioned and selected. The cast read like an all-star list of Asian American male actors: Mako, Soon-Tek Oh, Sab Shimono, Yuki Shimoda, Alvin Ing, Ernest Abuba, Gedde Watanabe, Ernest Harada. A total of thirty Asian Americans plus one non-Asian American actor (Isao Sato, a Japanese actor) made up the company.[36] According to Harold Prince, it took "a year and half and three different people making seven different trips to the West Coast" to put the company together.[37] The casting director Joanna Merlin had the difficult task of seeking out talent and leaving "no stone unturned in hunting for Asian Americans."[38] They saw about 250 actors around the country and continued to audition after the show opened because some actors were coming down with the flu during the run. Despite the difficulties and suggestions that he audition Puerto Rican actors "who look Oriental," Prince stayed committed to keeping the cast Asian American: "This is an American musical done by Americans playing Asian roles, and that's intentional."[39]

The critics and audiences did not know how to respond to *Pacific Overtures*, and the musical never gained popularity like previous Prince-Sondheim shows. But, for Asian American actors, it was a landmark opportunity. Some were nonprofessionals who performed on stage for the first time, Gedde Watanabe was "found" on a street in San Francisco

[35] "Roy Pannell Talks to Composer and Lyricist Stephen Sondheim," *The Stage and Television Today* (London), November 27, 1975, 10.
[36] According to some actors, James Dybas was not Asian American but claimed that he was in order to be in the show. Asian American actresses included Kim Miyori, Diane Lam, and Susan Kikuchi.
[37] Lillian Ross, "Meetings," *New Yorker*, March 22, 1976, 24.
[38] Ibid.
[39] Ibid., 27.

Figure 2. The casting director Joanna Merlin (left) with the cast of *Pacific Overtures* in front of the Winter Garden in 1976. At the front of the line is Mako with Soon-Tek Oh behind him.

where he was making a living as a street singer.[40] (Watanabe would go on to have a successful career as an actor, appearing for instance in the film *Sixteen Candles* and the television drama *ER.*) Harold Prince stated that the musical was the hardest show he had had to cast, but the audition process had brought to the surface many Asian American actors. Prince practiced his artistic freedom to reverse the racial hegemony in American theatre by having Asian Americans play all roles, Asian and non-Asian. And all this happened only three years after the State Division of Human Rights had ruled that Asian American actors did not have a case against the Repertory Theater of Lincoln Center.

Asian American actors had reason to celebrate, but they also knew better than anyone else that, as a group, they were small in number and weak in experience and training. The fact that only one of them showed up to the original Equity call for auditions for *Pacific Overtures* demonstrated their defeatist mentality. According to Alvin Lum (who was at the time chairman of the Ethnic Minorities Committee of Actors' Equity Association) the reason for this poor showing may simply have been that Asian

---

[40] Edward Hausner, "Overtures Opens Door for Orientals," *New York Times*, March 2, 1976, 24.

American actors had given up. Because so many Asian roles had gone to non-Asians, they did not think they had any chance; many had stopped trying and simply left the profession. Those who performed in *Pacific Overtures* knew that the show was an once-in-a-lifetime opportunity to jumpstart the careers of Asian American actors. More than ever, they had to support each other and be sure they were ready professionally.

"Asian American Actors"

After *Pacific Overtures* closed, the members of Oriental Actors of America decided to take a different path with their protest. They continued to challenge the ruling of the State Division of Human Rights but decided to change the name of the organization to Theater for Asian American Performing Artists (TAAPA). While the name "Oriental Actors of America" remained on paper in the continuing appeal case against the Repertory Theater of Lincoln Center, it became obvious that "Asian American" had become a more appropriate identifier. Like OAA, TAAPA focused on protesting racial stereotypes and promoting job opportunities for Asian American actors. Led by Alvin Ing and Catherine Okada Robin, the group was best known for performing a series of skits during the US Commission on Civil Rights hearings in New York City.[41] Skits were created in collaboration with the Asian Americans for Fair Media and depicted racial stereotypes of Asians and Asian Americans. TAAPA eventually developed a revue titled "Asian American Blues" based on the skits performed at the hearings. The group performed the revue in the outdoor plaza of Lincoln Center, the Japan Society, and other venues in New York City. TAAPA had the potential and ambition to grow into a company similar to the East West Players in Los Angeles, but in its developing years internal conflicts plagued the unity and eventually caused the breakup of the group in 1977.[42]

---

[41] A report titled "Window Dressing on the Set" came out in 1977 from the hearings. It looked at employment data of women and minorities in television shows and commercials from 1975 to 1977. The report concluded: "The virtual absence from the television screen of minorities other than blacks suggests to the general viewing public that these minorities constitute an insignificant presence in this nation." It also pointed out, "With few exceptions, Asian and Pacific Island Americans are seldom seen as continuing characters in dramatic roles." See Tom Shales, "Unlocking Doors To Those Rooms at the Top," *The Washington Post*, August 21, 1977, F1

[42] Members of TAAPA are still upset about the events that led to the breakup, and most of them would not speak about what actually happened. I could only gather from various sources that it all started when some actors from Hollywood joined the group. They "took over" the group by bringing their friends to a meeting and voting out the founding members, including Alvin Ing

Mako's presence during and after the run of *Pacific Overtures* had significant influence on the creation of TAAPA and other organizations in New York City. He saw that the musical inspired younger Asian Americans to enter the profession of theatre. He remained committed to training actors as he had done since the early years of the East West Players. In New York City, while he was appearing in *Pacific Overtures*, he co-founded a group called the Basement Theater Workshop at the Basement Workshop's loft on Lafayette Street. At the request of interested Asian Americans, Mako taught acting to both experienced actors and young hopefuls for six months. One of the participants, David Oyama, wrote in 1977 that the members worked to create "a program of Asian American scenes, mainly conceived and written by workshop participants" and presented their work in August 1976.[43] Mako subsequently left New York City to perform in the national tour of *Pacific Overtures*, and the acting workshops were conducted by Randall Duk Kim and Ernest Abuba. The workshop also collaborated with other artists, including members of the Asian American Dance Theater in New York City. However, several factors led the group to disband in 1977. For one, the landlord of the Basement Theater Workshop's seventh-floor loft enforced a clause in the lease that did not allow any elevator usage in the evenings. Adding to the problem was the cancellation of the socialist drama *Roar China* by the Russian playwright Sergei Tretiakov. Led by Ernest Abuba, the ambitious production required over thirty actors. The workshop did not have the resources (lacking even enough actors to fill the parts) to mount the play, and the cancellation, along with the elevator problem, led to the closing of the workshop.

Around the same time that the Basement Theater Workshop closed, the Theater for Asian American Performing Artists (TAAPA) had also disbanded, and many Asian American actors in New York City decided to move to Los Angeles to seek opportunities in film and television. According to Sab Shimono, the decision came easily because the Hollywood actors in *Pacific Overtures* had agents and some idea of where their next jobs would be. At the time, Shimono had no agent and never imagined life outside of theatre. After talking to actors such as Soon-Tek Oh, he found

and Sab Shimono. They then took possession of the group's checkbook and budget and disappeared. I have not heard all sides of the story, so I have no way of verifying this version. However, the group did break up when the new members from the West Coast joined.
[43] David Oyama, "The New York Scene: Varied But Clear," *Bridge: An Asian American Perspective* 5.2 (1977), 12.

an agent in Hollywood. By the end of the 1970s, many New York City Asian American actors and former members of OAA had gathered in Los Angeles. Some went on to found their own groups with purposes similar to the Oriental Actors of America, while others used the East West Players as their base. And some, like Ernest Abuba, remained in New York City to continue the mission of OAA in groups like the Pan Asian Repertory Theatre.

In two decades, the 1960s and 1970s, actors such as Mako and Sab Shimono shed the label "oriental actors" and took on "Asian American actors." As the new generation of Asian American actors emerged in the late 1970s and early 1980s, they had already paved the ways for better employment opportunities, professional training, and community support. They had also let the country know that yellowface was offensive to Asian Americans. Although demeaning stereotypes of Asians continued to appear in theatre and on film, and television (and many Asian American actors played those roles), they found ways to balance their long-term goals and immediate financial stability. Many acted the stereotypical roles in order to learn enough to act in bona fide Asian American plays. Experienced in both picketing and acting, these actors managed to stay in the industry by understanding what they needed to do and how. They were not always political and some did compromise their integrity, but as a group, their activism never ceased. Asian American actors had become the fuel that would empower the movement of Asian American theatre.

3

The first four theatre companies

[Asian American Theatre Workshop] is the first Asian American theater to start with a vision of Asian American theater. And to be quick and dirty about it, we started with a vision of Asian American theater because I started this group.

Frank Chin[1]

I started Asian American theatre in New York.

Ellen Stewart[2]

THE FIRST FOUR ASIAN AMERICAN THEATRE COMPANIES WERE the East West Players (Los Angeles), Asian American Theater Company (initially called Asian American Theatre Workshop, San Francisco), Northwest Asian American Theatre (initially called Theatrical Ensemble of Asians, Seattle), and Pan Asian Repertory Theatre (New York City). Each company has a unique history because of the specific sociocultural environment and geographical location. The founders' distinct visions of Asian American theater also contributed to the differences. The East West Players (EWP) has continued to focus on the advancement of Asian American actors while the Asian American Theater Company (AATC) has honored its founder, the playwright Frank Chin who wanted the company to function as a writers' workshop. The Northwest Asian American Theater (NWAAT) found a niche in Seattle as a community-based group, and the

---

[1] Frank Chin, Letter to the Board of Directors (November 16, 1976), 1. The Asian American Theater Company Archive, California Ethnic and Multicultural Archives at the Special Collections Library, University of California, Santa Barbara.

[2] Quoted in Alvin Eng, "'Some Place to be Somebody': La MaMa's Ellen Stewart," in *The Color of Theater: Race, Culture, and Contemporary Performance*, edited by Roberta Uno and Lucy Mae San Pablo Burns (New York: Continuum, 2002), 135.

Pan Asian Repertory Theatre (PART) has been shaped by its founder, an artistic director who wanted to establish Asian American theatre in the competitive theatre capital of the United States, New York City.

All four companies have had the same goal: to create a space for the development and expression of Asian American theatre. The specific ways to achieve that goal have differed, however. The founders and subsequent leaders of the companies have debated the fundamental questions about Asian American theatre. What is its purpose? Does it exist to train Asian American actors? Should an Asian American theatre company produce only Asian American plays or could it also present Western canonical works? Should Asian Americans avoid Asian theatre, traditional or contemporary, and push to be part of American theatre? Is the ultimate goal of Asian American theatre total inclusion into American theatre (which implies the eventual disappearance of Asian American theatre)? Which community does Asian American theatre serve: established communities such as Little Tokyo in Los Angeles or recent immigrant communities? What is gained or lost by subscribing to the agendas of multiculturalism?

There are no simple answers to these questions, and the companies have had to constantly adapt and evolve over three decades. At one point or another, all four companies faced difficult times when survival was on the line, and the questions often led to intense disagreements among members. Many left, hurt or burned out (or both), and many gave everything they had, including youth, time and money. Some who worked together no longer talk to each other, and some vow never to work for another Asian American theatre company. But some have become best friends, spouses, and successful collaborators.

Asian American theatre became established as an institution because of the first four companies. Their continued existence for over three decades further demonstrates the significant influence they have had on shaping the direction of Asian American theatre. A comprehensive history of the four companies requires a separate book-length study. In this chapter, I provide a brief overview of the companies with a focus on founding agendas, major leaders, key challenges, and the ways in which they shaped the emerging definitions of Asian American theatre in the 1960s and 1970s.

East West Players, Los Angeles

In 1967, the EWP officially became a nonprofit cultural organization. First, an honorary board was established, and the members elected themselves to the new board of directors as well as to the artistic staff. Beulah Quo was elected president of the board, which also included Mako, Guy Lee, Soon-Tek Oh, Yet Lock, and Yuki Shimoda. For the artistic staff, Mako was elected the artistic director, Guy Lee the business manager, Rae Creevey the technical director, Beulah Quo the audience development officer, and Jeanne Joe the workshop coordinator. Soon-Tek Oh served as the executive director. Once the company settled on an organizational structure, albeit a loose one, the EWP began what the members called the "church basement period" from 1967 to 1971. They rented the basement space of the Bethany Presbyterian Church on Griffith Street, which was led by a young liberal-minded minister who welcomed the EWP to use the space. According to Mako, the basement space was the EWP's "playground" for about six years. In exchange for low rent, the members agreed to do maintenance work. This period was both beneficial and damaging to the company: while the church provided an affordable space for the company to establish itself, it limited the group in many ways such as not allowing Sunday performances. More-over, a church basement was not an ideal place for theatrical perfor-mances. For one, the company had to spend much time and money letting people know of its existence.

But, most importantly, it was during this period that the EWP found its production style. With Asian American plays virtually nonexistent, the EWP members debated play selection, especially in terms of the artistic style that would become associated with the company. In keeping with the name of the company, the members decided to take advantage of theatres from both Eastern and Western traditions. Of the fourteen productions during the church basement period, five were Western plays, four Japanese classic pieces in English translation, three original plays, and one collaborative piece from the acting workshops. Generally, the repertory had three stylistic categories: (1) intercultural interpreta-tions of canonized Western plays in either Western or Eastern settings, (2) Japanese classics in traditional settings but performed in English, and (3) original plays by Asian American writers in English. The first cate-gory included *The Servant of Two Masters* by Carlo Goldoni with the setting changed from Venice to an imagined Chinatown in the city. The second category included two canonized Japanese plays, *Twilight Crane* by Junji Kinoshita and *Lady Aoi* by Yukio Mishima. Also included in the category were Kyogen plays, which were easier for actors to learn than Noh or Kabuki. For the third category, Soon-Tek Oh wrote *Martyrs Can't Go Home* (a play about the Korean War which Oh submitted as his master's thesis). Oh also adapted *Camels Were Two Legged* in China, a renowned Chinese novel.[3]

Soon-Tek Oh, the executive director, summarized the accomplishments and goals of the EWP as of December, 1967:

> The company has been introducing a unique theater to the western world – the amalgamation of East and West in its ultimate form, as well as providing opportunities for Orientals to extend the scope and depth of their theatrical talents. It is now well-known fact that the nation's only all-Oriental acting company, through its remarkable achievements since 1965, has been a decisive influence in amending the debasing [the] Hollywood image of Oriental actors.[4]

As Oh states, the EWP was a showcase theatre for actors, so the repertory had to be diverse and even international to optimize the demonstration of their "theatrical talents." At the same time, the member of the EWP wanted to turn their racial identities into assets, rather than liabilities. For Mako, the intercultural element of the repertory was a strategy that played to the casting director's expectation: "Casting directors see you only as 'Oriental.' The more 'Oriental' things you know the more jobs you'll get."[5] In other words, the actors rejected stereotypical images of "orientals," but at the same time, they projected a new version of Asianness that was packaged as intercultural and artistic. The ultimate goal was to be showcased for possible casting in film and television.

However, the dual goals of the EWP (to be showcased and to take advantage of being "oriental") did not always work together. In fact, the members continued to disagree on the interpretation of the goals throughout the church basement years. Some members saw the EWP as a stepping-stone towards a better acting career while others saw a potential that was more aligned with the emerging rhetoric of the Asian American Movement. Moreover, the questions of a goal and a vision were dictated by the realities of managing a new theatre company. Namely, the sources of funding that shaped the evolution of the EWP. Mako began to notice that other cultural groups were receiving funding at both state and federal

---

[3] See Yuko Kurahashi, *Asian American Culture on Stage: The History of the East West Players* (New York: Garland Publishing, Inc., 1999) , 29–42 for descriptions of the three types of shows. Also see Appendix B in her book for a complete list of productions from 1965 to 1998.

[4] Soon-Tek Oh, Letter (December 15, 1967), 1. The East West Players Archive, Arts Library Special Collections, University of California, Los Angeles.

[5] Mako, Personal interview, July 22, 1999. All quotes by Mako without citation are from this interview.

level. He initially resisted requesting government funding because he thought "guidelines, rules, regulations, and stipulations . . . would block our energy." But he soon realized that the EWP could not survive without outside funding. With the help of Jack Jackson who was leading the Inner City Cultural Center, Mako and others at EWP learned about the available funding resources, including the Ford Foundation, whose guidelines were not restrictive.[6]

In 1968, the EWP received a $38,500 grant from the Ford Foundation, which required that the money be spent between June 1968 and May 1970 to: (1) prepare and stimulate original plays; (2) train actors in a workshop situation; and (3) develop each season's productions.[7] For the first requirement, Soon-Tek Oh proposed an annual playwriting contest. The first was held in 1968 with a first prize of $1000. The EWP placed ads in literary magazines and newspapers and solicited Asian American writers to explore playwriting. According to Mako, the EWP received only half a dozen submissions, and the quality of writing was generally mediocre. The winner of the first contest was Henry Woon whose play, *Now You See, Now You Don't*, dealt with racism in the workplace and a Chinese American man's personal activism. The play was the first EWP production to address issues unique to Asian Americans, and it is considered the first Asian American play to receive staging. The production, directed by Mako, featured white characters played by Asian American actors wearing white half-masks. The Chinese American protagonist, played by Soon-Tek Oh, wore a similarly shaped yellow mask which he takes off at a critical point when he finally succeeds in forcing his white co-workers to submit to his wishes.

The second playwriting contest was held in 1970, and Soon-Tek Oh's *Tondemonai – Never Happen* won first prize. In the following year, Frank Chin's *Chickencoop Chinaman* and Momoko Iko's *Gold Watch* shared first prize. However, because the EWP decided to move out of the church basement space in the same year, neither of the winning plays was performed at the time. Instead, *Chickencoop Chinaman* premiered at the America Place Theater in New York in 1972, and *Gold Watch* had its first performance at the Inner City Cultural Center in Los Angeles, also in 1972.

---

[6] Inner City Cultural Center was founded in 1965 in Los Angeles. It is a multiethnic, multi-disciplinary cultural institution recognized for providing programs in theater, music, dance, and visual arts to poor communities in the Los Angeles area.

[7] Kurahashi, *Asian American Culture*, 49.

Figure 3. A scene from the 1968 production of *Now You See, Now You Don't* by Henry Woon, the first play to win the East West Players Playwriting Competition. Pat Li (left) plays the girl friend of the protagonist, played by Soon-Tek Oh (right), who wears a yellow half-mask symbolizing his disguise in a white-dominated world.

The end of the church basement period began when the young minister who had welcomed the EWP resigned, and the new minister who replaced him formed the Building Committee to partly oversee EWP's activities. The Building Committee frowned upon nudity and vulgar language and started to censor productions. One day, a church deacon walked into a rehearsal of Soon-Tek Oh's *Tondemonai – Never Happen*, a play that dealt with risky topics such as nudity, homosexuality, concentration camps, and interracial marriage. According to Mako, the actors were almost naked, and one of the actors got out of bed and put on his underpants in dim light when they were visited. Not surprisingly, the church leaders found the play inappropriate and demanded to review all plays before rehearsals. The church also responded by calling the fire inspector who made expensive demands. According to Mako, he could not even think of approaching the Building Committee with Frank Chin's play because of the strong language. With the possibility of censorship looming, the EWP could not continue its residence, and the problems came to a head when the church congregation voted to evict the company.

The period between 1970 and 1972 was the most challenging time for the EWP since its foundation. On top of the eviction, the Ford Foundation grant was not renewed due to "a lack of growth."[8] With the survival of the company on the line, the members had to deal with fundamental questions about the past accomplishments and future identity of the company. The difficulty was exacerbated by another major disappointment. The Los Angeles Civic Light Opera decided to cast a white actor in the role of Okinawa in the musical *Lovely Ladies, Kind Gentleman*. As noted in Chapter 2, the EWP joined the Oriental Actors of America in publicly opposing the casting choice and declaring their objections to the stereotypic roles. This casting controversy frustrated the EWP members because their five-year effort seemed to have made "no dent on the industry."[9]

The layers of trouble started to put a strain on the infrastructure of the company, causing internal disagreements and financial instability. Mako and other founding members were pressured to reevaluate the existence of the EWP. Around this time, Soon-Tek Oh resigned as the executive director and officially left the company. He would return on occasion to act and help behind the scenes, but he never took on an administrative role after his resignation. Oh, like other founding members, had worked without pay for several years, during which his acting career was virtually on hold. He was, in short, burned out. Moreover, he had fundamental disagreements with Mako about the repertory of the EWP. Oh wanted to produce showcase works, especially canonized Western plays such as Shakespeare or Tennessee Williams, but Mako wanted to focus on original plays: "I felt we weren't ready for it because we would be compared immediately and that would have hurt us at that time. I kept pushing original, original."[10] Another disagreement Oh had with Mako was over the kind of space the EWP was to obtain. Oh wanted a bigger space, while Mako and the Board of Directors chose the small storefront space of 4502 Santa Monica Boulevard.

Both Mako and Soon-Tek Oh, who have remained good friends, were committed to improving the status of Asian American actors, but their

[8] Irvin Paik, "The East West Players: The First Ten Years are the Hardest," *Bridge: An Asian American Perspective* 5.2 (1977), 14–17.
[9] Ibid.
[10] Ibid., 16.

differing views on the direction of the EWP could not be negotiated. Oh decided to continue his version of activism by making changes within the industry and pursuing a full-time career in Hollywood. Mako, on the other hand, did not want to give up on the EWP. He enlisted help from other core members such as Beulah Quo and Rae Creevey, who willingly spent their personal time and money to get through the tough times. Quo was especially indispensable during this time. For instance, Mako was in Japan when the core members found out that the landlord had lied about the structural condition of the Santa Monica space, which they were renting for $300 a month. They could not use the space, and some talked of closing the EWP. Without Mako, the members relied on Beulah Quo to save the company by finding financial and legal resources.

The experience of near-disaster strengthened the loyalty of the core members. The sense of loyalty was essential to the continuation of the EWP during the early 1970s. Many of the original or early members recall the EWP as a family. The model was indeed like a family with Mako as the father figure and breadwinner, as he did not hesitate to use his own money to pay the company's bills. More than once, Mako used the money he earned by playing stereotypical roles in Hollywood films to produce Asian American plays that criticized the very same stereotypes. However, as self-sacrificial as his actions were, Mako's administrative practices back-fired on him in the late 1980s when the board of directors, accusing him of practicing nepotism, forced him to resign. In hindsight, the problem started in the early 1970s when Mako and others saw the EWP as a family, an insular group who built the company "out of love."[11]

In 1972, Mako returned from Japan, and the members found a ninety-nine seat theatre space at 4424 Santa Monica Boulevard, which would become the home of the EWP until 1998. The space was initially designed as a small supermarket, and the members of the EWP had to furnish it with used theatre chairs. The space was, however, ideal for the purpose of the EWP. According to Mako, workshop was the "only thing that was keeping us alive." Focusing on workshops for actors in the new space, the EWP began a new era. Kathleen Freeman, who taught acting at the EWP,

[11] The phrase "out of love" was used by Mako in a meeting on March 22, 1971. The full quotation is: "I recommend that whatever people owe in back dues be dropped as of now – only the people who have worked here day and night. We have spent roughly $1500 remodeling so far. This place is built out of love. This will be the last time such compromise will be made on dues. This is yours, not mine – it belongs to all of us." East West Players, Meeting Minutes (March 22, 1971). The East West Players Archive, Arts Library Special Collections, University of California, Los Angeles.

assisted on starting workshops as soon as possible. On December 8, 1972, a production of Bill Shinkai's *S.P.O.O.S.* premiered at the new space, opening doors to other original plays by Asian American writers.[12] The production featured Mako, Clyde Kustasu, Shizuko Hoshi, Alberto Issac, and Pat Morita – all of who would become major actors both within the EWP and as mainstream actors. For the first time since its foundation, the EWP produced a show that directly questioned and addressed the problems of Asian stereotyping and representation. Moreover, the play set the tone for the new kind of repertory in the new space: the EWP would produce, on the average, four shows a year with an emphasis on original Asian American plays.

In 1973, the EWP pursued and received two major grants. The first was a National Endowment for the Arts Grant ($20,000) that allowed the company to continue workshop-based productions. The second grant came from the Rockefeller Foundation, which gave the company $3,500 for an Asian American playwright-in-residence ($2,500 to the playwright-in-residence and $1,000 to the EWP). As one of the most important grants in the history of the EWP, it continued annually until 1980. This combination of workshop and playwright-in-residence grants provided fertile conditions for emerging Asian American playwrights. Between 1972 and 1980, the EWP premiered over twenty original Asian American plays in addition to producing several European and Euro-American plays.

The EWP increasingly became an artistic home for many first-wave Asian American playwrights. These writers included Jon Shirota, Momoko Iko, Dom Magwili, Wakako Yamauchi, Karen Tei Yamashita, Perry Miyake, Bill Shinkai, Paul Stephen Lim, Jeffery Paul Chan, Frank Chin, and Edward Sakamoto, many of whom were new to playwriting. For instance, Wakako Yamauchi was solicited by Mako to adapt her short story, *And the Soul Shall Dance*, into a play. She admits that she was "sort of pushed into playwriting – blind and unaware."[13] Similarly, for Momoko Iko, the East West Player's playwriting competition was the "catalyst" that encouraged her to experiment with plays.[14] *Chickencoop Chinaman*, another

---

[12] The play satirized "Oriental" stereotypes in film and television with exaggerated Asian characters ranging from a militant student activist to opportunistic Asian American actors who would play anything for money. Asian characters in the play fight against the S.P.O.O.S. agents (Society for the Preservation of Oriental Stereotypes) who perpetuate "media images of Asians such as the bucktoothed, four-eyed, and acquiescent types." See Kurahashi, *Asian American Culture*, 53–55, for an extensive description and discussion of the play.

[13] Velina Hasu Houston, ed., *Politics of Life* (Philadelphia: Temple University Press, 1993), 36.

[14] Roberta Uno, ed., *Unbroken Thread: An Anthology of Plays by Asian American Women* (Amherst: University of Massachusetts Press, 1993), 107.

EWP competition winner, was also Frank Chin's first attempt at playwriting. For these first-wave Asian American playwrights, the EWP provided a forum for experimentation and a place to develop a new dramatic canon of Asian American plays.

The 1977 premiere of Wakako Yamauchi's *And the Soul Shall Dance* was a ground-breaking production for the EWP and put the company on the map in the Los Angeles area. The production was not only the most profitable in terms of the box office but also ran for fifty-three extended performances. It received positive reviews and three Los Angeles Drama Critics Awards: lighting (Rae Creevey), directing (Mako and Alberto Isaac), and acting (Shizuko Hoshi). With the success of the production, the EWP began to grow towards a mid-size theatre company. Beginning in the late 1970s, the company found its stability with a large Nisei (second generation Japanese American) subscription base in Los Angeles. The Nisei theatre goers sympathized strongly with *And the Soul Shall Dance*, which is about two Japanese immigrant families in California's Imperial Valley during the Great Depression. The Nisei audience identified with the play's themes, which include assimilation, cultural conflict, generational gaps, and the pre-internment camp innocence of Japanese Americans. The EWP was encouraged to produce more plays about Japanese Americans, and during the 1981–82 season, it devoted the entire season to the internment of Japanese Americans during World War II. And during the 1980s, the majority of the produced plays dealt with Japanese American issues.

Another major shift during the late 1970s and the 1980s was the addition of musical theatre to the repertory. With the success of *And the Soul Shall Dance*, the EWP increased its budget to include larger productions of musicals. The repertory included both popular musicals such as *Pacific Overtures* (in 1978) and *A Chorus Line* (in 1987) and original Asian American musicals such as Philip Kan Gotanda's *The Avocado Kid* (in 1979). Musicals were profitable in many ways. The Nisei subscribers enjoyed and supported popular musicals produced at the EWP with all-Asian actors, dancers, and singers. In turn, the EWP welcomed the profit-making musicals. It also provided a training ground for Asian American actors in musical theatre. Another reliable type of production were Hawaiian plays. Every time the EWP staged a play by Hawaiian playwrights such as Jon Shirota and Edward Sakamoto, Hawaiians living in the Los Angeles area were mobilized to attend the productions, giving the EWP the incentive to produce at least one Hawaiian play per year.

With a solid subscription base, profit-making musicals, an increasing number of original works by Asian American writers, and strong financial support, the EWP in the 1980s became not only the first and largest Asian American theatre in the country, but also a major mid-size theatre company in Los Angeles. However, as the funds for multicultural theatre began to dwindle towards the end of the 1980s, the EWP faced the most painful administrative predicament since the early 1970s. For one, the company increasingly became identified as a Japanese American theatre, not as the pan-Asian American theatre company it professed to be. Also, the company continued to run as an ensemble with auditions open only to the EWP members. The EWP board accused Mako of practicing nepotism, casting his family members whenever possible. The board also attributed financial problems to Mako. Some blamed his closest collaborators, especially his wife Shizuko Hoshi, for perpetuating the insular culture of the EWP. The chasm between Mako and the board members began to appear in the mid-1980s, and it culminated in Mako's forced resignation in January 1989.

Nobu McCarthy, who had worked in theatre and film as an actress, became EWP's artistic director soon after Mako's resignation. She shifted the company's focus from Japanese American to pan-Asian American and multicultural issues. She envisioned the EWP as an inclusive regional theatre where artists of all ethnic backgrounds could find opportunities. For instance, McCarthy hired non-Asian Americans in major staff positions, including the literary manager position, which was filled by Brian Nelson, a European American. She also increased the board members and organized several major fundraising events to improve EWP's financial situation which, like those of other regional theatres in the USA, suffered subsidy cuts in the late 1980s and early 1990s.

In July 1993, Nobu McCarthy resigned due to poor health, and Tim Dang became the artistic director. Under his leadership, the EWP grew in both size and diversity. He made efforts to reach out to Asian American communities in the Los Angeles area beyond Little Tokyo by diversifying the season and creating new conservatory programs. In 1998, the EWP moved to a new theatre space, the former Union Church building. Based in the heart of Little Tokyo, the building had been selected by Mako as the ideal location during his administration, but it wasn't until 1995 that the EWP had enough money to begin renovation. In this new space, the EWP has led Asian American theatre in new play development, actor training, fundraising, and audience development.

What started in 1965 as a modest attempt to change the perception and status of "oriental actors" had grown into a major Asian American theatre company by the early 1990s. While play development and community service have been top priorities, the EWP has remained an actor's theatre. The primary goal of the company has not changed: to train and provide opportunities to Asian American actors. The actors at the EWP have performed in musicals, European American plays, adaptations of Asian plays, and Asian American plays. In 1999, the EWP reported that "Over 75% of all Asian Pacific performers in the acting unions have worked with EWP."[15] No other company in the country can claim such an influence. The history of the EWP is not without administrative problems and personal clashes, but it has managed to survive and thrive as the first and largest Asian American theatre company.

Asian American Theatre Company, San Francisco

When Frank Chin submitted his first play *Chickencoop Chinaman* (originally titled *Chickencoop Chinaman's Pregnant Pause*) for the East West Player's playwriting competition in 1971, the judges could not decide on the winner. Many plays had been submitted, but none pleased all of the judges. One judge in particular argued for the cancellation of the competition and criticized the submitted plays as "[un]performable" and "lectures," but another judge, Jack Jackson, felt Chin's play was "worthy of a prize."[16] They postponed the decision and waited until the artistic director and the executive producer looked into the matter. After serious consideration, the East West Players announced two winners: Chin's *Chickencoop Chinaman* and Momoko Iko's *Gold Watch*. The concern over Chin's play wasn't with its literary or artistic merits but with its contentiousness. One judge warned that the EWP "should not get into a bag similar to the Blacks, i.e. lamenting that [Asian Americans] are yellow."[17] The judge's concern was not totally unfounded because the main character of the play, Tam Lum acts, talks, and moves like a black man and has a best friend named Kenji, a Japanese American with the nickname "Black Jap." Tam's goal in the play is to make a documentary film about the life of a black boxer and former light heavyweight champion, Ovaltine Jack Dancer, whom he admired as a child. Although Tam ultimately becomes disillusioned with the project and his childhood hero, his angry rhetoric is unmistakably an echo of the poets and playwrights of the Black Arts Movement and the cultural

---

[15] "About East West Players," www.eastwestplayers.org/aboutus.html.
[16] East West Players, Meeting Minutes (April 21, 1971). The East West Players Archive, Arts Library Special Collections, University of California, Los Angeles.
[17] Ibid.

nationalism of the 1960s and 1970s. Frank Chin applied the same rhetoric in founding the Asian American Theater Workshop in San Francisco by claiming his theatre is "real" and "authentic," as did the leaders of the Black Revolutionary Theater.[18]

Whether Frank Chin should be considered as the Asian American version of Amiri Baraka or Larry Neal – as the intellectual and literary leader of the civil rights movement – is questionable but worth exploring. There are, of course, many similarities, including the hyper-masculinization of colored men and the framing of American racism as a form of cultural imperialism. Although there is no direct evidence of Chin participating in the Asian American Movement as an activist, he could have not missed the protest scenes, especially in Berkeley, California, where he was born.[19] Also, the Bay Area at the time, like other parts of the country, witnessed a renaissance of alternative culture as artists freely expressed their views with poetry, theatre, and music. Many saw the new cultural activities as participating in the "American version of the decolonization movement."[20] Moreover in 1968, the Asian American Movement emerged, partly out of students' protests at San Francisco State University over the inclusion of ethnic studies in the curriculum. Chin's surroundings were filled with what Harry J. Elam calls "the explosion of social antagonism" that erupted in the forms of the antiwar movement, the civil rights movement, the farmworkers movement, and the student protest movement, all of which created their own social protest theatre.[21]

Although Chin himself refuses to be called a cultural nationalist, it seems sensible to consider Frank Chin as a literary and intellectual voice

---

[18] I'm using the term "Black Revolutionary Theater" as defined by Harry J. Elam in *Taking It to the Streets: The Social Protest Theater of Luis Valdez and Amiri Baraka.* (Ann Arbor: University of Michigan Press, 1997). As Elam describes, Amiri Barak (LeRoi Jones) was the founder of the Black Revolutionary Theater (BRT) during the period 1965 through 1971. Elam compares BRT to El Teatro Campesino, the farmworkers theatre founded by Luis Valdez in 1965, as the "direct and confrontational" social protest theatre movements.

[19] Frank Chin was born in Berkeley, California in 1940 to a Chinese immigrant father and a fourth generation Chinese American mother. He was raised in the Chinatown of "Motherlode country" (the Sierra Nevada) and in the Chinatown of Oakland, California. Between 1962 and 1965, he worked as a clerk around the Western Pacific Railway's Oakland Yard. He later returned to the railroads, after graduating with an AB in English from the University of California, Santa Barbara, where he worked as a brakeman, becoming the first Chinese American brakeman on the Southern Pacific since the railroads were completed.

[20] Mike Sell, "The Black Arts Movement: Performance, Neo-Orality, and the Destruction of the 'White Thing,'" in *African American Performance and Theater History: A Critical Reader,* edited by Harry J. Elam and David Krasner (Oxford: Oxford University Press, 2001), 60.

[21] Elam, *Taking It,* 22.

from the Asian American version of cultural nationalism. Tam Lum's emulation of blacks can be read as an acknowledgement of the influence of the Black Arts Movement on Frank Chin. Indeed, some have credited Frank Chin as a leader of Asian American cultural nationalism and radicalism. But others, often the majority, have found Chin's formulation of cultural nationalism problematic and exclusionary. Central to his idea of an Asian American culture is "real vs. fake," a binary concept that has extended not only to his definition of a "real" Asian American theatre but also to his relationships with other writers and colleagues. For Chin, the binary concept begins with what he calls a "real Chinaman" who, in the most simplistic terms, is not "Chinese" (foreigner) or "Chinese-American" (assimilated sell-out). Chin refuses to identify with China (the "country of origin") and does not see a convergence between Asian nationalism and Asian American cultural nationalism.[22] Moreover, as Lisa Lowe argues, Frank Chin represented "cultural nationalism" and assimilation in polar opposition: "cultural nationalism's affirmation of the separate purity of its culture opposes assimilation of the standards of dominant society."[23]

Such a separatist Chinaman identity is articulated in the first scene of *Chickencoop Chinaman*, in which Tam describes himself as a synthetic byproduct of racist history and "no more born than nylon or acrylic." When the character of Hong Kong Dream Girl asks Tam "Where were you born?" Tam answers: "Chinamen are made, not born, my dear. Out of junk-imports, lies, railroad scrap iron, dirty jokes, broken bottles, cigar smoke, Cosquilla Indian blood, wino spit, and lots of milk of amnesia."[24] Frank Chin uses "Chinaman," a term that has historically been a derogatory and racist one, in order to empower a separatist identity that does not depend on race (biological birth) but on historical memory and amnesia.

In 1972, *Chickencoop Chinaman* premiered at the American Place Theatre, an Off Broadway theatre known to produce unconventional plays. Chin's play was the first Asian American play to be produced in New York City. The founding artistic director of American Place Theatre, Wynn Handman, remembers the original script as "fat as the Queens or Brooklyn

[22] David Palumbo-Liu, *Asian/American: Historical Crossings of a Racial Frontier* (Stanford: Stanford University Press, 1999), 307.

[23] Lisa Lowe, *Immigrant Acts: On Asian American Cultural Politics* (Durham: Duke University Press, 1996), 75.

[24] Frank Chin, *The Chickencoop Chinaman and The Year of the Dragon: Two Plays by Frank Chin* (Seattle: University of Washington Press, 1981), 6.

phone book."[25] He invited Frank Chin to New York City and asked him to cut the play to a manageable size, but Chin was not easy to work with. "He had and still has so much talent and anger and fury in him and such a wild imagination that it creates a turbulence that just keeps exploding. So when you ask him to change something in a scene, he comes back with a long prologue when you don't need a prologue."[26] Handman's description of Chin foreshadowed the legacy of the talented but volatile writer. No one doubted Chin's talent, but many found him impossible to work with.

The comments and reviews of *Chickencoop Chinaman* at the American Place Theatre varied, but all agreed on the play's significance in American theatre history. For the first time, an original Asian American play was produced in New York, and a conversation about Asian American drama had begun. Comments by Clive Barnes of *The New York Times* seem to best describe the general reaction (admittance of ignorance and cultural shock) felt by the mainstream white audience: "To be honest, I did not much like the play, but it showed me an ethnic attitude I had never previously encountered. It is difficult to understand a prejudice when you don't subscribe to it, but I can see that the American Oriental, in some fashion like the American Indian, must feel very underprivileged and threatened."[27] Moreover, the New York critics were unanimous in praising Randall Duk Kim, who played the role of Tam Lum. Frank Chin credits Kim for making his writing sharper and fast-paced. For Chin, Kim is the only actor who could play his Chinaman characters to his satisfaction. With Kim's notable performance, an angry Chinaman appeared on the American stage, and the theatre community began to take notice of Frank Chin.

After *Chickencoop Chinaman* closed at the American Place Theatre, Edward Hastings, executive director of the prestigious American Conservatory Theater (ACT) in San Francisco, approached Chin about starting an Asian American theatre program at the ACT. The two agreed to start an experimental program, the Asian American Theater Workshop (AATW), as part of the ACT's Summer Training Congress program in 1973. Initially, the purpose was to provide a laboratory setting for playwrights to develop new Asian American plays, but they quickly realized that there were no trained Asian American theatre artists to participate in the workshops. It

[25] Alvin Eng, ed., *Tokens?: The NYC Asian American Experience on Stage* (Philadelphia: Temple University Press, 1999), 410.
[26] Ibid.
[27] Clive Barnes, "Stage: Identity Problem," *New York Times*, June 13, 1972, 53.

was imperative to first provide basic training to cultivate Asian American actors, designers, and technicians.

By 1973, San Francisco was ready for such an experiment. Because the city had one of the highest Asian populations, including fourth and fifth generation Chinese Americans who were descendents of the first-wave of Chinese laborers in the mid-nineteenth century, both Edward Hastings and Frank Chin recognized the cultural vitality and potential of Asian Americans in San Francisco. The combination of successful political activism, cultural maturity, and sheer numbers made the city an ideal setting for a new Asian American theatre workshop.

The goal of the workshop was to produce an "Asian-American production" by the end of the summer. In May 1973, ACT gave ten special tuition scholarships of $600 each to Asian American actors and actresses for the company's Summer Training Congress in San Francisco. A press release announced the pilot Asian American Theater Workshop program: "Asian-American talent has been virtually untapped for decades, with no professional outlet for growth and development on its own terms. The result is a widely-noted scarcity of Asian-American performers and playwrights, even in San Francisco where 17% of the population is Asian-American."[28] The workshop allowed the recipients of the scholarships to attend the full curriculum of courses taught by ACT directors and actors. Frank Chin also organized evening workshops, which were open to Asian American writers. Chin wanted Randall Duk Kim to lead the acting workshops, but when Kim could not take on the responsibility, Janis Chan stepped in as the acting instructor. Janis Chan was a white actress, an acting teacher by profession, and wife of Jeffery Paul Chan, writer and friend of Frank Chin.

Frank Chin had a clear vision of what he wanted to accomplish with the workshop. In an undated letter (probably early 1973) to Randall Duk Kim, Chin described his plans to create what he tentatively called "The Chinatown Theatre Workshop" with the help of ACT and the Chinese Cultural Foundation. The letter included a draft of the "Prospectus" that Chin later incorporated into the proposal for a "Theater Workshop for Asian-Americans," submitted to Edward Hastings. In the Prospectus, Chin lamented the lack of "self-statement" in Asian American culture, especially in the theatre arts. Chin wrote in the Prospectus: "[T]he total absence of an artistic voice from a minority group that has had seven

[28] Cheryle Elliott, American Conservatory Theater Press Release (May 3, 1973), The Asian American Theater Company Archive, California Ethnic and Multicultural Archives at the Special Collections Library, University of California, Santa Barbara.

generations of evolution is unnatural."[29] Chin emphasized that theatre is
the best way to satisfy the cultural needs of the Asian American communities in San Francisco because of the medium's "intrinsic collaborative
nature" that combines "both the literary and performing aspects." He
ended the letter on a humorous note: "Hopefully, if all goes well, we don't
lose our hearts or minds, we will shut down the swordshow for a night or
two, and end the summer with a play or two, put up on a big Chinatown
stage."[30]

Chin had the idealism and ambition to advance Asian American culture
by producing theatre works that would have literary and artistic merit
equal to that of the best of Asian, European, and American dramatic
traditions. And he always emphasized the writer as the central visionary.
He felt Asian American plays should reflect the emotion and language of
the culture, similar to the plays of the Irish playwright Sean O'Casey. One
way to develop such plays, for Chin, was the oral history project he had been
working on since the late 1960s. He had personally collected many oral
history tapes in Seattle and San Francisco and had founded the Combined
Asian American Resources Project (CARP) in San Francisco that archived
the tapes and other historical documents. Chin found in these tapes invaluable sources of emotion and language for Asian American plays. With the
AATW, he envisioned actors helping the writers to develop dramatic
characters from the tapes.

But before he could achieve his greater vision, Chin's immediate goal was
to start a workshop. When the first Asian American Theater Workshop
opened in the summer of 1973, twenty-five members, most of whom were
new to theatre, joined the first classes that began on June 18 and continued
through August 25. Chin's idea for the workshop was a four-week rehearsal
after which participants would present their work to an audience. In
August, they presented scenes from the summer workshop at ACT's Playroom: on August 16, 18, and 25, the presentation consisted of "The Lone
Ranger Scene" from *Chickencoop Chinaman*, excerpts from *The Year of the
Dragon* by Chin, *Portrait of Three Chinese-American Women*, which was
"developed by the director [Janis Chan] and actresses from taped interviews

[29] Frank Chin, "Prospectus" (1973), The Asian American Theatre Company Archive, California
Ethnic and Multicultural Archives at the Special Collections Library, University of California,
Santa Barbara.
[30] Frank Chin, "Letter to Randall Duk Kim" (1973), The Asian American Theatre Company
Archive, California Ethnic and Multicultural Archives at the Special Collections Library,
University of California, Santa Barbara.

made for CARP," and on August 17 and 24, the entire first act of *Chickencoop Chinaman* was performed.[31]

At the end of 1973, the group began to work on a full-length show, "Freddie Eng's Chinatown Tour" which was based on a new play Frank Chin was working on, *The Year of the Dragon*. The play is about Fred Eng, a Chinese American travel agent and tourist guide who fakes his accent for "authenticity" while giving tours to visitors in Chinatown. Members used the oral history tapes and their personal experiences to create the show, which included monologues, skits, and agitprop techniques. Around this time, two faculty members of Sacramento High School approached the AATW to request a performance at their school. The invitation encouraged the AATW to complete the development of "Freddie Eng's Chinatown Tour." More requests by schools, colleges, and community groups came in, and in March, April, and May of 1974, the AATW performed "Freddie Eng's Chinatown Tour" at eight different venues in San Francisco, Sacramento, Santa Cruz, and San Jose. The sponsors of these performances varied but indicated a demand for Asian American theatre, especially in educational venues.[32]

In the same year, 1974, Chin's full-length play *The Year of the Dragon* premiered at the American Place Theatre on May 22. Around this time, the members of AATW increasingly worked with each other, rather than with Frank Chin or Janis Chan. Chin was often out of town, working on other projects, and when he returned, he "directed" what the AATW

[31] Asian American Theater Workshop, "Program for The Asian American Workshop at ACT" (1973), The Asian American Theatre Company Archive, California Ethnic and Multicultural Archives at the Special Collections Library, University of California, Santa Barbara. The cast of the "Lone Ranger Scene" included John Ng (Tam), Kathleen Chin (Kenji), Frank Chin (Lone Ranger), and Peter Fong (Tonto). The director was Janis Chan. In the excerpt from *The Year of the Dragon* (directed by Frank Chin), the cast was Marion K. Yue (Fred), Viki Chang (Sissy), Gloria Choi (Ross), Joanne Matsui (Ma), Lulula Lee (Pa), and Eva Chan (Johnny). *Portrait of Three Chinese-American Women* included Judy Seto (left position), Kathleen Chan (center position), and Jean Wong (right position). And in Act One of *Chickencoop Chinaman*, the cast included Gil Chooey (Tam Lum), Jean Wong (Hong Kong Dream Girl), Cliff Yosa (Kenji), Mary Dacumos (Robbie), and Arika Dacumos (Lee). Set and light designers were Michael Brooks and Eric Hayashi.

[32] For instance, on March 22, AATW's performance at Sacramento High School was sponsored by two school groups: Asian American Awareness and The Thespians. The April 9 performance at the Calvary Presbyterian Church was sponsored by the Christian Careers Forum. And on May 4, AATW performed at the University of California, Santa Cruz and was sponsored by Merrill, Covell, Stevenson, Oaks, and VIII Colleges. On April 19, the performance at San Francisco State University was sponsored by Association of Students for Third World Cultural Fair, and at Pine Methodist Church on May 17, the show was sponsored by San Francisco Center for Japanese American Studies.

members had already created. More often than not, Chin was critical of their work. Increasingly, the younger members of the AATW were personally hurt by Chin's sharp comments (and many left for that reason) and began to clash with him. Some felt uncomfortable with Janis Chan (a white woman) teaching and directing them. They felt Chan did not understand the Asian American sensibility, and this distrust eventually led to Chan's resignation in 1975.

By the end of spring in 1974, the Asian American Theater Workshop had produced nearly thirty trained Asian American theatre artists who had performed for hundreds of spectators. Most of the audiences were Asian Americans who, for the first time, saw glimpses of their own lives on the stage. The popularity of AATW in the community demonstrated the need for such cultural outlets. When the 1974 summer classes were announced, over eighty potential members showed up at the first meeting. Janis Chan, for the last time, led the acting classes, and instructors from ACT volunteered to teach voice and movement classes. Also, Eric Hayashi and Nathan Lee, who had effectively designed and toured "Freddie Eng's Chinatown Tour" shows, taught new classes in "scene study" and technical theatre.

During the fruitful year of 1974, Frank Chin and AATW members articulated their objectives in "An Overview of the Asian American Theatre Workshop":

1. To provide a training ground for Asian American actors, directors, and technicians.
2. To mount an easily toured production to present to groups in the area.
3. To continue to develop an oral-history archive through taped interviews of Asian Americans of all ages and walks of life.
4. To continue to create theatre pieces from these tapes, using the actual words (and duplicating the actual accents) of the individuals recorded.
5. To develop and encourage Asian American playwrights

   a. By having advanced actors work with playwrights in creating new plays.
   b. By setting up writers' workshops and conferences.
   c. By helping Asian American playwrights obtain grants.

6. To collect, edit, and publish anthologies of Asian American writings, including fiction, poetry, essays, and drama, specifically designed to be used as textbooks in both elementary and secondary curricula.

7. To set up a physical plant for a workshop-theatre, self-contained and housing ancillary services.

8. To integrate our activities with others in the Asian American community that are aimed at raising the level of consciousness concerning the history and condition of Asians in America.

9. To obtain financial support from local sources.[33]

With these goals, the AATW made plans to leave the ACT in 1975 and establish itself as an independent company.

During the transition in 1975, members often gathered at Eric Hayashi's apartment to discuss the future of AATW. By this time, Frank Chin was not actively involved with details of AATW administration, and Janis Chan had resigned. The members revisited the objectives of AATW without them. In numerous meetings, the members discussed what they called "vision questions," which boiled down to "what is the objective of the Workshop?"[34] The members spent numerous hours in meetings discussing and debating the questions. Some sided with Frank Chin's original vision, and others wanted revision. Chin was still nominally the artistic leader, but administratively, younger members such as Eric Hayashi and Karen Seriguchi led the group. While Chin was busy with the Asian American Writer's Conference and other projects away from San Francisco, AATW members gradually began to define their own vision of AATW in many of the long meetings.[35]

---

[33] Asian American Theater Company, "An Overview of the Asian American Theater Workshop," (1974). The Asian American Theater Company Archive, California Ethnic and Multicultural Archives at the Special Collections Library, University of California, Santa Barbara.

[34] Other questions were: "What are we individually in it for?; What direction would we like to see it go?; What end result or final goal would we like to see?; How does the Workshop fit into the Asian Community?; How can I individually contribute to the Workshop?" Asian American Theater Company, "Vision Questions" (October 30, 1975), The Asian American Theater Company Archive, California Ethnic and Multicultural Archives at the Special Collections Library, University of California, Santa Barbara.

[35] Frank Chin increasingly identified himself as a leader of Asian American literature by co-organizing the first Asian American Writers' Conference in San Francisco in 1975. In 1974, Chin established himself as a pioneer Asian American writer when he and three other male Asian American writers (Jeff Chan, Lawson Fuaso Inada, and Shawn Wong) co-edited *Aiiieeeee!: An Anthology of Asian-American Writers*, the first anthology of writings by Asian Americans. It included excerpts from novels, short stories, plays, and poems by Chinese, Japanese, and Filipino Americans from the early years of the century to the 1970s. The anthology addressed "fifty years of [Asian American] voice" which had been "so long ignored and forcibly excluded from creative participation in American culture" (viii). The editors proclaimed: "Asian America . . . is wounded, sad, angry, swearing, and wondering, and this is his AIIIEEEEE!!!" (viii). The emerging Asian American writers were more than ready to reclaim their cultural identity by developing a body of literature for and about Asian Americans. And as Chin claimed his vision of theatre as the "authentic" and "real" Asian American theatre, he argued that the writings in *Aiiieeeee!!!* represent the "real" literary tradition of Asian America.

One undisputed need and requirement for the AATW was an Advisory Board that would reflect the Asian American community in San Francisco. By the end of 1976, sixteen members from the community had joined the Board.[36] The Advisory Board brought much needed legitimacy and financial stability. Between August and October of 1976, the AATW obtained a $20,000 grant from the San Francisco Foundation. With the grant, the members of the Workshop stabilized the administrative structure and obtained a rehearsal and performance space in a building (4344 California Street). The Asian American Theater Workshop was now a formal theatre company. During the first season as an independent company, AATW produced one of the most successful and significant plays in Asian American theatre history: *Honeybucket* written by Mel Escueta and directed by Frank Chin and Chris Wong. The play was the first Asian American play to address the Vietnam War and the experiences of Asian Americans in the US Armed Forces.

While the quality of the productions was impressive, the administrative aspect of AATW remained unfocused. All members shared administrative and artistic responsibilities, but the members decided to appoint Marianne Li as the first named artistic director of AATW. However, within a few months, Marianne Li left her position as artistic director. Surprisingly (or perhaps not so surprisingly), Frank Chin, who had been in the background during the season administratively, stepped in and nominated himself as the new artistic director. In a letter to the Board, Chin blamed it for not filling the position of artistic director vacated by Marianne Li. He criticized Li's performance as artistic director as "miserable, confused and lacking in guts" without a "vision of Asian American theater." With criticisms targeting the staff and the board, Chin reclaimed his responsibility as the leader of AATW:

> I have, in effect, if not in fact, been the artistic director of the AATW from the start. I'd like the title and power laid on me up front so no one, including myself, will be confused anymore. As artistic director I will fix and direct artistic policy. I will be in charge of play productions, script development, anything affecting the artistic quality of our work . . . from the physical plant to the casting of specific parts. I will set

---

[36] Some of the most active members of the first Advisory Board included Danilo Begonia (acting dean of the School of Ethnic Studies at San Francisco State University), Jeffery Chan (chairperson of Asian American Studies at San Francisco State University) Darrell Knouye (deputy public defender), Jeff Mori (director of JCYC), George Woo (lecturer in Asian American Studies at San Francisco State University), and Antonio Grafilo (member of the Human Rights Commission).

Figure 4. Frank Chin (center) performs the role of Fred in his play *Year of the Dragon* in the 1977 production at the Asian American Theater Workshop. Kathleen Chang (left) plays Sissy, and Wayne Mattingly (right) plays her husband Ross.

the season, select the directors, coordinate the set design, construction and painting, costuming, casting, directing, stage managing and technical servicing of the productions. All the normal stuff of all Artistic Directors.[37]

With Frank Chin as the artistic director, AATW produced his play *The Year of the Dragon* in the 1976–77 season. Chin acted the lead role and directed the production. The 1977–88 season included *Manila Murder* by Dom Magwilli (directed by Frank Chin) and *Lady is Dying* by Amy Sanbo and Lonny Kaneko (directed by Frank Chin).

With Chin at the helm, AATW continued to develop new Asian American plays and train new artists. However, his autocratic style of leadership did not please everyone. Tension had been building up since the beginning in 1973, and Chin had upset many people with his explosive temper and sharp tongue. Among many complaints directed towards

---

[37] Frank Chin, "Letter to the Board of Directors of AATW" (November 16, 1976), 1. The Asian American Theater Company Archive. California Ethnic and Multicultural Archives at the Special Collections Library, University of California, Santa Barbara.

Frank Chin, the most frequent was the fact that Chin conceived and operated the group as a "Writers Workshop" and refused to address community outreach and other potentials for the group. Chin, on the other hand, complained that some of the pieces created by members without his help (i.e. without the guidance of a writer) were "illegitimate." Furthermore, he felt that AATW should not go out to the Asian American community to perform, but that the community should come to the theatre. In 1977, for instance, some members performed agitprop pieces before the Asian Law Caucus and at Hayward State University, receiving positive responses. The members used such performances for "fundraising, publicity, the promotion of Asian consciousness [and to provide their] actors with experience."[38] The Board fully endorsed such projects, but Chin opposed them for lacking "artistic control" and "advanced planning."

Throughout his appointment as the artistic director, Chin's style of theatre management clashed with that of others in the company, and AATW suffered from the odd triangular relationship between Chin, veteran members, and new members. There were, of course, exceptions. For instance, Bernadette Cha, a founding member of AATW who did the stage makeup for Frank Chin in the 1976 production of *The Year of the Dragon*, experienced no difficulty in working with Chin. She remembers Chin as forming a better interpersonal relationship with those whom he could trust and understand. She also notes that many younger members were unnecessarily intimidated by Chin, and such intimidation led Chin to distrust and misunderstand them.[39] Most members, however, found Chin's approach problematic. Founding members such as Eric Hayashi, who had received his apprenticeship from Chin, began to challenge Chin's authoritarian method. Hayashi, for instance, suggested a newer model of theatre management that would allow the staff to have some power in the decision-making process. To their credit, veteran members knew Chin's style and understood ways of communicating with him. New members, on the other hand, could not cope with Chin's style. For instance, Chin had a reputation of yelling at members when he did not like their work. The veteran members had learned to dismiss such outbursts and to confront Chin when necessary. The new members, however, were intimidated by Chin. Often, a new member would leave AATW with an emotional

[38] Glenn Kubota, "Internal Memo from Board of Directors" (March 24, 1974), The Asian American Theater Company Archive, California Ethnic and Multicultural Archives at the Special Collections Library, University of California, Santa Barbara.
[39] Bernadette Cha's recollection of Frank Chin is from an informal conversation with the author. Cha did not want to give a formal, tape-recorded interview.

wound, and the staff would have difficulty finding a replacement. Also, new members shied away from Chin and avoided any direct conversation with him. This caused Chin to disapprove of new members even more. Caught in between, the veteran members continually pushed Chin to restructure AATW's administrative organization to be more inviting and democratic. Chin remained adamant about his vision and style as artistic director, and when staff opposition (by both veteran and new members) grew, he resigned.

The dispute that led to Chin's resignation began as a small disagreement over a set design. It culminated during the rehearsal for Jeff Chan's new play, *Bunnyhop*, in early 1978. (Ironically, *Bunnyhop* was the first comedy produced by AATW.) The play required a wall that would make a loud noise as it fell flat on the ground. In one scene, the wall was to fall while a character stood at its open door. Frank Chin wanted the wall to fall like the real thing and make a believable noise. He insisted on building an actual wall on the stage. Technical director Raymond Ju and managing director Eric Hayashi disagreed, preferring a set wall that would be lighter and therefore safer for the actors. Chin, as artistic director, felt that he could direct and design the show himself as he had done during the earlier years of AATW. Chin went ahead and started to build the wall as he wished, but Ju and Hayashi were just as unrelenting. They argued that the technical crew was responsible for implementing the set design. The dispute escalated, and Chin responded by demanding the board to fire the entire staff, threatening to leave if his demands were not met.

The board asked Chin to reconsider. On March 1, the board sent a letter to Chin, essentially siding with the technical director. The board did not think that Chin would actually quit, but to everyone's surprise, he was not bluffing. Considering the board's letter an ultimatum, Chin resigned four days later. However, Jeff Chan, the author of *Bunnyhop* and a board member, would not allow the play to continue without Chin as director. Two days later, on March 7, the board rehired Chin to direct *Bunnyhop*, giving him full authority. But when Chin saw that the set he had constructed had been "kicked" (according to Chin) and dismantled, he left, never to return to work with AATW. According to an article in *The San Francisco Journal*, Raymond Ju, Eric Hayashi, and assistant director Marc Hayashi had, with the Board's permission, disassembled the triggering device that collapsed the wall. They felt it was "too damn heavy" and therefore dangerous.[40]

---

[40] Randall Yip, "Chin Quits AATW," *The San Francisco Journal*, April 12, 1978, 1.

To make things more complicated, AATW had recently received a large grant from the Rockefeller Foundation, and such mainstream recognition could not have been possible without Frank Chin's reputation. After a long meeting, the board decided that AATW had a better future without Chin: "It is our belief that, while the Workshop will possibly be financially poorer in the immediate future, the present offers a rich opportunity to develop acting, directing, and technical skills for many people."[41]

Those who welcomed the decision expressed disapproval of Chin's insistence on making the company an Asian American playwright's workshop. They felt the company had to explore other directions. But others, like Ben Tong of the University of California, Santa Cruz, defended Chin and asked to be disassociated from AATW:

> Suffice to say that Frank did not deserve to be treated in the way that he was. He may not have been the easiest Artistic Director to live with but his wholehearted, sacrificial efforts should have counted for something … All I can say at this point is that those in AATW who have resented Frank for the glory that was not theirs can have it all now. I imagine AATW will become a nightclub act, doing a lot of instant flashy things like poetry readings and the like, which will be nice. Too bad it will never be a theater again and live up to what it might have been.[42]

Those who defended Chin's style of leadership were generally avid supporters of Chin's vision of AATW. Supporter like Ben Tong and Jeffery Paul Chan were also invested in researching and creating an Asian American culture, and Chin's interpersonal and leadership skills were the least of their concerns.[43]

After the resignation, Chin went to Seattle and worked briefly with Bea Kiyohara and the Asian Exclusion Act during its difficult times. There, Chin continued to work on his third play, *Oofty, Goofty,* which is about the

---

[41] Asian American Theater Workshop, "Letter from the Board of directors" (March 16, 1978). The Asian American Theater Company Archive, California Ethnic and Multicultural Archives at the Special Collections Library, University of California, Santa Barbara.

[42] Ben Tong, "A letter to Karen Seriguchi, President of the Board of Directors" (March 19, 1978). The Asian American Theater Company Archive, California Ethnic and Multicultural Archives at the Special Collections Library, University of California, Santa Barbara.

[43] Following Chin's departure, Jeff Chan's *Bunnyhop*, Chin's new play, *Oofty, Goofty,* and a third "unnamed original play" were withdrawn from the season. No play was produced in 1978, but in 1979, the Workshop produced four original Asian American plays: *Point of Departure* by Paul Stephen Lim, *Coda* by Alberto Isaac, *A Play by Bill Yamasaki* by Adrian Kinoshita-Myers, and *Intake-Outtake* by Judi Nihei, Marc Hayashi, Diana Tanaka, Adrienne Fong and others. The 1979 season showcased the new artistic style of AATW that would continue until the mid-1980s.

Japanese internment camps. He has since not returned to Asian American theatre (except on minor occasions) and focused on writing novels, short stories, and essays. The experience of resignation was bitter for Frank Chin: "I've been slapped in the face twice, humiliated and lied to by the Board . . . They [Hayashi and Ju] played on resentment, jealousy, and fear."[44] To this day, Chin calls the Asian American Theater Workshop a failed experiment.

Some conjecture that had his temper and autocratic style not gotten in the way, Frank Chin could have led the Asian American theatre movement as did Amiri Baraka for Black theatre and Luis Valdez for Chicano theatre for many more years. Perhaps the administrative organization and artistic style of the Asian American Theater Workshop were too similar to American regional theatre for it to be truly original and experimental as Frank Chin envisioned. Or it could be that the Asian Americans occupy a different space demographically, politically, culturally, and economically than do African Americans and Chicanos, and Frank Chin and his "real" Asian American theatre could not find a niche. The more plausible reason may be that the urgency and vigor of cultural nationalism and the movements of the 1960s and 1970s began to wane in the late 1970s. As Glenn Omatsu describes, the "winter of civil rights" began in the late 1970s, leading many to ask: "why did a society in motion toward progressive change seem to suddenly reverse direction?"[45] Frank Chin's agenda had not changed for almost a decade, and the sudden conservative turn in the national politics may have accelerated the jettisoning of his rhetoric and style.

All things considered, it would be fair to state that Frank Chin is a talented writer with a clear agenda who has many supporters and enemies. His role in Asian American culture and theatre history is that of an eccentric and infamous gadfly. He may have failed to rally everyone to believe in his vision, but he has managed to stir up controversies and discussions, forcing people to think and argue. In fact, over two decades after his resignation, Chin's vision of a "real" theatre for Asian Americans still dominates the discussions of what Asian American theatre should be.[46]

[44] Yip, "Chin Quits AATW," 5.
[45] Glenn Omatsu, "The *Four Prisons* and the Movements of Liberation: Asian American Activism from the 1960s to the 1990s," in *The State of Asian America: Activism and Resistance in the 1990s*, edited by Karin Aguilar-San Juan (Boston: South End Press, 1994), 89.
[46] For instance, Alvin Eng, in *Tokens?: The NYC Asian American Experience on Stage*, edited by Alvin Eng (Philadelphia: Temple University Press, 1999), features Frank Chin prominently in the "Verbal Mural" section of the anthology.

He is also central to the discussion of Asian American literature. While Frank Chin diligently sought out the "real" Asian American writers (such as John Okada, author of *No No Boy*), he viciously criticized the "fake" ones, especially those Chinese American writers who, in his opinion, misrepresented Chinese myths or Chinese American history. As early as 1976, Chin began a highly publicized debate with Maxine Hong Kingston after she published *The Woman Warrior: Memoirs of a Girlhood Among Ghosts* (1976) and received national recognition by winning the National Book Award. The editors of *Aiiieeeee!!!* found Kingston's book and its success disturbing and even damaging to their new literary movement. Frank Chin wrote severely critical letters to Kingston and described her book as catering to white readers and providing "prayers to white supremacy and white manhood."[47] In the letter, he calls her a "yellow white racist" for misrepresenting traditional Chinese mythology and reinforcing the stereotypes of Asian males as emasculate and chauvinistic. "The China and Chinese America portrayed in these works are the products of white racist imagination, not fact, not Chinese culture, and not Chinese American literature."[48] Chin described himself as "authentic" and Kingston as "fake" in their portrayal of traditional Chinese culture and Chinese American experience. As Kingston (and later Amy Tan) gained more popularity in the mainstream, Chin relentlessly attacked what he called "autobiographies by yellow women" written to satisfy the "white racist" readers.[49] In the 1980s, he would extend the criticism to David Henry Hwang for representing an effeminate Asian man on stage in *M. Butterfly* and thus fulfilling the "white" fantasy.[50]

Since the early 1980s, Chin has virtually stopped writing plays and turned to novels. His publications include *The Chinaman Pacific and Frisco R. R. Co.* (1988), a collection of eight short stories and novels, *Donald Duk* (1991) and *Gunda Din Highway* (1994). As in theatre, Chin is a controversial figure in Asian American literary and cultural communities. Some

[47] Frank Chin, "Letter to Maxine Hong Kingston" (1976), 1. The Asian American Theater Company Archive, California Ethnic and Multicultural Archives at the Special Collections Library, University of California, Santa Barbara.

[48] Ibid.

[49] Frank Chin and others rearticulate the argument in their Introduction to *The Big Aiiieeeee!: An Anthology of Chinese and Japanese American Literature* edited by Jeffery Paul Chan, Frank Chin, Lawson Fusao Inada, and Shawn Wong (New York: Meridian, 1991).

[50] Frank Chin's latest attack on David Henry Hwang appeared in an undated letter titled "Chin on Hwang" which Chin wanted the *Los Angeles Times* to publish. The paper wouldn't publish and, instead, he published the letter in Ishmael Reed's *KONCH*, an online magazine. Frank Chin, "Chin on Hwang," *KONCH* (March 14, 2001), www.ishmaelreedpub.com/articles/chin.html.

recognize him as the godfather of Asian American writing, while others describe him as acrimonious and misogynist. Although he has refused to participate in Asian American theatre since 1980, he has continued to dabble in drama, including a docudrama based on the court documents from the Japanese American internment camp period. According to Chin, he no longer writes plays for production, but at the same time, he does not dismiss the possibility of staging work at Asian American theatre companies in the future.

After his resignation, the AATW continued to honor Chin's vision of the writer's theatre. As I discuss in Chapter 5, a number of second-wave Asian American playwrights, including Philip Kan Gotanda, were produced by the company. However, the administrative side of AATW never stabilized after Chin's resignation. In fact, the 1980s was notable for a new kind of experimentation. With Chin, most veteran members left, creating a vacuum that provided the remaining members an opportunity to make artistic and managerial decisions. The remaining members were young and diverse: Eric Hayashi, Marc Hayashi, Lane Nishikawa, Judi Nihei, Bernadette Cha, Emilya Cachapero, Amy Hill, Dennis Myers, John Ng, and Dennis Dun. Eric Hayashi, who had played a central role in the resignation of Frank Chin, was one of the more veteran members of the new group and played a leading role in formulating a new model of management. Hayashi imagined a committee modeled after the United Artists Studio in which members could represent "different factions of the whole production, the whole theatre, including actors, directors, production people, administrators, and writers."[51] In 1979, after much debate, the group agreed to form what they called an "artistic committee" that would replace the artistic director position vacated by Frank Chin. Until 1986, the artistic committee managed the artistic aspects of productions including season selection and casting.

The artistic committee was as talented and passionate as it was daring and volatile, and the members were the best of friends and worst of enemies. The committee members practically lived together in the theatre, devoting everything to both administration and creation. Every member of the committee directed, designed, taught, wrote, and ran the theatre in the way he or she envisioned. Their visions clashed most of time, but that made the process even more creative and exciting. The complex relationship between the members of the artistic committee generated a

---

[51] Eric Hayashi, Personal interview (June 24, 2000), Los Angeles. All quotes by Eric Hayashi without citation are from this interview.

tremendously powerful artistic energy that has yet to be matched in Asian American theatre history. They produced over forty productions (most of which were new Asian American plays) and helped launch the careers of many actors, playwrights, and producers.

With the official formation of the artistic committee came the name change from "Asian American Theater Workshop" to "Asian American Theater Company," signifying a departure from Frank Chin's original vision of the group as a playwright's workshop and laboratory. The newly named group strived to become a major theatre company in the San Francisco area. They also wanted to build a stronger relationship with the audiences and the community in San Francisco and revise the company's image associated with Chin. No longer a playwright's laboratory, the Asian American Theater Company (AATC) began a new era with the first artistic committee that consisted of Eric Hayashi, Marc Hayashi, Amy Hill, Dennis Myers, John Ng, and Judi Nihei. As it can be expected from an organization run by young, inexperienced administrators, the artistic committee often faced irresolvable disagreements and loss of focus. However, as unstable as it was, the AATC managed to resurface with strong seasons in 1979 and 1980. A total of eight shows were produced in 1979, and three more shows followed in the first half of 1980.[52] Most were new Asian American plays, but some were revivals of previously produced plays such as Mel Escueta's *Honey Bucket*. The artistic committee also strengthened the training programs, which included classes in voice, movement, acting, improvisation, political theatre, tap dancing, musical theatre, and theatre management. Some of the classes were part of the professional training programs at the American Conservatory Theater in San Francisco, and some were offered to teach a variety of theatre styles to anyone who was interested. The space on 4344 California Street was open to anyone who was interested in participating in Asian American theatre.

While the artistic energy was palpable, the administrative experiment in the form of the artistic committee did not go smoothly. Ironically, despite the stressful management and unpredictable future, the AATC's repertory of new Asian American plays grew more numerous and diverse than ever before. The artistic committee managed to produce R. A. Shiomi's *Yellow Fever* at the YWCA on Sutter Street from October to December 1983. Other plays of the 1983–84 season included David Henry Hwang's

---

[52] See the AATC website for a complete season listings. www.asianamericantheater.org/archives. html.

FOB and *The Dance and the Railroad*, Ernest Abuba's *An American Story*, and *Not My Fault*, an ensemble improvisational comedy. In 1984, the AATC became a resident company of the People's Theater at Fort Mason Center, and soon after, moved its offices into a historic landmark building (formerly a Buddhist temple) on the edge of Japantown in San Francisco.

In November 1984, the AATC hired David Fong as its new executive director, but he left a few months later.[53] Like other members of the staff, he was expected to sacrifice everything and devote almost all of his time and energy to the company. The AATC, by this time, had too many problems to be solved by one person, but Fong was essentially hired to do exactly that. Despite Fong's resignation, the company had another impressive season. The season also had two benefit events: "In Celebration of Women: A Theater Party to Honor the Performance of *Tea*" in April 1985; and "An Evening of Elegance: Fashion Show and *Not My Fault* Performance" in November 1985.

However, it became obvious that hiring an artistic director could no longer be delayed, as artistic preferences clashed regularly and many bills went unpaid. The division of labor became a major issue for the artistic committee, and gender began to play a role in the growing tension. Judi Nihei, Amy Hill, and Emilya Cachapero, who took charge of administrative details, were close friends and trusted each other professionally. Cachapero, in particular, did most of the administrative work such as grant-writing and organizing committee meetings. But in public, men were the visible "leaders" of the company with their own close friendships. Also, the board of directors had a better relationship with the male members of the committee. The group, divided by gender, often disagreed on play selections and public relations strategies. Their professional relationships were also complicated by personal and sometimes intimate relationships. When a decision had to be made on an artistic director, the endgame began.

The board of directors finally decided to choose an artistic director from the artistic committee when it could not find an outside person. The female members thought that one of them deserved the job since they had taken care of much of the administrative work. Cachapero was an

---

[53] David Fong had been a volunteer with the company in the mid-1970s and had taken its acting and writing classes, he had just completed his MBA in New York City. He had excellent credentials for the job, but he joined the company in the midst of many transitions and internal disputes.

especially strong candidate. However, the board of directors chose Lane Nishikawa as the new artistic director, beginning with the 1986–87 season. Unhappy with this decision, Amy Hill, Judi Nihei, and Emilya Cachapero left AATC.[54] With Nishikawa as artistic director, Eric Hayashi was hired as the executive director in October 1986. Consequently, the "artistic committee period" ended at the AATC, and the "Nishikawa-Hayashi period" began. (After Nishikawa, Hayashi served as the artistic director from 1989 to 1993.)

During the next three years, Nishikawa and Hayashi implemented several changes, including obtaining, in January 1989, a new permanent space after being without one for six years. The new space, the Asian American Theater Center, was fulfillment of a dream for everyone. With a 135-seat mainstage, sixty-seat second stage, a dance and rehearsal studio, and administrative offices in the ethnically diverse Richmond district, it was the best place any Asian American theatre company had ever obtained. However, by the end of the 1980s, because of a combination of poor management and misfortune, the AATC lost the space and went into a financial downfall that still affects the company today.

According to Nishikawa and Hayashi, their plan was to obtain the performing space with borrowed money and to pay back using the profits from large-scale productions. However, the plan was destroyed along with the building when on October 18, 1989, an earthquake hit San Francisco. The earthquake caused the new space's mainstage fire sprinklers to trigger and break, flooding the theatre with 12,000 gallons of water. The space was fully renovated in ten months, but the reconstruction put the company in further debt. Before one season could be completed, the company had incurred an unmanageable amount of debt, including unpaid taxes. Moreover, grant sources found out about the company's financial situation, and cancelled their support. Also, in 1990, Nishikawa, with his lawyer, made a formal request for payment of about $33,000 in back salaries. To make things worse, the board of directors began to doubt the very survival of the company and hesitated to assist it financially. Unlike other periods in AATC history, very few documents from the Nishikawa-Hayashi period can be found in the company's archive. Some critics of this period allege that most administrative decisions were made at a bar which

---

[54] The details of the selection process and the subsequent resignation of some members were quite elaborate and dramatic. As anyone can imagine there were tears shed and damaging words spoken. In fact, many members still refuse to talk to each other and remain bitter about what happened.

Nishikawa and Hayashi frequented and that they rarely took minutes of their meetings. According to Hayashi, however, he still possesses most of the documents and has not yet donated them to the archive. A fair assessment of the period cannot be made until these documents have been examined.

In 1990, an accountant was hired to reconstruct records for the period of 1986–89, and the Business Volunteers for the Arts of the San Francisco Chamber of Commerce got involved in the inquiry. The details of this topic remain to be researched further when documents become available, but in short, the company faced near-bankruptcy in 1990. In 1993, Eric Hayashi resigned in order to work for the National Endowment for the Arts and asked Pamela Wu to take the position of executive director. Under the leadership of Wu, the personnel changes were frequent. Karen Amano and Diane Emiko Takei briefly served as artistic directors, and numerous others filled various administrative positions only to leave after short tenure. Many cited Wu's artistic vision and management style as the reasons for leaving. Moreover, the company's growing debt and lingering culture of mismanagement made it impossible to maintain a steady staff. According to Wu, she was not told the disturbing facts of the AATC's financial situation or that the company might need to close down. Making the best of a worst situation, Pamela Wu has managed to make deals with the IRS and other agencies to reduce back payments.

However, the AATC lost its space in the Richmond district, and the status of the company was diminished both in size and reputation. Some gave up on the company, and others (including Pam Wu) predicted its closing in a few years. The one thing that has kept it going has been the legacy of Frank Chin and memories of the exciting and "crazy" times under the artistic committee's management in the first half of the 1980s. Meanwhile, what remains is a blame game that continues to be divided along the gender line. (Pamela Wu is a good friend of Judi Nihei, Amy Hill, and Emilya Cachapero, who collectively blame Nishikawa and Hayashi for running the theatre to the ground. Nishikawa and Hayashi, on the other hand, do not agree with some of Wu's administrative decisions.)[55]

In 1999 when I spoke to Pamela Wu, she was pessimistic about the future of AATC. Productions were mounted sporadically, and it seemed

---

[55] Many former members of the artistic committee went on to pursue careers in theatre as administrators. Experienced and wiser, they led Asian American theatre through the 1990s and into the twenty-first century. Judi Nihei, for instance, served as the artistic director of the

impossible to get out of financial debt. In 2004, however, the AATC was revived with a new managing artistic director, Sean Lim, who put life into the company with his youthful vision. By producing plays that speak to a younger generation of Asian Americans, the AATC seems to have entered a "hopeful stage," as described by Robert Hurwitt of the San Francisco Chronicle. Hurwitt, in reviewing the 2004 production of *Rental Car* by Alex Park, was most impressed with the audience: "It isn't just that the theater is packed on a Saturday night. It's the youth and enthusiasm of a crowd that appears to represent an even broader cross section of the Asian American community than that onstage."[56] It remains to be seen whether AATC will indeed find financial and administrative stability. With a new generation of Asian Americans who may or may not know who Frank Chin is, the company may finally become the theatre he had envisioned: a cultural center for Asian Americans.

Northwest Asian American Theater, Seattle

In the early 1970s, a group of Asian American students at the University of Washington wanted to find acting opportunities. Led by Stan Asis, the group included Marilyn Tokuda, Yolly Irigon, Henry Tonel, Gloria Pacis, Larry Wong, and Maria Batayola. Before meeting Tokuda in a drama class at the University of Washington, Asis led a group called Dulaan Ng Mga Tao, Theatre of the People, a Filipino American theatre group in Seattle. As drama majors at the university, Asis and Tokuda felt the "loneliness of being nonwhite and having to play roles or learn about theatre which did not honor [their] culture."[57] They agreed to form an Asian American drama group on campus.

The first public show in 1974 was *Marginal Man* written and directed by Tokuda at the University of Washington. It was a musical comedy revue about the Asian American experience, emphasizing what was then a new concept of "Asian American" as "not Asian," and "not American." The sketches depicted "difficult situations and racist circumstances faced by the

---

Northwest Asian American Theater from 1994 to 1998, and Emilya Cachapero moved to New York City and worked as the director of artistic programs at the Theatre Communications Group. Eric Hayashi left the AATC to work at the National Endowment for the Arts and later for the Japanese American Cultural Center in Los Angeles.

[56] Robert Hurwitt, "Asian American Theater Enters a Hopeful Stage," *San Francisco Chronicle*, November 16, 2004, D1.

[57] *Dreams and Promises: Northwest Asian American Theater 20th Anniversary* (Seattle: Northwest Asian American Theatre Company, 1992), 14.

Chinese, Japanese, and Filipinos since they [had] arrived on the Western shores of the United States."[58] At the time, there were only a few Asians among over 300 drama majors in the University of Washington, School of Drama. Thus, most actors in the show were non-majors who were acting for the first time. The reception of *Marginal Man* was positive. The group was invited by other campuses to perform the show. Within a year, the group was touring not only around the Seattle area but also in Oregon.[59] During this time, the most important sponsor of the group was the Asian Multi Media Center.

The creation of the Asian Multi Media Center in Seattle was initiated by young Asian American actors and activists, Tim Cordova, Nemesio Domingo, Jr., and Douglas Chin. In March 1972, they conceived the idea of creating a permanent Asian American acting group that would resemble a local African American company, Black Arts West. After spending 1972 seeking supporters and possible funding sources, the three realized that their concept of an acting group had to include other art forms in order to receive community support. Community leaders advised them to create a multimedia group that could train youth in media for employment. They proposed a multimedia center for "photography, graphic arts, and journalism with a training program that would encourage inner city youth to enter the mass communication field."[60] After writing a grant to the Washington State Arts Commission, they received $14,500 from Model Cities for Youth Services Projects, and in late January 1973, the Asian Multi Media Center (AMMC) opened under the umbrella of Filipino Youth Activities. Cordova, Domingo, and Chin asked Alan Scharer, who had been active in the Filipino community and had expertise with youth programs, to direct the center.

By focusing on multimedia instead of acting, the center was able to tap a wide range of grant sources, thus situating itself as a community-

[58] Northwest Asian American Theater, "Proposal" (1974), 16. This Proposal and other documents cited in this section were available at the Northwest Asian American Theater Company (NWAAT). When I was researching, the materials were in transit to be archived. I give immense thanks to Bea Kiyohara for moving the boxes of materials to the Nippon Kan Theater in Seattle for me to access. Days of sorting through the boxes allowed me to piece together the history of Theatrical Ensemble of Asians, Asian Exclusion Act, and NWAAT, only some of which I detail in this section. Once formally archived, a more in-depth study of the Asian American theatre history in Seattle will be possible.

[59] Performance sites included: Seattle University, Gonzaga University, Washington State University, Shoreline Community College, the 1973 Bumbershoot Festival, the Asian Education West Coast Conference, and the Child Welfare League Multi-racial Conference in Eugene, Oregon.

[60] *Dreams and Promises*, 5.

centered organization for Asian Americans in Seattle. One of the main goals of the center was to train Asian youths for employment in media. In a grant proposal written in 1974, the center stated that the Asian communities in the Northwest had been confined to low-income jobs. The proposal also reported "the median income for Washington Filipinos, in 1970, was 62% of white male median income; for the Chinese, 68%; and for the Japanese, 86%."[61] According to the proposal, one way to develop Asian communities economically was to "encourage young Asians to enter occupational fields from which they traditionally have been excluded, so that they may draw upon the economic resources of the larger society to augment the resources of their own peoples."[62]

The primary goal of the center was to empower Asian American youths by providing occupational training and a cultural education. In addition, specific objectives included artistic training and media awareness. Free classes in photography, graphic arts, drama, and silk screening were taught by experts who volunteered to teach for a small stipend. Instructors included Steve Suzuki, Gary Wong, Rick Wong, and Hugo Louie, who were professionals in the community.

In the first year, a drama workshop titled "Creative Dramatics, Acting, Theater Games" was taught by Richard E. T. White, Stan Asis, and Marilyn Tokuda, drama students at the University of Washington. The 1974 grant proposal described the workshop as a coming together of "disjointed groups of Asian individuals doing a play here and there." Comprised primarily of Asian American high-school and college-age students who met two or three times a week, the classes provided training in basic acting and directing. One of the first public presentations of the drama workshop was a staged reading titled "If You Want to Know What We Are: Voices of Asians In America," directed by Richard E. B. White. It featured dramatic adaptations of novels and short stories by Lawson Inada and Carlos Bulosan, and other Asian American writers. Workshop students also presented staged readings at local high schools and colleges.

With the support of AMMC and encouraged by the success of *Marginal Man*, Tokuda, Asis, and other students began to contemplate the idea of forming a semi-independent Asian American acting group that would be part of AMMC. Their agenda was not to create just an acting group. They wanted to use theatre as a vehicle to address several problems:

---

[61] Northwest Asian American Theater, "Proposal," 2.
[62] Ibid.

-Negative stereotyping of Asian Americans in the mass media as depicted [by] such one dimensional characters as Charlie Chan, Fu Manchu, Lotus Blossom, and Susie Wong.
-The use of non-Asian actors and actresses to portray Asian characters.
-The lack of a forum to describe the true Asian American experience.
-Lack of local performance opportunities for Seattle's Asian American actors, directors, and playwrights.[63]

The members named the group Theatrical Ensemble of Asians (TEA) and began their first season in November 1974 with a dramatic adaptation of works by writer and poet Carlos Bulosan. Directed and adapted by Stan Asis, it was presented at the Ethnic Cultural Center at the University of Washington.

According to Tokuda, TEA gave artistic freedom and creative energy to its members who were in their early twenties: "Because we were young and full of energy and passion, fulfilling our visions left no room for the word, 'no.' We did what we had to do in order to get things done. As tiring and frustrating as it was at times, it was always a challenge and taught us self-sufficiency; it gave me the confidence to produce something independently."[64] For the members of TEA, theatre was a new world where they found the opportunity to act, write, produce, and participate as audience members. Also, most of them considered themselves both artists and activists. According to Stan Asis, "theater [in Seattle] was a hub of activity for Asians, Blacks, Chicanos, and Indians – for all people of color. Each group was developing theater which reflected the pain, anger, aspirations, and hope of its people."[65]

The founders of TEA were aware of the East West Players in Los Angeles, the Asian American Theatre Workshop in San Francisco and the Oriental Actors of America and often exchanged information and worked toward a common goal. For instance, in 1974, TEA joined EWP and OAA to make a formal proposal to the Actors' Equity Association to end the practice of yellowface in American theatre. TEA modeled itself after the EWP and the AATW in its administrative and artistic decisions. But more importantly, TEA established strong local relationships with the Asian Multi Media Center and other community resources in the International District in Seattle.

[63] *Dreams and Promises*, 6.
[64] Ibid., 12.
[65] Ibid., 14.

In 1975, TEA moved off campus and formally joined AMMC. In November of the same year, Garrett Hongo was hired as the managing director of AMMC's drama program and changed the name from TEA to Asian Exclusion Act (AEA), to which some objected. The first meeting, as Hongo recalled, took place in a loft space on South Rainier Street:

> At that first meeting, we stood in a circle in the loft space down on South Rainier. There was no heat and we wore our winter coats indoors. We were all kids in our early 20s, wanting something. I felt there was a powerful spirit among us, even though most of us were socially tentative, even a little gloomy giving suggestions . . . I took an intellectually radical stance and changed the name of the theatre group from Theatrical Ensemble of Asians to The Asian Exclusion Act – after the Chinese Exclusion Act of the late 19th Century, after the Alien Land Laws of the early 20th Century, after the Japanese American exclusion orders sending 120,000 Americans to concentration camps during WWII.[66]

Reflecting this new spirit of "radical stance," the first play by the Asian Exclusion Act was Frank Chin's *The Year of the Dragon*.

Garrett Hongo admits that other people in the group and the Board of Directors did not like the name change from "TEA (a kinder, gentler name)" to the Asian Exclusion Act. Some people in the community reacted negatively to the change. They also disapproved of the "ostensible subject of Chin's play."[67] According to Hongo, "A few folks [in the community] were angry, that they heard there was a character in [Chin's play] who was a stereotype, who used 'chop-suey English,' who played Asian ethnicity for laughs."[68] Chin's rebellious, biting critique of racism has always been controversial in the Asian American community, and Seattle was no exception. Before the play opened, rumors of protest from community activists – who threatened to picket the play on opening night and shut it down – worried the members of the Asian Exclusion Act. However, in late January 1976, the play opened without any trouble or disruption. The house had about sixty or seventy members in the audience which, for Hongo, "seemed enough of a beginning to keep on keeping on."[69]

---

[66] Ibid., 32.
[67] Ibid.
[68] Ibid.
[69] Ibid.

The 1975–76 season, which included a workshop of Wakako Yamauchi's *And the Soul Shall Dance* and Garrett Hongo's *Nisei Bar and Grill*, reflected Hongo's commitment to producing full-length plays rather than skits and readings. *And the Soul Shall Dance* was presented in a workshop format while Yamauchi continually rewrote the script. (In the following season, the East West Players premiered a full production of the final version of the play in Los Angeles.) *Nisei Bar and Grill* was directed by Frank Chin with a cast that included Bea Kiyohara, Judi Nihei, Stephen Sumida, Frank Abe, Richard Eng, and Maria Batayola.

The Asian Exclusion Act produced full-length Asian American plays in its 1976–77 and 1977–78 seasons. During Hongo's tenure as artistic director, most plays produced by the company were imported from San Francisco and Los Angeles. For instance, the 1976–77 season included Momoko Iko's *Gold Watch* which received first prize in the East West Player's playwriting competition, and Mel Escueta's *Honeybucket* which premiered at the Asian American Theater Workshop in the 1975–76 season. The members of the Asian Exclusion Act had a close relationship with artists at the Asian American Theater Workshop. Actors such as Marc Hayashi and directors such as Frank Chin from San Francisco visited Seattle regularly to assist Hongo and to participate in productions.[70] In the 1977–78 season, the Asian Exclusion Act produced Jeffery Paul Chan's *Jackrabbit* and Lori Higa's *Lady Murasaki Rides the Wild, Wild West*.

However, around this time, the Asian Multi Media Center began to lose financial stability, and the Asian Exclusion Act lost many of its key members, including Hongo. Also, many actors, directors, and writers who had come together for TEA and the Asian Exclusion Act wanted to move to San Francisco, Los Angeles, and New York City for greater opportunities. And, indeed, many did become leaders of Asian American theatre – Ken Narasaki would later serve as the literary manager of the East West Players, and Amy Hill, Marc Hayashi, and Judi Nihei served in the Artistic Committee of the Asian American Theater Workshop in San Francisco. (In 1992, Judi Nihei would return to Seattle to serve as the artistic director of NWAAT.)

Those who remained desperately wanted the theatre group to survive. The artists and staff agreed to work as unpaid volunteers to keep the Asian

---

[70] In 1976, the second Asian American Writers' Conference took place in Seattle. Frank Chin, who had organized the first conference in San Francisco in 1975, led the second conference as well. Participants of the conference included Frank Chin, Garrett Hongo, Stephen Sumida, and Wakako Yamauchi.

American theatre group in Seattle. The survival of the theatre group would not have been possible without Bea Kiyohara. "I wanted to keep the drama program alive. With Garret Hongo leaving, I became the Artistic Director of the Asian Multi Media Center, more by default than anything, but a position I . . . held for the [next] fifteen years."[71] Having lost the performing space in the Asian Multi Media Center, Bea Kiyohara with a few others such as Chris Wong and Maria Batayola utilized every possible resource. They performed at the Ethnic Cultural Center at the University of Washington and the historic Nippon Kan Theater, which was being renovated at the time. Bea Kiyohara found help and inspiration in Frank Chin who had moved to Seattle after resigning from Asian American Theater Workshop. With his help, Kiyohara and others continued with their mission. In the 1979–1980 season, three simplified productions were presented: staged readings of excerpts of John Okada's *No-No Boy*, Mei-Mei Bressenbrugge's *One, Two Cups* (directed by Frank Chin), and Frank Chin's *The Year of the Dragon* (directed by Mako). Kiyohara remembers this production of *The Year of the Dragon* at the Nippon Kan Theater as one of her "acting highlights." She was "sharing the stage with Mako, Frank Chin, Pat Suzuki, and Tina Chen, all of whom [had] been [her] role models in acting and performing."[72]

However, Frank Chin abruptly left when opportunities were found in other cities. The following years were tremendously challenging for Bea Kiyohara and other remaining members. In 1981, Bea Kiyohara renamed the Asian Exclusion Act the Northwest Asian American Theater (NWAAT) "to reflect both its regional and ethnic identity."[73] The first priority for Kiyohara and others was obtaining a permanent space. They continued to rent spaces that required the company to strike the set every night. The lack of permanent space on top of fluctuating budget made only bare survival possible. The remaining staff of NWAAT, led by Kiyohara, had identified, in 1977, an old garage in the International District as a possible site for a theatre. According to Kiyohara, she spent eight years on the board of the International District Preservation and Development Authority to convince others to renovate the garage into a cultural center that would house NWAAT. Her plan was raise enough money to build a structure that could be shared by various groups. She did everything in her power, playing politics and visiting every council

---

[71] *Dreams and Promises*, 11.
[72] Ibid.
[73] Ibid., 7.

member in the city. Her garage was storage space for equipment (including over a hundred cushioned seats) to be used in the new space. She found support from politicians, including Gary Locke, who would later become the governor of Seattle and the first Asian American governor in the United States history. After ten years of strenuous effort, Kiyohara's wishes were fulfilled: NWAAT moved to the lower floor of the newly renovated building, and The Wing Luke Asian Museum occupied the upper floor.

On January 27, 1987, NWAAT's new home, Theater Off Jackson, opened with the world premiere of *Miss Minidoka 1943*. The opening was dramatic in more than one way: only hours before the curtain went up, Kiyohara was negotiating with the fire and building inspectors to obtain a certificate of occupancy. *Miss Minidoka 1943*, an original musical comedy written by Gary Iwamoto and directed by Bea Kiyohara and Stan Asis, was a hit.[74] The musical takes place in Minidoka Internment Camp, Idaho in early 1943. Based on an actual beauty pageant to select the camp "Sweetheart," the story of the musical portrays Japanese Americans who were doing their best to make the best of an atrocious situation. The musical was a hit, and it provided much needed stability. Funding became more available, new artists joined, and the audience base increased.

The Northwest Asian American Theater has since become the flagship Asian American theater company in the Northwest region and a community-based theatre in Seattle's International District. After fifteen years as the artistic director, Kiyohara resigned in 1993, and Judi Nihei took the helm until 1998. During the five years, Nihei raised the quality of NWAAT productions to rival that of other Asian American theatre companies. After Nihei's resignation, Chil Kong (1998–99) and Rosa Joshi (1999–2000) also worked as the artistic director, and in 2000, Chay Yew came on board to lead the company in a new direction. Yew initially created much excitement with a season that catered to the gay community in Seattle, but his tenure did not last long. He left Seattle in 2004, and NWAAT has not hired another artistic director as of 2005.

During the 1970s and 1980s, many Asian American theatre artists left Seattle to find better opportunities in Los Angeles, San Francisco, and New York City. Those who remained devoted themselves to the theatre as a community-based organization and refocused their agenda to serve Asian Americans in the International District. During the 1990s, however, Seattle has become a major locale of regional American theatre, and many

---

[74] Others credited for music and lyric are: Richard Lewis, Stan Asis, Erin Flory, Brian Higham, Ken Kubota, Lisa Pan, and Diane Yen-Mei Wong.

Asian American artists have relocated to the city to pursue their careers. The talent pool in Seattle has been solid since, but NWAAT has had difficulty finding artists to serve in the leadership position. During his tenure at NWAAT, Chay Yew kept his residency in Los Angeles and the directorship position at Asian Theatre Workshop at Mark Taper Forum (Los Angeles). The continuation of NWAAT will depend on successful fundraising and the hiring of a next artistic director. Meanwhile, Bea Kiyohara, now as a member of the Board of Directors, will once again do everything possible to establish NWAAT as a community-serving organization central to the International District in Seattle.

Pan Asian Repertory Theatre, New York City

As the founding artistic director of Pan Asian Repertory Theatre, Tisa Chang's goal from the start was to compete with other professional theatre groups in New York City. Chang wanted to present a "blend" of Eastern and Western theatre styles and worked towards mainstreaming her version of intercultural theatre. She envisioned an intercultural theatre that would be inclusive of all Asian traditions. For Chang, Asian American theatre is a subcategory within pan-Asian theatre. In the 1960s, Tisa Chang was a Broadway actress and appeared in popular revivals of *The King and I* and *Flower Drum Song*. Chang eventually became interested in directing and creating her own work. Like many minority artists in New York City, Tisa Chang sought support from Ellen Stewart, the founder of La MaMa Experimental Theater Club (E. T. C.).

Founded in 1961, La MaMa E. T. C. has promoted multicultural theatre in a global context, supporting scores of artists of all backgrounds both nationally and internationally. Stewart is an African American woman and has been called the "mother of Off-Off Broadway."[75] She also credits herself for starting Asian American theatre in New York City. Her claim puzzles many because her name is associated with avant-garde, experimental theatre, not with minority theatre in the USA. In fact, she rejects the label "African American" and would be the first to say that such racial "boxes" do not belong in her company.[76]

---

[75] See Gussow, "Off and Off-Off Broadway," in *The Cambridge History of American Theatre: Volume Three: Post-World War II to the 1990s*, edited by Don B. Wilmeth and Christopher Bigsby, 3 vols. (London: Cambridge University Press, 2000), 198.

[76] Alvin Eng, "'Some Place to be Somebody': La MaMa's Ellen Stewart," in *The Color of Theater: Race, Culture, and Contemporary Performance*, edited by Roberta Uno and Lucy Mac San Pablo Buns (New York: Continuum, 2002), 138.

When Stewart says she started Asian American theatre in New York City, she is referring to Tisa Chang's group that started at La MaMa and eventually became the Pan Asian Repertory Theatre, but she is also recalling La MaMa Chinatown, a group that was formed before Chang joined La MaMa. Stewart has always had passion for diversity and experimentation and produced works from all corners of the world. But, in 1970, eight years after the foundation of La MaMa E. T. C., she had yet to figure out a way to extend her artistic vision to the local Chinese community, the largest Chinatown in the country. The New York City Chinatown in the early 1970s was bustling with new immigrants who had arrived after 1965, when restrictive immigration quota laws were abolished.[77] Despite the geographical proximity of New York City Chinatown and the theatre centers (Broadway, Off Broadway, and Off-Off Broadway), the types of theatre produced in the two communities had been worlds apart. Theatre in Chinatown had evolved separately from the rest of the city, and Chinatown remained foreign to the New York City theatre communities. As Alejandro Portes has put it, "Chinatown is in the city, but not really of it."[78] In Chinatown, traditional Cantonese opera had been the main theatrical attraction since the nineteenth century. But, for Stewart, Chinatown signified infinite potential as the site for a new kind of theatre in the twentieth century.

The opportunity to include Chinatown in La MaMa came to Stewart when she met Ching Yeh, a director from Hong Kong. Yeh had worked at La MaMa the previous year as a resident director: in 1969, he wrote and directed *Wanton Soup* and subsequently directed other works, including

[77] In the 1970s most Chinese immigrants were from mainland China and settled in Chinatown while the "elite" immigrants from Hong Kong and Taiwan came as students, professionals, or artists and resided in uptown. The first Chinatown appeared in San Francisco in the nineteenth century, but racism led the Chinese (who were mostly unmarried male laborers) to scatter to other cities around the country, including New York, Philadelphia, Chicago, Baltimore, and Boston. New York settlers chose the Lower East Side of Manhattan, which at the time was an undesirable place to live. According to Min Zhou, Chinatowners were "sealed off from the outside world and were forced to conduct marginal economic activities to sustain their daily survival needs" (32). They worked in laundromats, restaurants, and domestic servitude. The segregated Chinatown functioned as an economic, social, and cultural center where Chinese could protect and support each other. With the repeal of the sixty-year-old Chinese Exclusion Act in 1943 and the passing of the War Brides Act of 1945, Chinatown's image as a bachelor society receded, and more Chinese Americans decided to make America their home for themselves and their families. In the late 1960s, the population of New York City Chinatown changed drastically as immigration laws such as the Hart-Cellar Act in 1965 opened doors to an influx of new immigrants from Asia. See Min Zhou, *Chinatown: The Socioeconomicc Potential of an Urban Enclave* (Philadelphia: Temple University Press, 1992)

[78] Quoted in Zhou, *Chinatown* xiii.

Heimskringla! Or the Stoned Angels by Paul Foster in March 1970.[79] Around
the same time, a group of New York City Asian American professional
actors formed a group called Asian American Repertory Theater to fight
racism in theatre. The actors invited Ching Yeh to direct the company and
their first project, *Three Travellers Watch a Sunrise* by Wallace Stevens.
According to Katy San, the play was written in the style of a Japanese Noh
play.[80] The performances ran through July and August of 1970 in the basement of the Transfiguration Church on Mott Street in Chinatown. Yeh,
with the intention of soliciting her help, invited Ellen Stewart to one of the
performances. According to Stewart, Ching Yeh and other artists, including Wu Gingi, approached her and told her "the only thing in Chinatown
was an occasional traveling troupe doing Beijing opera and not really anything else." She joined them to create "something" in Chinatown.[81] Stewart
began by inviting them to rehearse and perform at La MaMa where she
provided training in experimental theatre and improvisation.

The group eventually acquired the name La MaMa Chinatown, a name
that has remained in the memories of most people, including Stewart. La
MaMa Chinatown's next production was *Cranes and Peonies* by Jing-Jyi
Wu and Ching Yeh, presented on December 30, 1970. For the next six
years, La MaMa Chinatown produced one show per year, including *Anti-
classical Presentation* (October 20, 1971, written and directed by Gustavo
Ames with music by Alvin Ing) and *Pomp-Eii* (November 1, 1972, written
and directed by Ching Yeh).

Tisa Chang went to Ellen Stewart in 1973 with the idea of directing a
project called *Return of the Phoenix* which was based on a Peking opera.
Chang did not find much commonality with Ching Yeh and his style of
theatre, so she decided to spearhead the project independently from La
MaMa Chinatown. First of all, Chang spoke Mandarin and Ching Yeh
spoke Cantonese, and Chang found their "artistic aesthetics" very different.[82] Also, Chang was born in Chungking, China, and grew up in New
York where her father, Ping-Hsun Chang was the consul general for

---

[79] Yeh was one of many international theatre artists who came to work at La MaMa in the late
1960s and early 1970s. The artists included Yugoslavian playwright Aleksandar Popovich,
French director and actor Antoine Bourseiller, Romanian director Andrei Serban, and Indian
playwright Jagga Kapur. For a listing of productions at La MaMa, see Barbara Lee Horn, *Ellen
Stewart and La MaMa: A Bio-Bibliography* (Westport, CT: Greenwood Press, 1993).

[80] Katy San, "The Asian American Repertory Theater," *Bridge: An Asian American Perspective* 2.3
(1973), 24.

[81] Eng, *Tokens?*, 408.

[82] Tisa Chang, Telephone interview (June 28, 2001). All uncited quotations by Chang are from
this interview.

Nationalist China. She was Chinese American, not an international artist like Yeh, and her family's political background was a sensitive issue to many (especially to those from Hong Kong and Taiwan). Chang credits her father for getting her interested in Western theatre, but while acting on Broadway, she found the definition of American theatre too narrow. She wanted to see it "expand . . . to also include the very enriching traditions of the master works of China, Japan, and India."[83]

When she began working on *Return of the Phoenix*, Tisa Chang knew early on that she was interested in bilingual works and storytelling. She wasn't drawn to the avant-garde experiments and foreign language productions that Ellen Stewart, Ching Yeh, and others at La MaMa were focusing on. Chang made sure that her show was accessible to all audiences. She advertised the play as a "Chinese musical fantasy . . . based on the story from the Chinese Peking Opera."[84] Adapted by Chang herself, the production used traditional Peking Opera movements and music while providing bilingual (Mandarin and English) narrative and dialogues. It also included musicians from the Yeh Yu Chinese Opera Association. The production was received favorably and subsequently shown at Fairfield University, the Smithsonian Institute, and Alice Tully Hall. It also aired on television as the first of a new series called the *CBS Festival of Lively Arts of Young People* on October 20, 1973.

The cast included Alan Chow, Lu Yu, Kitty Chen, Lynette Chun, Eddie Chen, Lori Chinn, and Eleanor Yung. Most of the cast members were members of the Actors' Equity Association, reflecting Tisa Chang's commitment to promote the casting of Asian American actors and pay them professional salaries. Unlike earlier intercultural production at La MaMa, Tisa Chang's show employed professional Chinese American performers and had popular appeal beyond the Off-Off Broadway experimental theatre community.

Using the momentum of the success of *Return of the Phoenix*, Chang formed a group within La MaMa and named it Chinese Theater Group. Chang continued her Broadway acting career during this time, but she found herself increasingly interested in intercultural theatre. Chang believed that her intercultural approach was different from both traditional theatre in Chinatown and American mainstream theatre. In the subsequent productions at La MaMa, Chang continued to integrate traditional

---

[83] Eng, *Tokens?*, 411.
[84] Pan Asian Repertory Theatre, "Program Note for *Return of the Phoenix*," 1973, author's personal collection.

Chinese theatre styles with bilingual dialogues. Those productions included *The Legend of Wu Chang* performed in "Chinese theatre style," *A Midsummer Night's Dream* set in China in 1000 BC, *Hotel Paradiso* set in turn-of-the-century France, and *Orphan of Chao*, an adaptation of a Chinese tragedy.[85]

As Tisa Chang's productions increasingly demonstrated her interest in narrative storytelling and popular accessibility, her style began to clash with Ellen Stewart's view of intercultural theatre as an avant-garde experiment. Stewart questioned Chang's artistic taste and preference for narrative story telling, but Chang did not want to be pigeonholed, producing what she describes as "one type of show with foreign language [and] costume." According to Chang, Stewart preferred exotic visuals and sound. Stewart, on the other hand, contrasted Chang's productions with those of other Asian and Asian American theatre artists such as Ping Chong and Jessica Hagedorn who were directly involved with the avant-garde movement at the time in New York City. Also, a growing number of artists from Asia (such as Ching Yeh) came to New York City and La MaMa to create experimental and intercultural projects that blended modern and Asian theatre styles. For Stewart, their works, not Tisa Chang's, corresponded solidly with the goals of La MaMa.

Tisa Chang had in mind a different kind of theatre. She preferred to produce intercultural theatre that told stories form both Western and Eastern cultures. For example, she adapted Shakespeare and Goldoni as well as Peking opera with the purpose of telling the stories to all interested audiences in an entertaining style. This interest intersected with her desire to promote acting opportunities for professional Asian American actors. For one thing, this meant that the group needed to produce profitable shows in order to pay the salary termed by the Actors' Equity Association. Secondly, the focus set the stage for a shift away from intercultural theatre to a multicultural and Asian American theatre, which Chang would begin

---

[85] In 1975 Tisa Chang received a Best Play Focus Award for *The Legend of Wu Chang*, which she adapted from *The Yellow Jacket: A Chinese Play Done in a Chinese Manner* by George C. Hazelton and J. Harry Benrimo. Produced in November 1912, at the Fulton Theatre on Broadway, *The Yellow Jacket* was one of the first American plays to dramatize an "Oriental tale" in the style of Chinese theatre. The play takes place in 900 AD in provincial China where the wicked governor orders his first wife and infant son to be killed. The son survives and grows up to unseat his half-brother and "ascend the throne of [his] ancestors." For more information on the reception of the play, see the introduction by Brander Matthews in George Hazelton and J. Harry Benrimo, *The Yellow Jacket: A Chinese Play Done in a Chinese Manner* (Indianapolis: The Bobbs-Merrill Company Publishers, 1913).

to incorporate in the late 1970s. It was clear to both Chang and Stewart that the Chinese Theater Group had a different agenda, and in 1977, it became an independent company. Yet, despite this separation, Stewart and Chang have maintained an amicable yet complex relationship (which some have compared to that of a mother and daughter). For example, La MaMa has continued to assist Chang by providing performance spaces and low rent office space.

Tisa Chang's independent group was now renamed Pan Asian Repertory Theatre (PART) reflecting its goal to include and reflect all Asian cultures. Tisa Chang articulated the agenda that she had been developing to Mel Gussow of *The New York Times*:

> I want to utilize my heritage to explore new theatrical forms – rather than to espouse ethnicity. I also want to provide opportunity for Asian-American performers to work on the highest professional level. Sometimes American audiences find it jarring to see Orientals in predominantly white companies. We're experimenting by doing Western classics with an Asian company. We already did *Hotel Paradiso* and *A Midsummer Night's Dream*, which I set in China.[86]

Chang did not call her company "Asian American" but emphasized that it was an "Asian company" exploring "new theatrical forms" based on Asian heritage. She wanted to include plays from East Asia, the Philippines, India, Southeast Asia, and even Hawaii. Moreover, intercultural theatre, for Chang, was to be performed by those professional actors who brought the whole spectrum of Asian background to the production.

Chang herself continued to perform as an actress and her earnings on Broadway "literally made it possible to fund [her] first production" at PART.[87] In May 1977, Chang was on Broadway playing Al Pacino's Vietnamese girlfriend in David Rabe's *The Basic Training of Pavlo Hummel*. In the same month, PART staged its first production, a revival of the La MaMa production, *The Legend of Wu Chang*. As director, Chang had to open at La MaMa downtown at 7:30 p.m. and hurry to Broadway for the second act of *The Basic Training of Pavlo Hummel* to replace her understudy who appeared in the first act. The production of *The Legend of Wu Chang* was funded in part by the New York City Department of Cultural Affairs and the Board of Education and Arts Connection. But the majority of the funding came from Chang's own pocket. According to Chang, "The

[86] Mel Gussow, "Pan-Asian Troupe Visits La MaMa," *New York Times*, October 14, 1977, Section 3, 5.
[87] Terry Hong, "Theatre," *Asian American Almanac*, edited by Susan B. Gall and Irene Natividad (Detroit: Gale Research Inc., 1995), 578.

founding of Pan Asian wasn't something whimsical. It was a culmination of skills and dreams. I had experience as a working professional in the field, so by the time I founded Pan Asian, I was very focused and purposeful, and ready for new challenges as a director and producer."[88]

The program note of *The Legend of Wu Chang* describes the show as a "thrilling tale of a young prince battling for his rightful throne against his evil half-brother . . . A Total Theatre Experience unfolding the magic and color, the music and dance, the slapstick comedy and lyrical drama of the rarely performed Chinese theatre style." Mel Gussow, who reviewed the production for *The New York Times*, described it as having "an unabashed childlike quality in both the play and the performance." He found the plot "easy to follow as a nursery rhyme" and the show "suitable for children as well as adults" with gongs, drums, "vivid panoplies of color," mime, dancing, martial arts, and cartwheels.[89] Also, unlike the original bilingual production, the revival was performed entirely in English.

Chang carried out her commitment to Asian American actors from the first season. The cast of *The Legend of Wu Chang* included Lynette Chun, Lu Yu, Henry Yuk, Arline Miyazaki, Alvin Lum, Ching Valdes, Michael G. Chin, Gusti Bogok, and Glenn Kubota. Ernest Abuba played the title role. Of these ten actors, eight were members of the Actors' Equity Association, and Chang paid her actors equity salary since the first season. Chang was the first Asian American artistic director to pay her actors as contracted by the Actors' Equity Association. While actors at other Asian American theatre companies were treated as volunteers or members, Chang's actors were paid full professional salary. Mako acknowledges Chang's accomplishment: "I must say, on behalf of Tisa, she was able to pay her actors way before us [the East West Players]. Unless we had grants to cover [the production] we couldn't pay actors."[90]

After *The Legend of Wu Chang*, in 1977, PART produced *Thunderstorm*, written in 1933 by Tsao Yu, a modern Chinese playwright whose play had been produced in Japan and the Soviet Union. Set in Peking, China in the summer of 1923, the play is a domestic drama written in Ibsenite dramatic style. Written when the author was twenty-three, the play was the first major mainland Chinese play to use Western dramatic conventions. The original script ran for four hours, but Chang edited the 1956 translation by Wang Tso-liang and A. C. Barnes into a two and half hour version. In his

---

[88] Ibid.
[89] Gussow, "pan-Asian Troupe," 5.
[90] Mako, Personal interview (July 22, 1999).

review, Mel Gussow of *The New York Times*, described the play as a "compendium of our own [Western] theatrical clichés" and "not exotic."[91] For him, the plot was confusingly complex and "exceedingly Western." The only production-related comment he made was about the actors who performed the play "unabashedly – as if for the first time" and with a conviction and enthusiasm that, he commented, was enough to "override even incipient amateurism."[92] The production was directed by Tisa Chang, and the cast included Ernest Abuba as Chou Ping and Mia Katigbak as Lu Ssu-feng.

In November of 1977, Chang rearticulated her goals in a mission statement in the program note for *Thunderstorm*:

1. To provide opportunities for Asian American performers to work under the highest professional standards;
2. To utilize the style, music and movement of our native origins in order to explore new theatrical forms;
3. To promote new Asian American playwrights and plays, particularly those plays with themes pertinent to our life in America today.[93]

The third agenda was added to the two previous goals as Tisa Chang began to identify herself and the company with other Asian American theatre companies on the West Coast. She began to diversify the play selections to include not only Asian and Euro-American works but Asian American works as well. In 1978, PART produced its first Asian American play, Wakako Yamauchi's *And the Soul Shall Dance*, which was East West Player's ground-breaking production in 1977. Just as it brought much needed visibility and financial profit to the EWP in Los Angeles, the play was by far the most successful production produced by Tisa Chang in the 1970s. Moreover, it was a naturalistic family drama of the kind that Ellen Stewart least supported. Encouraged by its success, Tisa Chang extended the production to the next two seasons. Other plays in the 1978–79 season included *The Dowager* by Ernest Abuba, a Filipino American writer, actor, and a founding member of PART, and *The Servant of Two Masters* by Carlo Goldoni. The 1979–80 season included *Sunrise* by Cao Yu and *Monkey Music* by Margaret Lamb.

[91] Mel Gussow, "Stage: Storm of Complex Currents," *New York Times*, November 10, 1977 Section 3, 17.
[92] Ibid.
[93] Pan Asian Repertory Theatre, "Program Note for *Thunderstorm*" (1977), author's personal collection.

Figure 5. Pan Asian Repertory Theatre's production of *And the Soul Shall Dance* by Wakako Yamauchi in 1990. From left to right: Carol A. Honda, Roxanne Chang, and Dawn Saito.

By the end of the 1970s, PART had managed to balance all three goals of the mission statement, and the popularity and success of *And the Soul Shall Dance* confirmed for Tisa Chang that Asian American theatre had to be included in her stipulation of "Pan Asian theatre." During the next three seasons, PART focused increasingly on Asian American plays. For instance, the 1980–81 season included Momoko Iko's *Flowers And Household Gods* and Edward Sakamoto's *Yellow is My Favorite Color*, and the 1981–82 season featured Philip Kan Gotanda's *Bullet Headed Birds*.[94] Tisa Chang maintained that the name "Pan Asian" evolved from "inclusive of all Asia" to include "all Asians in America."[95] Whereas the Asian American Theater Company in San Francisco purposely used the term "Asian American" to distinguish it from "Asian," PART used "Asian" to imply both terms. For Tisa Chang, "Pan Asian" included not only all Asians in America, but also all Asians in the world.

[94] Also in 1981, PART was officially established with four artists' signatures: Tisa Chang, Lu Yu, Ernest Abuba, and Hsueh-tung Chen.
[95] Mel Gussow, "A Stage for All the World of Asian-Americans," *New York Times*, April 22, 1997, C16.

As the only remaining founding artistic director of an Asian American theatre company from the 1970s, Chang has received both praise and criticism for her approach to intercultural and Asian American theatre. Some, including Ellen Stewart, found her style not experimental enough and too geared towards popular entertainment while others criticized Chang for commercializing "Asianness" as foreign and exotic. More and more, a younger generation of writers and performers resisted Tisa Chang's request to keep focusing on their Asian identity and felt limited by the company's repertory. Also, Tisa Chang's strong personality and determination often led to personnel conflicts and disappointments. However, the most difficult challenge for Tisa Chang was keeping her promise of professionalism, especially because she wanted to present productions with the same caliber and quality as the best of other New York City theatres. The Pan Asian Repertory Theatre was not a community-based Asian American theatre company (like the Four Seas Players discussed in Chapter 4) but one that ambitiously sought to be included in mainstream Off Broadway and Broadway theatre. As some have pointed out, many of its productions came short in quality. However, in a city where most new theatre companies close after a few seasons, the Pan Asian Repertory Theatre has continued for almost three decades to play the role of the flagship Asian American theatre company in New York City while maintaining its unique agenda of including Asian American theatre as part of its "pan-Asian" theatre project.

4

Diversification of Asian American theatre

In the case of my own theater, I have tried to create a space for artists of color in the theater which would not reduce us to representative categories, but would create, through an expanded dramaturgy and deep relationships with communities, a new site of production.

Roberta Uno[1]

As DISCUSSED IN THE PREVIOUS TWO CHAPTERS, ASIAN Americans during the 1960s and 1970s made efforts to build a theatrical culture of their own by forming coalitions and theatre companies. The organizational structure of the companies was modeled after regional theatres in the United States, typically with an artistic director who would produce written plays on proscenium stage with actors trained in the style that emphasized psychological realism. With productions based on realism and narrative storytelling, the first four companies became home base for the majority of Asian American theatre artists. There were, however, artists who did not feel comfortable with the regional theatre model. Some were activists who preferred a less structured, agitprop style (such as street protest theatre), while others participated in the experimental arts movement that rejected American realism. Many wanted to incorporate poetry, music, dance, media arts, and non-European theatre traditions. In this chapter, I use the term "diversification" broadly to describe their works. It is not, however, my intention to connote a center-margin binary. The artists discussed in the following sections are central to the history of Asian American theatre. I'm using the term "diversification" as an

[1] Roberta Uno, "Introduction: Asian American Theater Awake at the Millennium," in *Bold Words: A Century of Asian American Writing*, edited by Rajini Srikanth and Esther Y. Iwanaga (New Brunswick: Rutgers University Press, 2002), 326.

umbrella concept to describe those works that have purposely resisted the
regional theatre model that privileges the written text.[2]

Asian American Movement, Third World Movement, and theatre as protest

On November 18, 1969, an antiwar activist group called Triple-A (Asian
Americans for Action) used a guerrilla theatre show to protest the Japanese Prime Minister Eisaku Sato's visit to the United States. Performing
in Dupont Circle in Washington, DC, the protesters argued that Japan
was the weaker partner in perpetuating imperialism in Asia, especially
Southeast Asia. They demanded the end to the US-Japan Security Treaty.
With twenty demonstrators arrested, the event caught the attention of
media outlets, including the *Washington Post* and *Washington Star*, both of
which gave the protest conspicuous coverage. According to the *Washington
Post*, the street theatre portrayed "Uncle Sam as a dragon 'swallowing up
third-world groups.'"[3] The dragon, made of cloth, featured a cardboard
head "resembling a malevolent imperialist Uncle Sam and a tail labeled
Sato."[4] The demonstration is one of many examples of street protest
theatre and guerilla theatre that were used during the late 1960s and early
1970s by Asian American activists.

The Asian American Movement began during the late 1960s as one of
the last ethnic-consciousness movements. The movement, as it is popu-
larly called, was not singular in its approach and form, and some of its aims
were not new (such as improving the community). But during the late
1960s, a younger generation of Asian Americans was inspired by the
antiwar movement and the Third World Movement that called for the
liberation of oppressed people worldwide. Asian American activists drew
connections between what they saw as an attempt to establish American
imperialism in Vietnam and racism in the United States. As William Wei
describes, Asian Americans found solidarity among themselves as well as
with other minority groups: "For Asian Americans, the antiwar movement
crystallized their understanding of racial discrimination against Asians in
America and convinced them that an inter-Asian coalition was an effective
way of opposing it."[5]

---

[2] I discuss solo performance, another aspect of the diversification, in Chapter 6.
[3] Martin Weil, "20 Held in March on Japan Embassy," *Washington Post* (November 18, 1969), A3.
[4] William Wei, *Asian American Movement* (Philadelphia: Temple University Press, 1993), 27.
[5] Ibid., 42.

Nobuko Miyamoto

Among the activists were writers, musicians, community leaders, and theatre artists. One of the most visible artists/activists was Nobuko Miyamoto. She created a version of Asian American theatre that has "eluded categorization".[6] A Nisei (second generation Japanese American), Miyamoto spent part of her childhood in internment camps during World War II. During the 1950s and 1960s, she acted, sang, and danced in Broadway musicals such as *The King and I* and *Flower Drum Song* and films such as the 1961 film version of *West Side Story*. She could have joined the Oriental Actors of America or the East West Players as did the majority of Asian American actors. Instead, during the late 1960s and 1970s, she used her theatrical talent to fight racism in political protests. She became an active member of the movement with the goal to "get involved in the community, [to] make revolution."[7] She found her situation different from the actors who founded the East West Players. Her concern was not about finding jobs in the mainstream acting industry. Her questions were directly related to her activism: "How do you make a voice for the community? How do you create cultural workers?"[8] She was interested in finding and training other Asian American artists who would use performance for political purposes.

In 1971, Miyamoto, along with Chris Iijima and "Charlie" Chin, recorded an album titled *A Grain of Sand: Music for the Struggle of Asians in America*, the first collection of contemporary Asian American music. As a group called A Grain of Sand, the trio sang on college campuses and at community-sponsored events across the country. She was reputed to be the most radical one of the trio. According to "Charlie" Chin, she was inspired by the Black Panthers: "she felt that the Asian [American] Movement, too, had to stand up around issues such as racism and US aggression in Viet Nam, that Asian Americans had to make their voice heard, to get off their knees and no longer be a quiet minority."[9]

---

[6] Roberta Uno, "Nobuko Miyamoto," in *Asian American Playwrights: A Bio-Bibliographical Critical Sourcebook*, edited by Miles Xian Liu (Westport, CT: Greenwood Press, 2002), 233.

[7] Lucy Mae San Pablo Burns, "Something Larger Than Ourselves: Interview with Nobuko Miyamoto," in *The Color of Theater: Race, Culture, and Contemporary Performance* edited by Roberta Uno and Lucy Mae San Pablo Buns (New York: Continuum, 2002), 199.

[8] Ibid., 200.

[9] Fred Wei-Han Houn, "An ABC from NYC: 'Charlie' Chin, Asian-American Singer and Songwriter," *East Wind* 5.1 (Spring/Summer 1986), 4–8. Quoted in Wei, *Asian American Movement*, 66.

Figure 6. Nobuko Miyamoto in her solo performance *A Grain of Sand* (1994).

In a solo performance Miyamoto created in 1994, titled *A Grain of Sand,* she described her participation in the movement during the early 1970s:

> Now, being in the movement was about change. Changing the injustices in our society, changing the system that ignored our history in this country. But the movement changed something else . . . my wardrobe . . . CHANGE . . . TALK ABOUT CHANGE . . . first you had an army jacket with lots of buttons on it then to complete the look . . . a beret . . . now blacks had black berets, Latino-brown berets, maroon was our color – better with out complexion . . . we were remaking ourselves, creating our own images and expressions.[10]

[10] Nobuko Miyamoto, *A Grain of Sand,* Unpublished manuscript.

Another change Miyamoto made during the early 1970s was her name. She had used the name Joanne Miya (an abbreviation of Miyamoto) when she performed on Broadway. Inspired by other activists and artists who had changed names to reflect cultural pride (such as LeRoi Jones who had changed his name to Amiri Baraka), Miyamoto found a new identity by reclaiming her Japanese name.

For Miyamoto and other artists who actively participated in the movement, "change" also meant the construction of what Chris Iijima describes as "a counter-narrative – an oppositional voice – to the white supremacist narrative [about] the inferiority of people of color and Asians in particular."[11] Like the African American and other minority counterparts, Asian Americans demanded to reclaim their histories, expose racism, and promote cultural pride. For Miyamoto, performance was the most effective tool to create this narrative. She did not distinguish between art and politics, between aesthetics and ethics.

In 1978, she founded Great Leap Inc., a multicultural arts organization in Los Angeles. While the organization began with a focus on Asian Americans, it has been inclusive of diverse ethnicities and artistic styles. Great Leap Inc. has toured extensively around the country, appearing at multicultural festivals and schools. It has promoted residency programs for artists in public schools and supported numerous artists engaged in both group and individual works. One of Great Leap Inc.'s most popular shows has been *A Slice of Rice, Frijoles, and Greens*, which was created during the 1990s partly as a response to the 1992 Los Angeles Riot. Miyamoto and other members of Great Leap Inc. were deeply affected by the riot. They realized that more effort had to be made to create a dialogue between different racial and ethnic groups. *A Slice of Rice* features "personal stories" as a way to "bridge the gap among different groups."[12] Artists who have told stories in *A Slice of Rice* have included Nobuko Miyamoto, Dan Kwong (Chinese-Japanese American), Chic Street Man (African American), Paulina Sahagun (Mexican American), and Arlene Malinowski (a white woman who was raised by two deaf parents). Using a flexible format in which each performer tells their stories individually, the show maximized its effectiveness with humor and accessibility to all audiences.[13]

[11] Steve Louie and Glenn Omatsu, eds., *Asian Americans: The Movement and the Moment* (Los Angeles: University of California, Los Angeles, Asian American Studies Center Press, 2001) 7.
[12] Burns, "Something Larger," 196.
[13] The version of *A Slice of Rice* I saw was presented in August 2001 at the University of California, Los Angeles as part of the orientation for incoming medical school students. The performance was to provide multicultural education on cultural sensitivity to the students.

Another major contribution Miyamoto has made to Asian American theatre was *Chop Suey* (1980), a musical theatre piece she co-created with Benny Yee (who wrote the music). Mako had encouraged her to write a musical, and the show included a number of actors from the East West Players. The show toured at colleges and parks along the coast of California and the Pacific Northwest. Other musicals created by Miyamoto include *Talk Story I and II* (1987–89). She has also created solo performances and helped launch the first Vietnamese American theatre group, Club O'Noodles in Los Angeles. Her involvement with Club O'Noodles was an extension of her antiwar activism of the late 1960s and 1970s. According to Miyamoto, she felt a sense of responsibility: "When I met Hung Nguyen [founder of Club O'Noodles] and some of the Club O'Noodles people, I said, 'Well, these are the kids we were talking about' . . . I wanted to bring out that part of the story."[14]

Miyamoto has maintained her interpretation of the movement as inseparable from global politics. Unlike Frank Chin who claimed his cultural identity through the history of Chinaman (who is neither the foreign Chinese nor the assimilated Chinese-American), Miyamoto has embraced her Japanese and Nisei heritage in less exclusive terms. The stories she has told have been inspired by her family's internment during World War II and racism she encountered as a female ethnic minority in the United States. But she has (especially since the 1990s) identified with Asian traditions and has incorporated them in her life and work. Her career as an Asian American artist has indeed eluded categorization, but in many ways, she is the quintessential Asian American theatre artist.

Roberta Uno

Nobuko Miyamoto has inspired and influenced numerous artists, but one person who has closely followed her career and has consistently admired and supported her is Roberta Uno. A Sansei (third generation Japanese American), Uno was born in Hawaii and grew up in a multiracial neighborhood in Los Angeles. As a child, her mother exposed her to the emerging multicultural theatre community in Los Angeles, including the East West Players and Inner City Cultural Center. In fact, she participated in the first East West Players workshop in the late 1960s. In the early 1970s, when she moved to the East Coast to attend college, Uno was shocked at the overt racism she observed around her. She articulated her

---

[14] Burns, "Something Larger," 201.

experience in a play she wrote and directed (titled *In the Rock Garden*) at Hampshire College in Amherst, Massachusetts. The play, which was her senior thesis, featured a multiracial cast with all Asian American female leads. Presentations of the play at not only Hampshire College, but also Smith College and University of Massachusetts positioned Uno as a leading spokesperson for multicultural theatre in the region.

In 1979, Uno was invited by the University of Massachusetts at Amherst to create "an arts program for students of color."[15] At the time, students at the university were protesting for inclusion of multicultural education on campus. The program she started was called Third World Theater, and its first production was a play by a South African playwright. Uno and other participants envisioned a group that was "very political [with a] global perspective": "We saw ourselves as an antiracist project, anti-apartheid project." Uno wanted to think about domestic issues in connection to global struggles over racism, classism, and sexism. In the early 1980s, the group changed its name to New WORLD Theater (NWT) because a new generation of college students identified less with the specific language of the Third World Movement but nevertheless believed in the overall vision of the company.

For Uno, NWT was different from other political theatres at the time. Instead of attaching "multiculturalism" to a white-dominated theatre structure, NWT strove to be diverse at its core. Additionally, Uno found the use of the term "multicultural theatre" by mainstream companies highly problematic. As Shauneille Perry describes, NWT has not been a company that defines "multicultural" as "having a potpourri of plays of predominantly European origin with one or two minority pieces, usually Black or Hispanic, thrown in for 'Color.'"[16] Instead, NWT's seasons in entirety have been filled with what mainstream theatres would call minority, multicultural, ethnic, and international works.

Moreover, Uno did not want NWT to become another ethnic theater, which for her often meant ethnic specificity without political agendas. Uno wanted to encourage dialogues between ethnic groups. In addition to producing plays by a diverse group of writers, the NWT has presented works created by ethnic theatre companies such as Negro Ensemble Company, the American Indian Dance Theater, and the Pan Asian Repertory Theatre. In terms of Asian American theatre, the NWT has

---

[15] Roberta Uno, Personal interview (June 27, 2000). All uncited quotations by Uno are from this interview.
[16] Shauneille Perry, "Celebrating the Tenth Anniversary of New WORLD Theater," *MELUS* 16.3 (Autumn 1989-Autumn 1990), 5.

invited numerous artists (including Nobuko Miyamoto) to Amherst, thus introducing them to the East Coast audiences. The NWT has also provided opportunities to those ethnic artists whose works were excluded by ethnic theatres. For instance, when some black theatre companies failed to include plays about homosexuality or feminism (which were seen as too radical), the NWT eagerly produced such "cutting-edge" works.

According to Roberta Uno, the support from the University of Massachusetts at Amherst provided the stability that allowed the company to produce financially risky works. The university support was especially crucial during the 1980s when major funding cuts affected the arts communities across the country. Also, Uno's archival collection, "Asian American Women Playwrights' Scripts Collection" at the university's W. E. B. Du Bois Library includes over 200 unpublished plays from 1924 to 1992. The archive initially began with a personal collection of plays Uno had gathered when she worked on the anthology of plays by Asian American women writers, *Unbroken Thread*. The archive was a targeted project to give voice to Asian American women, to provide a place where their work could be made known.

Because the NWT could not be easily categorized (as, for instance, an ethnic theatre), it had difficulty obtaining grants. According to Uno, funding sources did not understand the mission of the NWT. Moreover, the fact that the company was tied to a university and was located in western Massachusetts made it even more difficult to convince funders of its significance. Uno has also found the academic culture resistant to the NWT's approach, which blurred the very boundaries that gave structure to academia. For example, while academia tended to promote separate ethnic studies programs (such as Asian American studies, African American studies), the NWT challenged the neat categorization of race and ethnicity, exploring multiracial identities.

For Uno, the first group to understand and welcome the NWT was the artists of color, many of whom told her, "That's what needs to be done." In 1989, just such a sentiment was reiterated in the special issue of the journal *MELUS*, which featured transcripts of the conversations that occurred on December 9 and 10, 1989 at the Conference and Play Festival sponsored by the New WORLD Theater. Titled "Ethnic Theater," the special issue includes statements made by a number of prominent artists and producers of color, including David Henry Hwang, Carlos Morton, Aishah Rahman, Cat Cayuga, Eric Hayashi, Woodie King, and Miriam Colón. In the issue, Roberta Uno situates the NWT at the forefront of the multicultural theater movement:

Ten years of New WORLD Theater have been marked by nearly 100 productions of the theater of the African diaspora, Asian America, Native America, and Latin America presented side by side. They are often unified by themes, but more often strikingly disparate in their range of artistic styles, aesthetic sensibilities, and social concerns . . . The Theater has sought to present each cultural expression as distinct, emerging from separate cultural traditions – leaving the audience to make comparative analysis and draw thematic and cultural relationships.[17]

Uno implies that the kinds of works produced by NWT are true reflections of America. As she does in other writings, Uno asserts in the special issue of *MELUS* that America and world are changing rapidly, but mainstream American theatre remains "conservative" and behind the times. Moreover, American theatre, according to Uno, has historically been "an ethnic theatre," that began with "ethnic self-consciousness of ethnic writers like Royall Tyler" (who wrote about the Yankee identity in the eighteenth century).[18]

After the tenth anniversary conference, Roberta Uno continued to pursue her goal to situate multicultural experiences and aesthetics at the center of a theatrical season. She also promoted dialogue between and among local communities (most recently, the Southeast Asian immigrants in Amherst), activists, scholars, and artists. In 2002, she left her position as Artistic Director of the NWT to work as a Program Officer for Arts and Culture at the Ford Foundation in New York City. She has served in other leadership positions in theatre organizations, including Theatre Communications Group and Women Playwrights International.

In the 1970s, Roberta Uno was an activist and artist for the Third World Movement. In the early twenty-first century, she is a central and influential figure in American theatre and an indisputable representative of the multicultural theatre movement. In my conversation with her, Uno noted that she has been asked on more than one occasion whether she is of a mixed heritage. The questioners were Asian Americans who could not understand why a Japanese American woman would work with blacks and Latinos unless she was "part them." For Uno, such questions indicated Asian American ethnocentrism and racism towards other people of color. (She added that such sentiment exists in all racially defined groups). According to Uno, her vision of the NWT has not "fit into what Asian

[17] Roberta Uno, "Preliminaries," *MELUS* 16.3 (Autumn 1989-Autumn 1990), 1.
[18] Ibid.

American is." Nor has she, as a theatre artist and administrator, found a neat category within Asian American theatre. At the same time, she is confident that the niche she has created and filled represents the future of American theatre. She understands that cultural nationalism was necessary in the creation of ethnic theatres during the 1960s and 1970s, but since then, it has been more effective to build coalitions between ethnic groups. And the NWT, led by Uno has impressively achieved that goal.

Transnationalism and intercultural theatre

In a broad sense, Asian American theatre is essentially and necessarily transnational and intercultural. The term "Asian America" in a literal sense demands a transnational explanation: "Asia" invokes the original geographical location consisting of multiple nations, and "America" is the destination nation to which Asian Americans or their ancestors immigrated. In this sense, various forms of exchange, travel, and transfer between nations (as in the case of foreign students, laborers, refugees, or artists) made "Asian America" possible. Moreover, if intercultural theatre is, in Patrice Pavis' words, "hybrid forms drawing upon a more or less conscious and voluntary mixing of performance traditions traceable to distinct cultural areas," we have to consider Asian American theatre as a form of intercultural theatre.[19]

However, the concepts of transnationalism and interculturalism are tied to a myriad of problems, controversies, and histories that complicate, rather than define, Asian American theatre. As I discuss in Chapter 8, the 1990s saw an increase in the number of Asian American theatre artists who traveled to Asia or worked with Asian artists, making transnationalism and interculturalism an essential part of the discourse of Asian American theatre. However, during most part of Asian American theatre history, cultural nationalism with focus on enfranchisement and inclusion in America motivated the majority of artists. The artists had reservations about identifying with "Asia" for the term can connote a number of problematic concepts, ranging from "exotic" to "homeland." They wanted to be represented as Americans onstage. As Karen Shimakawa puts it, on the stages of Asian American theaters, "it was possible to see a kind of Americanness that was visible nowhere else in the US popular

---

[19] Patrice Pavis ed., *The Intercultural Performance Reader* (London: Routledge, 1996), 8.

representation."[20] Moreover, Asian American theatre has had a love-hate relationship with Asian theatre, which some artists have embraced and others rejected. Many also objected to the ways in which Asian theatre had been appropriated by Western directors, who viewed it as a viable alternative to realism and naturalism and found inspiration in its theatricality.[21] Daryl Chin, in criticizing such directors, has described interculturalism as having a "hidden-agenda of imperialism."[22] And Una Chaudhuri asks: "Is this kind of interculturalism a sophisticated disguise for another installment of Orientalism or worse, of cultural rape?"[23]

Despite the reservations, there have been Asian American theatre artists who worked within the framework of transnationalism and

[20] Karen Shimakawa, "(Re)Viewing an Asian American Diaspora: Multiculturalism, Interculturalism, and the Northwest Asian American Theatre," in *Orientations: Mapping Studies in the Asian Diaspora*, edited by Kandice Chuh and Karen Shimakwa (Durham and London: Duke University Press, 2001), 46.

[21] Artaud, for instance, criticized modern European theatre as text-based and used Balinese theatre as an example of a "pure theater" that can restore theatre to its "original destiny." Antonin Artaud, *The Theater and Its Double* (New York: Grove Press, Inc., 1958), 52. Artaud's ethnographic fascination with Balinese theatre informed other European artists such as Jean Genet and Jerzy Grotowski, who interpreted theatre as a form of "ritual." By the 1950s and the 1960s, the discipline of anthropology instructed and perpetuated what Julie Stone Peters calls the dualism of "post-1950s neo-imperialism: anthropologist/primitive, writing/ritual, subject/object, observer/observed." Julie Stone Peters, "Intercultural Performance, Theatre Anthropology, and the Imperialist Critique: Identities, Inheritances, and Neo-Orthodoxies," in *Imperialism and Theatre: Essays on World Theatre, Drama and Performance*, eidted by J. Ellen Gainor (London: Routledge, 1995), 203. Since the 1960s, Richard Schechner, Eugenio Barba, Lee Breuer, Peter Brook, and Ariane Mnouchkine have used forms of Japanese, Chinese, Indian, and Balinese theatre to interpret Greek tragedies, Shakespeare, and even Asian classics such as the *Mahabharata* (directed by Peter Brook, 1985). All of these directors have justified their use of Asian theatre by advocating its "sacred," "formal," and "ritualistic" characteristics that are lacking in Western theatre. In other words, their goal is not to imitate Asian theatre, but rather, to borrow certain (mostly visual and technical) elements in order to reinvigorate Western theatre. The founder of the Théâtre du Soleil, Ariane Mnouchkine, has been drawn to Asian theatre (especially Noh and Kabuki) because she finds "a simple ceremonial quality which seems . . . indispensable in the theatre": "I remembered recently that Artaud said: 'The theatre is Oriental.' I know what he meant. From Asia comes what is specific to theatre, which is the perpetual metaphor which the actors produce. [. . .] The moment one uses the word 'form' in connection with theatre, there is already a sense of Asia." Ariane Mnouchkine, "The Theatre is Oriental," in *The Intercultural Performance Reader*, edited by Patrice Pavis (London: Routledge, 1996), 97.

[22] Daryl Chin, "Interculturalism, Postmodernism, Pluralism," in *Interculturalism and Performance: Writings from PAJ*, edited by Bonnie Marranca and Gautam Dasgupta (New York: PAJ Publications, 1991), 87.

[23] Una Chaudhuri, "The Future of the Hyphen: Interculturalism, Textuality, and the Difference Within," in *Interculturalism and Performance: Writings from PAJ*, edited by Bonnie Marranca and Gautam Dasgupta (New York: PAJ Publications, 1991), 193.

interculturalism since the early 1970s. They may or may not have identified themselves as "Asian Americans," and their understanding of theatre may have been drastically different from that of the majority of artists in American theatre. However, they form a historical link to those artists of the 1990s and the twenty-first century who have embraced a more globally defined Asian American theatre.

During the 1970s, when the first four theatre companies were defining the styles and agendas of Asian American theatre, a number of individual artists and organizations formulated a different type of theatre, one that purposely looked beyond the geographical boundaries. In terms of ethnic groups, Filipino Americans were most mobilized. Lucy Mae San Pablo Burns, in her dissertation, argues that Filipino American theatre is part of larger "transnational formation of Pilipino American culture, through its dynamic ties with Philippine culture, politics, and society, and with Pilipinos in various diasporic sites."[24] As Burns's study reveals, Sining Bayan (meaning Filipino People's Performing Arts) was formed in 1973 as a subgroup within the Filipino American political group, the Katipunan ng mga Demokratikong Pilipino/Union of the Democratic Pilipinos (KDP). Sining Bayan was a political theatre group that articulated "Pilipino American identity formation as historically linked to the strug-gles of the working class – globally and amongst Pilipino in the [USA], Philippines, and other parts of the world."[25] Moreover, Sining Bayan's productions readily incorporated Filipino dance, music, and drama.

Similar to Sining Bayan, other ethnic-specific theatre groups existed since the 1970s to serve the community by presenting works that reminded the audience of the homeland. For instance, Soon-Tek Oh, who co-founded the East West Players in 1965, also founded the Korean American Theatre Ensemble in 1978 in Los Angeles. Oh had attended the produc-tion of a Korean play, *Bae-bi-jang-jun*, in Los Angeles and noticed that the audience consisted of first generation immigrant Korean adults and that their children were conspicuously absent. Oh was concerned with the 1.5 generation (those born in Korea and raised in the United States) and

[24] Lucy Mae San Pablo Burns, "Community Acts: Locating Pilipino American Theater and Performance," (PhD dissertation: University of Massachusetts, 2004), 16.

[25] Ibid., 40. There was also a short-lived Filipino American theatre group in Seattle in the early 1970s named Teatro ng mga Tao. As Lucy Burns's research indicates, Filipino American theatre is a subject that deserves much more attention than the brief mention I give in this book. One of the reasons for this lack is the fact that Burns and I were researching and writing concurrently, and she had much better access to the materials. Because her work is recent and reliable, I point to her writings for details on Filipino American theatre.

with second-generation Korean Americans, who did not speak Korean and had trouble communicating with their parents, who did not speak English.[26] In 1979, Oh produced a show titled *Ka-ju-ta-ryung* (literally "Ballad of California"; titled *Have You Heard* in English). It was a bilingual production about Korean American youths done in a style that featured traditional Korean theatre such as *Madang-nori* (arena play or outdoor yard play) and traditional dance, music, and folktales, as well as components of contemporary American popular culture. Oh wanted to demonstrate that Korean culture, as tradition, is "not something you only see in museums." The show was produced annually until 1991, and Oh witnessed the young Korean Americans' preference for popular culture change: "twist in the 1970s, break-dance in the 1980s, and rap in the 1990s." The following section describes the work and career of Joanna Chan as a more detailed case study of transnationalism and interculturalism in the context of Asian American theatre. The most accurate descriptor for Chan would be a leading theatre artist of the Chinese diaspora. But she also has numerous other roles, including Catholic nun, published playwright, and recipient of PhD in theatre, to name only a few.

Joanna Wan-Ying Chan

When she arrived in New York City in 1969, Sister Joanna Chan's goal as a theatre artist was to promote social well-being in the community, and the result was an unintended and unexpected form of intercultural theatre, or as she prefers to call it, a hybrid theatre. Chan, who grew up in the southern city of Kwangzhou in China, came to the USA as a Maryknoll sister, and attended the Art Institute of Chicago and earned her doctorate in theater at Columbia University. Her 1977 dissertation, *The Four Seas Players: Toward an Alternative Form of Chinese Theatre; A Case Study of a Community Theatre in Chinatown, New York City*, details her experience as a co-founder of the Four Seas Players, which at one time was the largest Chinese repertory company in the USA. She has also had an extensive career as a playwright and director both in the USA and in Hong Kong. In 1992, she founded the Yangtze Repertory Theater of American, Inc. in New York City in order to provide performance and exhibition venues to artists of Asian (primarily Chinese) descent within and beyond the USA. For example, in the 1990s, Chan and Yangtze Repertory Theater produced

[26] Soon-Tek Oh, Personal interview (August 2, 2001). All uncited quotations by Oh are from this interview.

the world premiere of *Between Life and Death* by Gao Xingjian, the recipient of the 2000 Nobel Prize for Literature.[27] Since the early 1970s when she founded the Four Seas Players, Chan has developed a form of intercultural theatre that is based specifically on community yet defined transnationally.

When she arrived in New York City, Sister Chan was assigned to work at the Transfiguration Roman Catholic Church at 25 Mott Street in Chinatown. The Transfiguration Church had helped New York City's immigrant poor since the nineteenth century, first serving Irish and Italian immigrants, and by the 1970s, the Chinese. Because Chan was an experienced math teacher (she was officially certified in Hong Kong), she tutored high school students, many of whom were in gangs and needed guidance. Another of Chan's first duties at the church was to explore ways to stage a play for the Chinese New Year celebration. Her wish was simple, and as she admits, naïve and ignorant of the complexities of the politics in Chinatown.[28] Since 1965, when the changes were made in the immigration laws to allow Chinese men to bring family to the USA, the New York City Chinatown had seen a steep growth in population. The majority of new immigrants were of what Chan calls "the peasant class."[29] Although Chan, who is not of the peasant class, grew up as a refugee in Hong Kong, she had never encountered the culture of the rural Chinese farmers who filled Mott Street. She was initially "shocked" at the intra-Chinese cultural differences she witnessed in Chinatown. Looking back, Chan states that she could not have accomplished what she did without the immigrants who with "their courage and selflessness" informed her. In fact, most of her plays feature characters and storylines of the "peasant" or "common" class.

On October 31, 1969, she and seven others in the community sent out a notice to various clubs and associations in Chinatown to announce their plan:

> We feel that a full-length play performed in Chinese would be most fitting [for the New Year celebration]. Not only would it provide an

---

[27] The 1997 production of Gao Xingjian's *Between Life and Death* at Yangtze Rep was the only play by the writer to receive production in the United States before he won the 2000 Nobel Prize for Literature. Gao also directed the production.

[28] Joanna Wan-Ying Chan, "The Four Seas Players: Toward an Alternative Form of Chinese Theatre; A Case Study of a Community Theatre in Chinatown, New York City" (PhD dissertation: University Columbia U, 1977), 57.

[29] Joanna Chan, Personal interview (March 22, 2002). All uncited quotations by Chan are from this interview.

evening of cultural interest for our community, but also an opportunity
for our many organizations to work together on a common project . . .
Please bring your ideas and scripts, if perchance you have any.[30]

The first meeting was held at the Transfiguration Church located in the
heart of Chinatown. At the ninth meeting, the group decided to perform
an adaptation of a popular Cantonese opera, *The Emperor's Daughter*.
Sister Chan had adapted the opera into simpler dialogue form and symbolic dance movements that were more accessible to untrained performers.
Like all of their subsequent shows, attention was paid not to the authenticity of the opera, but to compatibility of their production to their group
and community. They freely experimented with available theatrical forms
and openly admitted that they were developing "an alternative form of
Chinese theatre."[31]

By November, the group had grown to sixty people of diverse backgrounds, including Puerto Rican and Italian Americans, high school
students, community leaders, young professionals, and clergy. Rehearsals
were held in the church basement, and all those who could perform did.
Others made costumes, constructed the set, made flyers, and sold tickets.
The performance, held on February 7, 1970, attracted much publicity and a
large group of spectators, many of whom were elderly residents of Chinatown. According to Sister Chan, the church basement, which seats about
three hundred people, was filled for three evening performances.[32]

Invitations for more performances began to come in, and discussions of
a new production quickly emerged, reflecting the excitement and dedica-
tion of the participants. The group had obviously filled a cultural need in
Chinatown, but Chan soon discovered that she had made a major mistake
with the elders of Chinatown, and, in particular the Chinese Consolidated
Benevolent Association that had been the accepted governing organization since the beginning of Chinatown history. She had not requested
formal permission to perform from the elders and soon found herself
ostracized by all major groups, including the local newspaper. The Chinese
Consolidated Benevolent Association had faced increasing problems with
the new wave of Chinese immigrants in the 1960s and the growing
number of Chinese youths had began to emulate the Black Panthers in
using confrontation to communicate their needs. Thus, the popularity

[30] Chan, "The Four Seas Players," 57.
[31] Ibid., 56.
[32] Ibid., 69.

of Chan's drama group was seen as another threat to the association's established power. And Chan's youth and gender did not help; it took Father Denis J. Hanly of the Church to appease the elders (Chan was not allowed to meet with them). Only after making formal apologies and recognizing the honor code of the Chinese community, did Chan and the drama group manage to reestablish their relationship with other Chinatown groups, opening the door to future productions.

On September 13, 1970, Chan and four other members of the group held a meeting and decided on the name Four Seas Amateur Players. They defined the purpose of the group: to cultivate the talents and skills of our Chinatown community, to promote a spirit of unity and cooperation, and to nurture an interest in dramatic arts. The name Four Seas represents the first two Chinese characters in the ancient saying: "Within the Four Seas, All Men are Brothers."[33] For their second production, again for the Chinese New Year celebration, the players decided to stage *The Tale of the Romantic Fan*, an eighteenth-century Italian story adapted by C. P. Woo and relocated to early seventeenth-century China as a three-act farce. The story revolves around a fan purchased by a young man for the woman he loves during the peaceful time of the Ming dynasty. The fan causes a series of comic misunderstanding but ultimately brings all characters together in a happy ending. The cast and crew of the production again included a diverse group of community members. Some were American-born Chinese students who spoke none of the Cantonese that was demanded of the actors in the production, while others were immigrants from Hong Kong who spoke no English. Danny Yung, an architect, volunteered to build the set with found objects on Mott Street and transformed the church auditorium stage into a small Chinese village.

Everyone involved in the production worked voluntarily making the best of the limited resources available. Because of the flexibility and informal nature of volunteering, the cast and staff were not always reliable. For example, during the second night's performance, two policemen visited the company, and the next day, three cast members (including one that played a lead part) disappeared unannounced, apparently to hide from the police. The show could not be cancelled, and the staff frantically tried to reassemble the cast. According to Chan, the production was saved when she ran into Alice Leung in the subway. Leung was a member of the Chinese Dance Company of New York and an interested observer of the Four Seas Players. After learning about the situation, Leung brought a

---

[33] Ibid., 79.

classmate, Tony Tam, to take over the lead part. With two additional volunteers from the community, the new cast rehearsed throughout the night and performed for another sold-out performance at three o'clock the next day.

Despite the challenges, the production provided the Four Seas Players with a sense of mission in the Chinese community, and the members came to the conviction that theatre was a tool to give people a sense of "belonging and self-worth."[34] It was more than a social service and gave both the performers and spectators "great pride." Chan experienced the power of theatre when she observed people "who would otherwise not so much as look at each other" laughing together: "For a few brief hours, all the frustration[s] and self-doubt[s] were put aside . . . Little people like us, who had been locked in our lonely struggle in a strange land, had come together in spite of everything and had accomplished something much larger than what one of us could have done alone."[35]

The style of the Four Seas Players productions was a blend of the traditional and contemporary, Chinese and European, past and the present. Although similar to other forms of intercultural theatre in many ways, Four Seas Players had a distinct purpose: to serve its community by providing cultural education, theatrical entertainment, and a sense of unity. In other words, form followed purpose. Material was written specifically for the available talent in the community, and the performances directly reflected the experiences of the community. Four Seas Players did not attempt to emulate the model of American regional theatre companies as did the East West Players and the Asian American Theater Workshop. Instead, it sought the specific needs of the New York City Chinatown community and took advantage of all those who could participate in the creative process. For example, when the actor Lu Yu (who had worked in film and television in Hong Kong and Taiwan) visited the Four Seas Players, Chan immediately adapted the production of *The Heirloom* to accommodate his talent. Often, productions depended on luck and coincidence, but the group's flexibility allowed diverse talents to participate and led to surprisingly successful shows.[36] The resulting style of Four Seas Players was a community-based intercultural theatre that used traditional Chinese theatre to reinforce cultural pride and self-expression and that

---

[34] Ibid., 89.
[35] Ibid.
[36] In the 1990s, Theater Mu in Minneapolis would use the same model of using local Asian talent to produce innovative and successful intercultural productions. See Chapter 8.

included contemporary forms and content to nurture the participants and spectators.

For the next three decades, Four Seas Players produced two to three full-length productions each year. The style of the productions continued to be intercultural, transnational, experimental, and based in the diverse Chinatown community. In its twenty-year anniversary, the Four Seas Players was recognized by Ruth W. Messenger, the president of the Borough of Manhattan, for making "contributions to the world of theater and to the Chinese-American community" and September 8, 1990 was proclaimed as Four Seas Players Day.[37] Chan's involvement with the Four Seas Players was intermittent, but her commitment to theatre was demonstrated transnationally. Between 1986 and 1990, she worked as the artistic director of the government commissioned national theatre, the Hong Kong Repertory Theater, and made a historical impact on Hong Kong's theatre. Her reputation as a director grew throughout this time, and her plays, including *One Family One Child One Door*, were produced internationally.[38]

In 1992, she returned to New York City and co-founded Yangtze Repertory Theater of America, Inc. in Chinatown. Unlike Four Seas Players, it began as a professional theatre company with the intention to produce works written in Chinese in the USA. As a Christian, Chan saw similarities between religion and theatre: both could affect individuals to work together towards a collective vision. Chan explains, "When the curtain goes up on the opening night, it has to be a common vision that we can own while in the meantime, each individual has made contribution. I think that's the most Christian process."

Moreover, according to Chan, both theatre and religion should serve the community. For Chan, both honor "the sacredness of each individual while forging a community in a common project." During the 1970s, Chan saw Four Seas Players serving the local Chinatown community, but with the Yangtze Repertory Theater of America, the word "community" is no longer limited to Chinatown. It encompassed the global sense of the word.

---

[37] Four Seas Players, "About Four Seas Players," www.4seas.org/about.html.

[38] Other plays by Joanna Chan include *Staged Lives, The Soongs*, and *The Story of YuHuan*. She is a member of the Dramatists Guild in the United States, and an English version of her 1985 play, *Before the Dawn-Wind Rises* is included in Martha P. Y. Cheung and Jane C. C. Lai eds., *An Oxford Anthology of Chinese Contemporary Drama* (New York Oxford University Press, 1997). Chan is also an accomplished painter and designer. For instance, her painting entitled *Jerusalem '98* was selected as one of the top sixty images of Jesus for the new Millenium by the National Cutholic Reporter and was exhibited at the Gallery at Pace University's Schimmel Center for Art in New York City.

Chan notes: "Theatre for me now is not a job I do but a state of mind . . . So, community theatre is not just limited to a bunch of people doing amateurish things, but it's holding this attitude, approaching this attitude." Chan maximized the global potential of the company by offering multilingual productions and casting artists across ethnic and cultural backgrounds. The company's repertory has consisted of plays by writers of Chinese descent (including Chinese Americans such as David Henry Hwang), and the style has been eclectic, ranging from interpretative Peking opera to Western naturalism and postmodernism.

Although Joanna Chan's theatre companies have been geographically close to mainstream theatres (Broadway, Off Broadway and Off-Off Broadway theatres), she has not been interested in what she perceives as "commercial theatre." According to Chan, "I was never interested [in mainstream theatre] from day one. But that became misleading. People would think maybe I didn't expect to be excellent in the arts, which is not true." Chan also believes "art should be a major part of anyone's life." As a director, playwright, producer, and painter, Joanna Chan has found a way to use theatre not for its own sake, but to serve others in the vastest sense.

Performance art, multimedia theatre, and alternative theatre

Performance art, multimedia theatre, and other forms of alternative theatre emerged during the 1960s and 1970s as part of what Theodore Shank describes as "a new cultural movement outside the dominant culture."[39] Influenced by experimental art and music, alternative theatre provided expressive tools to those who chose not to participate in the text-based, fiction-based traditional theatre. Works like John Cage's 4'33" (1952) were inspiration to many artists of the new form. Participation by Asian American artists in alternative theatre was notable, but they are rarely included in the scholarship on the topic. As Shank does in his book, *Beyond Boundaries: American Alternative Theatre*, Ping Chong is often featured as the representative Asian American. There have been, of course, many others including Jessica Hagedorn, Winston Tong, Nicky Paraiso, Sandra Tsing-Loh, and Muna Tseng. Moreover, numerous artists from Asia have infused much energy and creativity to the new form of theatre. Such international artists have blurred the Western demarcations of theatre by radically redefining what theatre, and in a larger sense art, meant. During

---

[39] Theodore Shank, *Beyond Boundaries: American Alternative Theatre* (Ann Arbor: The University of Michigan Press, 2002), 1.

the 1960s and 1970s, artists such as Yoko Ono and Nam June Paik were leading figures in new forms of art such as the Happenings and Fluxus.

Alternative theatre has been central to the development of minority theatres, including feminist theatre. For instance, Elin Diamond, in discussing feminist theatre, argues that "highly personal, theory-sensitive performance art, with its focus on embodiment (the body's social text), promotes a heightened awareness of cultural difference, of historical specificity, of sexual preference, of racial and gender boundaries and transgressions."[40] In reacting against patriarchal, hierarchical structures of traditional theatre, feminist artists created a more egalitarian form of performance in which an individual artist would not have to depend on an authorial figure (which usually meant a dead white man). Similarly, African American theatre and Chicano theatre have used alternative forms of theatre in rejecting traditional forms.

Asian Americans have been the most excluded racial minority group in the United States. Asians were the last ones to be accepted as legal citizens, and the stereotype of the "perpetual foreigner" continues to operate in the imagination of what America is or should be. Traditional theatre has been even more exclusive, insisting for instance, that white actors in yellowface makeup suffice in Asian roles. Alternative theatre was often the only opportunity for Asian American actors who could not access traditional theatre. Some scholars argue that Asian American theatre as a whole is an alternative theatre because it occurred outside the dominant culture. In this section, however, I focus on artists who found Asian American theatre (as led by the first four companies) as limiting as the dominant theatre. For these artists, political coalitions of ethnic theatres did not matter as much as the freedom to experiment in terms of form and style. Two case studies are presented in the following section: Ping Chong and Jessica Hagedorn. Since the early 1970s, Chong and Hagedorn have been identified as artists who work across multiple boundaries. They have provoked Asian American theatre to expand its scope beyond reactive racial coalition.

Ping Chong

Ping Chong, a multimedia director, choreographer, and performer, grew up in New York City Chinatown and felt like a tourist in Times Square, a

---

[40] Elin Diamond, "Introduction," in *Performance and Cultural Politics*, edited by Elin Diamond (London: Routledge, 1996), 3–4.

place he rarely visited. He understood the Great White Way and all of its connotations: "Western theatre was something I had no real connection to."[41] Ping Chong left Chinatown to become a nationally and internationally recognized artist. He did not go to Time Square, but he did go to La MaMa E. T. C. and other alternative venues outside of Chinatown. In 1972, the same year that Frank Chin's *Chickencoop Chinaman* premiered in New York City, Ping Chong presented his first independent piece, *Lazarus*, at the Daniel Negrin Studio Theater (NYC). Stylistically, the works by Frank Chin and Ping Chong were diametrically different. Chin used textual language to express the rhetoric of the Asian American Movement and emphasized the importance of literary work in theatre. Chong, on the other hand, used visual language influenced by the avant-garde art movement in the 1960s and the 1970s and worked with artists of all racial backgrounds.

For the past three decades, Ping Chong has occasionally addressed specific Asian American issues in his work, but most of his performance pieces deal with the broader issues of culture: the Other, displacement, and alienation. Whereas writings by Frank Chin and other Asian American playwrights mostly dramatize realistic situations for Asian Americans, Chong chooses more abstract and metaphoric approaches. Yet, as Chong admits himself, his sensibility as an artist stems from his Chinese background, specifically, his grandfather and parents who were Cantonese opera performers. Chong has never denied this important distinction from other Asian American theatre artists and calls his work partially disguised autobiography. It is precisely this unique combination of avant-garde art and personal Cantonese opera influence that has placed Ping Chong as one of the most distinct and distinguished figures in Asian American theatre.

Ping Chong's childhood set the stage for such combination. His parents came to North America as Chinese opera performers on tour. They first landed in San Francisco and decided to stay when they saw the opportunities in the new land. They moved from the Bay Area to Vancouver and then to Toronto, where Chong was born in 1946. When Chong was a year old, the family moved to New York City, where he grew up in the city's Chinatown. His childhood experience gave him an early lesson on cultural differences and the sense of being an "Other": "I grew up in Chinatown

[41] Misha Berson, ed., *Between Worlds: Contemporary Asian American Plays* (New York: Theatre Communications Group, 1990), 3.

and went from public school that was 99 percent Chinese kids to a junior high school that was half Chinese and half Italian kids, to a high school where I was the only Chinese kid and graduated as one of only four Asian kids."[42] While living in Chinatown, Chong regularly attended Cantonese opera, which was his primary exposure to theatrical entertainment. Chong admits his theatrical sensibility was formed during this period of his life; he accepted the theatrical language of Cantonese opera and took for granted its uses of movement, sound, image, and metaphor.

In fact, text-based Western theatre (which he calls "talking heads") was foreign and dull to Chong. He was more interested in avant-garde film and attended the Pratt Institute and the School of Visual Arts to study film and graphic design. Instead of pursuing a career as a film director (his initial wish), Chong turned to stage directing and to the emerging experimental performance art and multimedia art movement in New York City. Although Chong remembers the 1960s, when he started out, as the period when "anything seemed possible," he fully understood the limitations that came with his being an Asian American.[43] Unaware of the emerging Asian American consciousness and of anyone like himself in the New York City arts scene, Chong felt "art was a way of surviving."[44] Chong survived the early years of his career by working with other experimental theatre artists, including Meredith Monk. He premiered most of his shows at La MaMa E. T. C. and has received unwavering support from Ellen Stewart, the founding artistic director of La MaMa.

In his first independent piece, *Lazarus* (1972), Chong tackled the issue of racial and ethnic identity by focusing on a Chinese American male character. He experimented with multimedia techniques and metaphorical and visual languages, but he also made the piece specifically about the Chinese American identity. With his subsequent pieces, Chong moved away from ethnic-specific topics, and instead, focused on the general notions of outsider and the Other:

> After [the first two shows] I had this realization that the role of the outsider was more universal. I began dealing more with the problem of how whole cultures are unable to interact harmoniously... In spirit I'm close to my Chinese roots but in practice I'm very far from them. As

[42] Eng, *Tokens?*, 409.
[43] John Dillon, "Three Places in Asia: Ping Chong Delves into the East-West Collisions of History," *American Theatre* 13.3 (Mar 1996), 20–21
[44] Ping Chong, "Notes for *Mumblings & Digressions*: Some Thoughts on Being an Artist, Being an American, Being a Witness," *MELUS* 16.3 (1989–90), 63.

Figure 7. Buzz, the gorilla, interacts with an American suburban girl Lulu in *Kind Ness* by Ping Chong, created in collaboration with Robert Babb, John Fleming, Brian Hallas, Jeannie Hutchins, Lenard Petit, Louise Smith, and Louise Sunshine.

another way of trying to feel positive about what I had lost when I left Chinatown, I began to think of the entire world as my culture. I've developed a commitment to the sense that we are all together on this one little planet. It's more and more important for us not to feel so foreign with one another.[45]

His later pieces, including *Humboldt's Current* (1977), *Nuit Blanche* (1981), *Nosferatu* (1984), *Angels of Swedenborg* (1985), and *Kind Ness* (1986), explored such themes of universal otherness, including alienation of humanoid and android races. Moreover, Ping Chong began to receive recognition in mainstream theatre, as well as prestigious awards, including an Obie Award for *Humboldt's Current* in 1977 and the USA Playwright's Award for *Kind Ness* in 1987.

Kind Ness was one of Chong's most accessible pieces and attracted both positive and negative responses from critics and audiences. *Kind Ness* is about a class of 1950s adolescents who live in an American suburb, or as Alan M. Kriegsman of *The Washington Post* called it, "a kind of cartoon

---

[45] Berson, *Between Worlds*, 3–4.

Our Town of the Eisenhower era."[46] Chong uses a gorilla character as a symbol of the outsider. "Buzz," a gorilla from Africa, is an exchange student in the local high school where he is popular with everyone. His friends don't notice his different looks, and this acceptance makes Buzz even stranger to the audience. At the end of the piece, Buzz is completely assimilated, financially successful, married to Daphne (the high school prom queen) with kids, living the ideal all-American life. The last scene takes place in a zoo where Buzz pushes his son in a stroller. They come to a cage with a gorilla inside who looks like Buzz, but Buzz fails to recognize any resemblance between him and the gorilla. The moment captures Chong's sense of irony in how he sees culture, assimilation, otherness, and America. As Suzanne R. Westfall describes, Buzz "serves as a sounding board for everyone's prejudices": "In Buzz we see all the strains of identity and allegiance that torment any assimilating ethnic group or subculture – Asian, female, Black, Jew, or Amerindian."[47]

Some took offense at Chong's use of the gorilla as the "Other" and "outsider" for its historically racist comparison to African Americans. Chong has claimed that such was never his intention and described Buzz as "not any different than the way Americans feel about Iranians."[48] As he did with earlier works, Chong was more concerned with an ambiguous and contradictory entity that could uncover xenophobia and fear of the Other. In *Angels of Swedenborg*, the character was the "fishhead" monster/stranger, and in *Fear and Loathing*, it was an Asian murderer, who was also monstrous and strange.

In 1990, Chong was commissioned by the Mickery Theater in Amsterdam to create a piece in commemoration of the centennial of the death of Vincent van Gogh. Chong created *Deshima*, named after the quarantined island that Japan opened up for trade with the Dutch in the sixteenth century. The piece covered the expansive story of the four centuries of contact between the West and Japan, including World War II, the internment of Japanese Americans, and the purchase of van Gogh's *Sunflowers* for a record $39.9 million by a Japanese investor in 1987. In *Deshima*, Chong continued to explore the issues of Otherness by centering on

---

[46] Alan M. Kriegsman, "Ping Chong's Wild, Weighty *Kind Ness*," *Washington Post*, (May 18, 1991), G7.
[47] Suzanne R. Westfall, "Ping Chong's Terra In/Cognita," in *Reading the Literature of Asian America*, edited by Shirley Geok-lin Lim and Amy Ling (Philadelphia: Temple University Press, 1992), 369.
[48] Ibid.

history and highlighting the universality of xenophobia, racism, commercialism, and historical amnesia. And as before, Chong played with the juxtapositions of contradictory images, sounds, themes, and aesthetics and blurred the audience's sense of time, space, and dimension. For example, in the last scene of *Deshima*, an African American actor (who, as the narrator, is dressed in an Armani suit) steps into an elaborate box set vividly painted to resemble the "inside" of van Gogh's *Crows in the Cornfield*. Once inside the set, the man takes off his suit and underneath is peasant clothing like the ones worn by figures painted by van Gogh. He then begins to sell postcards of van Gogh's paintings to the audience. This last tableau becomes an abstract commentary on globalization, capitalism, the commodification of art, and the irony of history.

Chong created three additional pieces on Asian countries, thereby completing what he calls the "East West Quartet": China (*Chinoiserie*, 1995), Vietnam (*After Sorrow*, 1997), and Korea (*Pojagi*, 1999).[49] The pieces addressed the critical points of contact between and within the East and the West, including the Opium War, colonization of Korea by Japan, and the Vietnam War, and in some cases, Chong related the international topics to the Asian American experience. For example, in *Chinoiserie*, he juxtaposed the 1792 British invasion of China with a scene from Henry Grimm's *The Chinese Must Go* (1879), an American play advocating Chinese exclusion. He also emphasized the universality of racism by having the mother of Vincent Chin (who was beaten to death by two white men) played by an African American actress, Aleta Hayes.[50] She sings a musical lament for her son, repeating that Chin was a "good Chinese" and "a good American." Ping Chong wanted to recognize the depth of pain caused by racism and hate crime in all mothers, especially those of African American descent who have endured it the longest.

---

[49] The quartet was published after I completed this chapter. See Ping Chong, *The East West Quartet* (New York: Theatre Communications Group, 2004). The publication includes an extensive interview with Ping Chong who describes how the quartet was created.

[50] In 1982, the two white men, Ronald Ebens and Michael Nitz, who were drinking in a bar in Detroit Michigan, mistook Vincent Chin, who was Chinese American, for a Japanese man and beat him to death with a baseball bat. The two men worked for General Motors and blamed the Japanese for the layoffs. On March 18, 1983, the two men pleaded guilty to killing Vincent Chin. Judge Charles Kaufman sentenced them to three years probation and fined them $3,780. Explaining the light sentence, Judge Kaufman stated, "These aren't the kind of men you send to jail . . . You fit the punishment to the criminal, not the crime." The men did not spend a single day in jail for killing Vincent Chin. Disillusioned with the justice system, Vincent Chin's mother left the United States and went back to China. Her words before leaving the US were: "There's no justice here."

Chong's East West quartet brought him closer to other Asian American theatre artists, some of who were excited while others were skeptical about his artistic turn towards Asian and Asian American themes. A few Asian American theatre artists criticized Chong for getting on the "multicultural bandwagon" in the 1990s. Reflecting the climate of competition amongst ethnic minority artists, Chong has been accused of "ignoring" Asian American issues and creating work for white, elite audiences. These critics have also alleged that when funding became available for multicultural projects, Chong began to incorporate Asian American themes in his work, thus taking money away from those artists who had focused on Asian American issues from the start. Although Chong received commissions and other financial benefits to create works about Asia, he has maintained that the Asia quartet is a continuation of his lifetime project to explore the themes of cultural Otherness.

Ping Chong's work undoubtedly differs from the theatrical works by those typically labeled as "Asian American" writers and directors such as Mako, Frank Chin, Wakako Yamauchi, Tisa Chang, Philip Kan Gotanda, and David Henry Hwang. Chong's work is not explicitly about Asian American issues, but rather, they function as metaphors. Moreover, Ping Chong's use of Asian theatre is not blatant or reductive as in the cases of some Western directors' intercultural theatre works. Instead, Chong seamlessly blends the sensibility of Cantonese opera and modern avant-garde dance and art. Ping Chong's intercultural theatre does not highlight the differences between the West and the East (as do most Western directors), and it does not create the binary systems of "Asia" versus "Asian American" or "Asian American" versus "American." Rather, Chong shows how the cultures mirror each other and how the self is often the Other. Daryl Chin recognized this quality of Ping Chong's work as early as 1978 when he compared him to Winston Tong (whom I discuss in Chapter 6), a Chinese American solo performer in the 1970s and one of the first original solo artists in Asian American theatre history. Daryl Chin asks, in his review of Tong's three solo pieces, "Beginning with the existential distinction of Self and Other, Tong's work as Chong's *Fear and Loathing* did before, hinges on the question posed by 'the alien,' which is: What happens when the Self *is*, in terms of cultural assimilation, the Other?"[51]

Ping Chong translates the psychology of "self as the Other" visually, theatrically, and sometimes literally. In an interview with Sally Banes,

---

[51] Daryl Chin, "Winston Tong: Three Solo Pieces," *Bridge: An Asian American Perspective* 6.2 (1978), 56.

Chong states, "The self is animal, primal. And my work is a way of moving toward that, looking at it, and understanding it – even if it only begins by visualizing it."[52] In looking at the self, he has found the outsider, foreigner, alien, stranger, criminal, beast, and monster. Chong has shown the self in all of its forms using a unique aesthetic sensibility that stems from Cantonese opera (which is, as Banes puts, "full of pageantry") and develops out of his training in film, visual arts, and modern dance. Because his style is difficult to categorize, Chong has been at the margins of both Asian American theatre and American avant-garde theatre. (For example, Arnold Aronson's book, *American Avant-garde Theatre: A History* does not include Ping Chong in the index.)[53] Both in theme and style, Ping Chong is an outsider all around, and as he admits himself he has "always been Other."[54] However, as David Oyama articulated in 1977, Chong has created a form of theatre that rejects the "conventional style of American realism," a style that has dominated Asian American theatre. Moreover, Chong's work represents the "startling and brilliant stylistic innovations" inspired by Asian theatre that can be exclusively claimed as Asian American.[55] David Oyama's description rings even truer in the twenty-first century, when more artists are emulating Chong by using racial and ethnic identity as a metaphor for the human condition.

Jessica Hagedorn

When Jessica Hagedorn moved to New York City in 1978, she received much inspiration from Ping Chong. In her Preface to Chong's *The East West Quartet*, she tells the story of how she first learned about Chong in "one of those 'hip' downtown papers": "a brief scene from the Obie Award-winning *Humboldt's Current* [by Chong] was excerpted . . . Intrigued, I clipped the page and tacked it on the wall by the rickety, multipurpose cardtable where I ate my meals and wrote. Ping Chong would be my funky new Role Model."[56] Hagedorn was intrigued and inspired because she

[52] Sally Banes, "The World According to Chong," *Village Voice* (February 28, 1984), 83.
[53] Arnold Aronson, *America Avant-garde Theatre: A History* (London: Routledge, 2000). Theodore Shank includes a section on Ping Chong in his revised version of a study on American alternative theatre. See Theodore Shank *Beyond the Boundaries: American Alternative Theatre* (Ann Arbor: The University of Michigan Press, 2002), 253–263.
[54] Eng, *Tokens?*, 417.
[55] David Oyama, "Asian American Theater – On the Road to Xanadu," *Bridge: An Asian American Perspective* 5.2 (1977), 6.
[56] Jessica Hagedorn, "Preface," in Ping Chong, *The East West Quartet* (New York: Theatre Communications Group, 2004), xi.

knew quite well how the arts world in the USA was "largely closed-off to artists of color."[57] Since then, she has become an inspiration to other artists both in and outside of the Asian American theatre community. Like other artists discussed in this chapter, Hagedorn is difficult – if not impossible – to pigeonhole. She is a playwright, poet, novelist, journalist, singer, rock-and-roll band leader, performance artist, and multimedia artist. She has also edited anthologies of Asian American writings.[58] Her novel about the Philippines, *Dogeaters* (1990), was critically acclaimed, receiving an American Book Award and a nomination for the National Book Award in 1991. She has, as Lucy Mae San Pablo Burns describes her, disavowed "strict artistic and community boundaries."[59] Ishmael Reed has called Hagedorn a "vanguard artist" who writes "the kinds of novels that will be written in the next century."[60] The same thing can be said of her plays and of her eclectic career as a theatre artist.

Born and raised in Manila, Hagedorn had immigrated to the USA when she was thirteen years old. She spent her teen years and young adulthood in San Francisco, where she attended the American Conservatory Theater's (ACT) training program instead of attending college. While she was at ACT during the early 1970s, she was "shocked" to see the establishment of the Asian American Theater Workshop led by Frank Chin.[61] She was especially interested in the production of *Manila Murders* (1977) by Dom Magwili, a play about the Philippines. She was the only Asian American student in her class at ACT and had an interest in participating in the workshop. However, she was too busy with the rigorous schedule of taking classes during the day and performing in ACT productions in the evenings. She met Frank Chin for the first time in 1976 in Seattle, at the second Asian American Writers' Conference, which was organized by Garrett Hongo. According to Hagedorn, the conference was informative, and she "got educated into the Asian American cultural history."

[57] Ibid.
[58] Jessica Hagedorn has edited *Charlie Chan Is Dead: An Anthology of Contemporary Asian American Fiction* (New York: Penguin Books, 1993) and *Charlie Chan Is Dead 2: At Home in the World* (New York: Penguin Books, 2004).
[59] Lucy Mae San Pablo Burns, "Community Acts: Locating Philipino American Theatre and Performance," PhD disseratation, University of Massachosetts, 2004, 97.
[60] Somini Sengupta, "Jessica Hagedorn: Cultivating the Art of the Mélange," *Nando Times* (December 4, 1996), www.english.uiuc.edu/maps/poets/g_l/hagedorn/about.htm.
[61] Jessica Hagedorn, Personal interview (September 19, 1999). All uncited quotations by Hagedorn are from this interview.

While she wanted to participate in Asian American theatre, she did not want to be "exclusively of it." Indeed, Hagedorn's artistic interests have always extended beyond Asian America. She identified with other female artists of color, the Third World Movement, as well as the beat poet culture in the Bay Area. For instance, her one-act play, *Chiquita Banana* (1972), addresses the exploitation of women of color. Hagedorn's writings during the 1970s in San Francisco have been anthologized in a number of publications. While her writing career had a solid beginning, she wanted to also perform. During her training at ACT, Hagedorn realized that the mainstream theatre had no place for an actress like her: "[ACT] taught me exactly what I didn't want to do: participate in so-called 'mainstream American theater.'"[62] She moved to New York City to explore opportunities in other forms of theatre and performance. For Hagedorn, the words theatre and performance were vastly inclusive. She was informed by the experiments in alternative theatre, performance art, and multimedia art. At the same time, her multiple roles (musician, actor, poet, and others) were often blended, making what Somini Sengupta describes as "art of the mélange."[63] For instance, Hagedorn often performed her poetry onstage, and her experience as a lyricist and lead singer in her band, The Gangster Choir, shaped the rhythm and style of her poetry. Such disregard for the traditional approaches to theatre and performance has been central to Hagedorn's career.

In 1977, Hagedorn collaborated with Thulani Davis and Ntozake Shange on *Where the Mississippi Meets the Amazon*, which was produced by Joseph Papp at the Public Theater. Papp also produced her first play, *Mango Tango* (1978). Her performances have also appeared in Off-Off Broadway venues, including The Kitchen, Franklin Furnace, the Danspace Project, PS-122, and Basement Workshop. Her shows in New York City during the 1980s include *Tenement Lover* (1981), *Peachfish* (1983), and *Ruined: A Beach Opera* (1985). In 1988, Hagedorn created *TeenyTown* with Laurie Carlos and Robbie McAuley. The trio was called Thought Music, a performance group they founded. *TeenyTown*, which has been anthologized in *Out From Under: Text by Women Performance Artists*, deals with "racism in pop culture in this country."[64] After premiering at the Franklin

---

[62] Jessica Hagedorn, "On Theater and Performance," *MELUS* 16.3 (Fall 1989), 13.
[63] Sengupta, "Jessica Hagedorn."
[64] Hagedorn, "On Theater," 15.

Furnace and a successful run at The Kitchen, the show toured to San Francisco, Los Angeles, and Atlanta until 1989. In each city, the trio invited guest artists and groups to perform in the show with them. Most famously, the show featured the dancers of the Urban Bushwomen.

TeenyTown explored the history of blackface minstrelsy in American theatre. It addressed a variety of issues of racism by tracing the lasting influences of minstrelsy in contemporary popular culture. In the first part of the show, the trio performed traditional minstrel songs and showed footage of what Hagedorn describes as "really racist cartoons and sexist cartoons." The second half of the show was presented in the format of a modern American talk show. Hagedorn played the role of Johnny Carson while Robbie McAuley played Ed McMahon. *TeenyTown* featured a number of guest artists who improvised and made the show different on each performance. For one of the shows in New York City, the trio of Thought Music invited the African American actor Samuel L. Jackson who was living in New York City and, at the time, working on Spike Lee's film *Do the Right Thing* (1989). According to Hagedorn, the trio invited Jackson to be a guest artist in their show at the Danspace Project, adding that they could not pay much. Jackson agreed. He appeared as a mock talk show guest along with the Filipino American actress Ching Valdes and Filipino American performance artist Nicky Paraiso. Jackson's character was called "Mr. Bones," who would tell "horrible jokes." His jokes were "really racist," according to Hagedorn. The jokes were "so bad" that "some nights, people would just get up and leave." However, Jackson's jokes were exactly the kind of provocation Thought Music wanted with *TeenyTown*. Hagedorn started to collect and tell racist Filipino jokes and eventually included racist jokes about Jews, Poles, and the white race. Audiences were offended and angry, but for Hagedorn, "that was the point." She wanted to explore what humor was and how it related to racism. For Hagedorn, "humor has to be tied with truth": "[Truth] is what makes you laugh because it hurts . . . Humor is about telling the truth."

After two years of performing *TeenyTown*, Hagedorn decided to focus on writing, finishing a novel titled *Dogeaters*. *Dogeaters* was published in 1990 and placed her at the center of Asian American literature. The novel is by far Hagedorn's best known work. In 1998, she adapted the novel into a play at the encouragement of Michael Greif, who was then the artistic director of La Jolla Playhouse. After premiering at La Jolla in 1998, the play opened at the Public Theater in 2001. The story of *Dogeaters* revolves around multiple characters whose lives are intertwined with each other and with the history of the Philippines.[65] The word "dogeaters" was used pejoratively by Americans to refer to native Filipinos when they colonized the Philippines after the Spanish-American War (1898). Don Shewey of *The New York Times* described the Public Theater production as a "portrait of Filipino life [. . .] a turbulent, exuberantly tacky post-colonial soap opera unraveling in the shadows of the superpowers."[66] With the success of both novel and play, Hagedorn has been identified as a prominent writer of the Filipino experience (both domestically and abroad) and a leading figure in Filipino American theatre.

In 1994, she had returned to her performance art roots with the multimedia piece, *Airport Music,* on which she collaborated with Han Ong, a "third wave" Filipino American playwright.[67] The piece was about the traveling bodies and identities of Filipinos who are lured by the promises of the American dream. Using beat poetry rhythms, stylized movements, and slide projections, the show was reminiscent of Hagedorn's earlier performance works.

In the early 1970s, Jessica Hagedorn found traditional theatre venues closed to artists of color, and she found ethnic theatres "often just as conservative and closed-off as white mainstream theater."[68] She turned to "art galleries, nightclubs, dance spaces, and other non-traditional performance venues" and worked mostly with other women of color.[69] Looking back, she sees that the closed doors forced her to create and open other doors. Before the terms "multicultural" and "performance" were used to describe what she and others were doing, Hagedorn created a "whole another kind of theatre" because she had to. She notes, "If you want to

---

[65] The play was revised multiple times, most significantly during the years between the La Jolla production in 1998 and the Public theater production in 2001. Hagedorn simplified the plot and limited the time span. The final version was published by Theater Communications Group in 2003.

[66] Don Shewey, "Filipino Life, Seen Through a Pop Culture Prism," *New York Times*, March 4, 2001, Section 2, 7. The production of *Dogeaters* at the Public Theater also highlighted what Don Shewey called "the maturation of a community of Filipino-American theater artists in New York City, which has been ripening for several years" (8). The cast included the "all-stars" of Filipino American actors: Ching Valdes-Aran, Jojo Gonzalez, Mia Katigbak, Ralph B. Peña, Raul Aranas, and Alec Mapa. I discuss Ma-Yi Theater Company, a Filipino American theatre company, in Chapter 8.

[67] I discuss the "third wave" playwrights in Chapter 8. *Airport Music* was presented at the Berkeley Repertory Theater, the Joseph Papp Public Theater, and the Los Angeles Festival.

[68] Hagedorn, "On Theater," 15.

[69] Ibid.

take yourself seriously as an artist, you have to create your own industry because they aren't going to do it for you." Hagedorn has created a whole another kind of theatre, one in which the boundaries of theatre, performance, literature, media, and nation are challenged and even ridiculed.

5

The second wave playwrights

I come from a specific place as a Japanese-American, but I want to make
sure audiences can meet me halfway. When you want to reach a lot of
people, your work should be inclusive enough for everyone to find its center.

Philip Kan Gotanda[1]

IN 1980, ASIAN AMERICAN THEATRE WAS VIRTUALLY UNKNOWN
outside its close-knit community, but by 1990, it was not uncommon for a
mainstream regional theatre company to produce an Asian American play.
In vast contrast to the early 1970s when the East West Players could not
find enough submissions for its playwriting competition, the 1980s saw a
number of playwrights receive national recognition. During the decade,
hundreds of original plays were written and produced. Most of them did
not receive more than one production, and some were quickly forgotten,
but the overall level of creativity and craftsmanship was impressive, and the
mainstream theatre took notice.[2] As Roberta Uno explains in her introduction to *Unbroken Thread*, productions of plays in regional and commercial theatres around the country during the 1980s led to the increased
visibility of Asian American theatre.[3] If the success of a minority theatre is

---

[1] Misha Berson, "Role Model on a Role: Philip Kan Gotanda's Work Grabs Mainstream
Attention and Inspires Younger Artists," *Seattle Times*, October 10, 1996, D1.
[2] The definition of mainstream varies in relation to what is considered central or marginal in
American theatre. Off-Off Broadway theatre, for instance, can be either mainstream or alternative depending on how the terms are stipulated. I'm using the term "mainstream theatre" in
contrast to "ethnic theatre." So, mainstream theatre in the United States includes Broadway
theatres, regional theatres, and alternative theatres that are not ethnic specific. The vast majority
of plays produced by mainstream theatre companies have been by male, European American
writers.
[3] Roberta Uno, ed., *Unbroken Thread: An Anthology of Plays by Asian American Women*, (Amherst:
University of Massachusetts Press, 1993) 8.

measured by the acceptance of its writers in mainstream theatre, then the 1980s brought out the best of Asian American theatre. The publication of three major multi-author anthologies of Asian American plays in the early 1990s also confirmed this text-centered version of success.[4] Many believed that Asian American theatre had finally achieved legitimacy and acceptance because its plays were being produced and published for mainstream American audiences.

After the premieres of Frank Chin's *Chickencoop Chinaman* in 1972 and *The Year of the Dragon* in 1974 at the American Place Theatre (New York City), no other Asian American play was produced by a major mainstream company throughout the 1970s. It took almost ten years before an Asian American play was once again produced in mainstream theatre. The most publicized production was the Broadway debut of David Henry Hwang's *M. Butterfly*, which also won a Tony Award for best play in 1988. Moreover, the Chinese American actor, B. D. Wong, who played the character of Song in the play, won a Tony Award for featured role. Both B. D. Wong and David Henry Hwang belong to the "second wave" Asian American theatre artists who were able to move towards the center of American mainstream theatre.

In using the term "second wave," I am referring to Velina Hasu Houston's reference to the term in her introduction to *Politics of Life*.[5] Similarly, Roberta Uno, in *Unbroken Thread*, distinguishes a "first generation" of Asian American playwrights from a "second generation".[6] I prefer "wave" to "generation" because the latter emphasizes the age of the participants; "wave," on the other hand, connotes artistic movement and style. It is true that most second wave artists were in their twenties and

---

[4] Misha Berson's *Between Worlds: Contemporary Asian-American Plays* (New York: Theater Communications Group, Inc., 1990) was the first anthology of Asian American plays to be published. Before Berson's anthology, the only published collection of scripts was Frank Chin's *Chickencoop Chinaman and The Year of the Dragon* (Seattle: University of Washington Press, 1981). Berson's anthology was followed by Velina Hasu Houston's *Politics of Life* (Philadelphia: Temple University Press, 1993) and Roberta Uno's *Unbroken Thread* (1993). Some of the published second wave playwrights include David Henry Hwang, Philip Kan Gotanda, Velina Hasu Houston, Jeannie Barroga, Genny Lim, Cherylene Lee, Elizabeth Wong, R. A. Shiomi, and Laurence Yep.

[5] Houston states: "The writers included in this anthology [*Politics of Life*] span two generations, two countries, and two cultures. [Momoko] Iko and [Wakako] Yamauchi (along with [Gladys] Li and Toishigawa Inouye) represent the first wave of Asian American women playwrights. [Genny] Lim and I are the early part of a second wave that also includes Akemi Kikumura, Karen Yamashita, Linda Kalayaan Faigao, Rosanna Yamagiwa Alfaro, and Karen Huie." Houston, *Politics of Life*, 23.

[6] Uno, *Unbroken Thread*, 7.

thirties (thus the "new" generation) in the 1980s, but more important than their youth was the attitude and preparedness that characterized the generation. The majority of them received professional training as actors, playwrights, and designers. For instance, unlike the first wave playwrights who got into theatre fortuitously, many second wave writers pursued MFA degrees in playwriting from major universities around the country. Moreover, second wave artists acknowledged the accomplishments of the first wave. David Henry Hwang, for instance, says that Frank Chin was a major influence and has considered him to be "a mentor of mine and an artistic father [. . .]"[7] When another second wave playwright Jeannie Barroga attended a production of an Asian American play for the first time, she felt as if "all of a sudden doors opened for [her]."[8] With formal training in playwriting and a tradition to follow, the second wave playwrights found the job title "Asian American playwright" not at all strange or novel, a contrast to the first wave writers who practically invented the term.

There were many moments during the 1980s that symbolized the passing of the torch from the earlier founding generation to the next generation of Asian American theatre artists. Of course, this does not mean that the first-wave artists disappeared or had less influence. On the contrary, many first-wave writers, actors, and producers have continually been instrumental in shaping Asian American theatre. What emerged in the 1980s was a network of a new generation of artists with optimism, intensity, and ambition to challenge mainstream theatre. Most of these artists met as friends with shared interest in Asian American issues. Some of them benefited from affirmative action in mainstream theatre while others chose to strengthen the margins. Some became award-winning artists while others simply burned out and quit theatre. And some, especially actors, had to make compromises to keep their careers.

Many second wave actors, writers, directors, and producers spent twenty-four hours and seven days a week in theatre, often living as pseudo families and blurring the boundaries of the professional and the personal. Together, they pondered new ways of expressing Asian American sensibilities, especially beyond the rhetoric of the cultural nationalism of the 1960s and 1970s. They were informed by the growing academic field of Asian American Studies. Some also responded to the renewed activism

---

[7] David Henry Hwang, Personal interview (Mar 16, 2000). All uncited quotations by Hwang are from this interview.
[8] Uno, *Unbroken Thread*, 204.

prompted by anti-Asian crimes such as the Vincent Chin incident.[9] Moreover, they were encouraged by mainstream successes such as that of the writer Maxine Hong Kingston and cheered the increasing popularity of Asian American independent films such as *Chan is Missing* (directed by Wayne Wang, 1981) and Asian American music made by artists like the rock band Hiroshima. Indeed, the second wave artists led the mainstreaming of Asian American theatre with optimism and confidence.

But a closer examination reveals that the so-called "mainstreaming" of Asian American theatre in the 1980s was not so simple. Many in the Asian American theatre community wondered how one should define mainstream success and whether it depended on individual success or group success. In other words, can we claim that the second wave as a group made a breakthrough when, in fact, only a handful of the artists (mostly playwrights) actually did? Can those individuals represent the entire group? These questions were even more pertinent in the context of the political climate of the 1980s in the USA. For instance, the Reagan administration endorsed the concept of a "color-blind" society as a model of race relations in America. Unlike the 1970s when race played a prominent role in defining the society, many Americans in the 1980s preferred to de-emphasize race. Instead, "culture" became the new keyword, and multiculturalism became the new American ideal. Often, the new concepts were contradictory. Both conservatives and liberals went back and forth arguing that differences should be irrelevant ("we should be color-blind"), and then arguing that they were crucial ("we should celebrate the different cultures"). All sides of the debate claimed that they were promoting social equality. For instance, neoconservatives of the 1980s argued that their opposition to affirmative action was consistent with the goals of the civil rights movement by asserting that individual rights and opportunities should be guaranteed by law whereas collective equality (or group rights) does not justify the granting of privilege.[10]

This dialectical conflict between the individual and the group affected Asian American theatre and made a determining impact on its second wave artists. The conflict had little meaning for "first-wave" artists of the 1960s and 1970s because individual ambitions were not distinguished from group agendas. They didn't have a choice. Often, the first-wave groups were formed in order to advance individual careers as was the case with the

---

[9] See footnote 50 in Chapter 4 for details on the Vincent Chin incident.
[10] Michael Omi and Howard Winant, *Racial Formation in the U.S.: From the 1960s to the 1990s*, (New York: Routledge, 1994), 130.

East West Players. In the 1980s, however, as multiculturalism became topical and even profitable, more second wave individuals found opportunities outside the group. Mainstream regional theatres commissioned Asian American plays in order to gain access to funding for multicultural art, perpetuating what many saw as tokenism and selective multiculturalism. Understandably, many second wave artists chose to move "up" to the mainstream route rather than staying "loyal" to the group. In some instances, Asian American theatre became a mere steppingstone to the mainstream theatre. While some worriedly predicted that such a talent drain would bring an end to Asian American theatre, others argued that Asian American theatre was finally finding its niche in mainstream American theatre.

The politics of defining Asian American theatre also complicated the choice second wave artists had to make. The first four companies, for instance, had to decide how they wanted to be identified in contrast to other companies competing for the same funding and audiences. For instance, the majority of the plays produced by the East West Players during the 1980s reflected the experiences of Japanese Americans, who formed the most reliable subscription base. Even within this narrow identification, the East West Players had to decide how inclusive or exclusive it needed to be. Should it select plays that discuss interracial marriage, for example? What constitutes the category "Asian American plays" or "Japanese American plays"? Often, such questions were burdened with interpersonal politics that had more influence on season selection than the formal mission statements that embellished grant proposals.

In the following sections, I examine three playwrights, David Henry Hwang, Philip Kan Gotanda, and Velina Hasu Houston, who have been representative of second wave writers working in mainstream theatre. My intention is not to provide comprehensive studies of their careers and plays.[11] Rather, I present specific illustrations of the ways in which they entered mainstream theatre and how they have maintained their relationships with Asian American theatre. All three playwrights have received numerous awards and have often spoken on behalf of Asian America. But at the same time, their careers have displayed more differences than similarities. Each career has displayed a unique version of mainstream success. Often, their move towards the center of American theatre resulted

---

[11] There are a number of sources that provide detailed examinations of the three writers' careers and works. For instance, see entries in Miles X. Liu ed., *Asian American Playwrights: A Bio-Bibliographical Critical Sourcebook* (Westport, CT: Greenwood Press, 2002).

from a set of fortunate (and sometimes unfortunate) factors that reflect how mainstream theatre does or does not prefer to include Asian American plays. The careers of the three writers are exceptional, but they also demonstrate the trails discovered by the second wave playwrights.

Affirmative action and David Henry Hwang (b. 1957)

As proud as Asian Americans are of David Henry Hwang's mainstream success, many are also uncomfortable with a thorny detail they hesitate to bring up: Hwang's most successful play, *M. Butterfly*, did not stem from Asian American theatre but, rather, came about directly as a result of his involvement with the mainstream theatre. Hwang did work briefly at the East West Players and the Asian American Theater Company early in his career, and he continues to work with other Asian American theatre artists. However, his road to mainstream success seemed to have very little to do with Asian American theatre. *M. Butterfly* premiered at the National Theatre in Washington, DC in 1988 and was directed by John Dexter, one of the best directors in modern theatre history. Also, as Hwang admits, he wrote the play at the encouragement of the producer Stuart Ostrow. In other words, the most famous Asian American play did not get developed at an Asian American theatre company or receive direct support from the community. Instead, the production's creative team consisted of non-Asian American artists from mainstream theatre.

Studies on *M. Butterfly* are numerous, and I do not wish to repeat them here.[12] I am, however, interested in the choices Hwang has made and the circumstances that gave Hwang an advantage, especially in the early part of his career. Certainly, Hwang's success did not happen overnight but through a series of negotiations, compromises, and risks Hwang and others have taken. Many point out the fact that Hwang had to leave Asian American theatre in some sense in order to have mainstream success. This was already apparent with his first play, *FOB*, which received its professional premiere at the Public Theater in 1980. The production foreshadowed what David Henry Hwang would accomplish and how he would achieve it in the mainstream theatre.

The debut of Hwang's *FOB* would not have been possible without David Oyama, a journalist, actor, and writer who actively participated in Asian American theatre in New York City during the 1970s and the early

---

[12] For a list of studies on *M. Butterfly*, see my entry on Hwang in Miles X. Liu's *Asian American Playwrights*.

Figure 8. From left to right. Eric Hayashi, Philip Kan Gotanda, David Henry
Hwang, Rick (R. A.) Shiomi, and Lane Nishikawa at Asian American Theater
Company Benefit at the Asian Arts Museum in San Francisco on November 12, 1988.

1980s.[13] For instance, his articles in the *Bridge* magazine on Asian
American theatre are rare and valuable records of its early history. On
February 18, 1979, Oyama led a group of actors (about twenty in number)
in a protest against the Public Theater for the "casting of non-Asian actors
in Asian roles without an equal opportunity for Asian actors to play non-
Asian roles."[14] It was a bitterly cold Sunday morning, but the actors

[13] I thank Jessica Hagedorn for bringing this to my attention and for encouraging me to interview
David Oyama. I also give special thanks to Mr. Oyama for agreeing to talk to me twice in an
effort to make sure I accurately tell this important part of Asian American theatre history.
[14] Fraser C. Gerald, "Asian-American Actors Get Pledge From Papp," *New York Times*, February
22, 1979, C26.

wanted to reveal the racist practices at the Public Theater. They claimed that between 1969 and 1979, ten or fewer Asian American actors worked at the Public Theater. In particular, in the production of Len Jenkin's *New Jerusalem* (1979), which was playing at the time of the protest, none of the Asian roles were played by Asian American actors. According to Oyama, he questioned the artistic director Joseph Papp's judgment to allow non-Asian actors to play all of the Asian roles: "[I don't know] why, when he [Papp] was a champion of other minority groups and minority actors, why he had this particular blind spot about Asian actors."[15] He wanted to show Papp that the practices needed to be corrected. It was a direct challenge to Papp, who many recognized as a leader of multicultural theatre in the USA.

Not surprisingly, the protest created bad publicity for Papp and the Public Theater. Papp immediately assured Oyama's group that they would "employ significant numbers of Asian-American actors, playwrights and directors in future productions at its Public Theater."[16] According to Oyama, Papp met with the group and explained "he [Papp] had already been pondering some possible projects because he could not help but be influenced by the large Chinese community in New York."[17] Either for positive publicity or because of a genuine interest (or both), Papp gave Oyama a staff position at the Public Theater. According to Jessica Hagedorn, who closely followed the protest and Papp's reaction, the position occupied by Oyama was essentially "a desk." Perhaps, Papp thought, the problem would just "go away" after a few months.[18]

Oyama did not go away. According to Oyama, he was the only person at the Public Theater responsible for developing projects for Asian Americans. Specifically, Oyama's position had two functions: (1) "develop awareness in the Public Theater of available Asian American talent"; (2) "explore and develop plays involving Asian American playwrights, actors, and other theater professionals."[19] The first phase involved the auditioning of over 125 Asian American actors with the help of Rosemarie Tichler, the casting director of the Public Theater. Next, Oyama then began to solicit and consider plays for productions at the Public Theater.

---

[15] David Oyama, Personal interview (March 17, 2002). All uncited quotations by Oyama are from this interview.
[16] Gerald, "Asian-American Actors," C26.
[17] David Oyama, "Asian-Americans Take Center Stage at the Public," *New York Times*, April 27, 1980, Section 2, 3.
[18] Jessica Hagedorn, Personal interview (September 19 1999).
[19] David Oyama, Email correspondence (April 7, 2003).

They eventually chose Wakako Yamauchi's *The Music Lessons* out of over forty submitted plays and later included David Henry Hwang's *FOB*. On April 30, 1980, about a year after the protest, Wakako Yamauchi's *The Music Lessons* premiered at the Public Theater on the Martinson Hall stage. David Henry Hwang's *FOB* was presented four weeks later in the same space. *The Music Lessons* is based on an actual widow Yamauchi knew as a child in California's Imperial Valley before World War II. The woman, Yamauchi remembers, "seemed so fragile yet drove a truck and ran a farm and raised children alone"[20] The character, Chizuko, embodies the suffering of many Issei (first generation Japanese American) women who came to America by arranged marriages and had to struggle with isolation, difficult labor, and the overwhelming challenges of a new culture. Hwang's *FOB*, on the other hand, portrays a lighter side of cultural assimilation. A second generation Chinese American, Hwang integrates the stories of the "FOB" (fresh off the boat) immigrants and "ABC" (American born Chinese) with traditional Chinese mythology by using a nonlinear dramaturgical style.

Hwang had written *FOB* as a senior project at Stanford University and had it performed at his dorm. Hwang then submitted the play to the Eugene O'Neill National Playwrights' Conference in Waterford, Connecticut in the summer of 1979. Much to Hwang's joy, the play was accepted. Constantly searching for good Asian American plays, David Oyama attended the O'Neill conference to see the reading of *FOB*. Upon returning to New York, he told Papp "we should consider the play very seriously."[21] Shortly after, the play received a reading at the Public Theater. The following year, Papp agreed to produce the play along with *The Music Lessons*. Oyama suggested Mako as the director of the play, and Mako, in turn, recommended actor John Lone to play the role of Steve, the unassimilated "FOB." Because Lone had an extensive training in Peking opera, it was decided that he would work with Hwang to add choreographed movements to the production. Subsequently, the revised draft of *FOB* featured Peking opera movements as visual metaphors for the character relationships.

The first productions of Asian American plays at the Public Theater were successful and were seen as a valuable fruition of the project that began with a small protest. Critics and audiences appreciated the historical focus of *The Music Lessons* and acknowledged the accomplishments of

---

[20] Uno, *Unbroken Thread*, 57.
[21] David Oyama, Email correspondence (April 7, 2003).

Yamauchi as a major first-wave playwright to emerge from Asian American theatre. Hwang, on the other hand, was unknown to many critics and audiences. He had shown early drafts of *FOB* to his friends at the Asian American Theater Company, including Judi Nihei and Marc Hayashi (who had encouraged him to rewrite after rejecting it in the season selection). But Hwang never had a play produced at a professional theatre company before *FOB*. The young playwright's career was definitely on a fast track. This perception was confirmed when *FOB* received extended performances and Hwang went on to receive an Obie award for best play, becoming one of the youngest playwrights ever to receive the honor.

Hwang's virtual overnight success surprised many in the Asian American theatre community. Some were curious, and others (especially his friends at the Asian American Theater Company) wondered how he could have achieved it without going through an Asian American company. Everyone agreed on his talent as a playwright, but some also wondered what other factors might have played in his fast-track success. In general, the success of *FOB* at the Public Theater can (and should) be attributed to the star-quality performance of John Lone and the direction of Mako. While I acknowledge these accomplishments, I am also interested in examining less obvious reasons behind the success of *FOB*. In my view, the success of Hwang's *FOB* resulted from a combination of at least three factors: (1) the play's accessibility for both Asian American and mainstream audiences; (2) visual Asian elements that fulfilled the mainstream expectation of an "Asian American play"; and most importantly, (3) the Public Theater's affirmative action that was implemented because of the tenacity of David Oyama and others.

Although David Oyama and the Public Theater partially succeeded in filling the seats with Asian Americans, the audiences for *The Music Lessons* and *FOB* were predominantly non-Asian American. Wakako Yamauchi was watchful of the differences in audience reception. More than once, she had been told by non-Asian Americans that "no audience exists for her work."[22] Her critics described her plays as too ethnically specific and even alleged that non-Asian American audience members would find it impossible to sympathize with her work. (In fact, such criticism has been quite common for all first-wave writers.) For instance, in reviewing *The Music Lessons*, Mel Gussow described the play as a "mood memory piece about Japanese-American farmworkers in California during the Depression."[23]

[22] Uno, *Unbroken Thread*, 57.
[23] Mel Gussow, "Theater: Nisei *Music Lessons*," *New York Times*, May 16,1980, C5.

Nisei audiences wanted to watch her plays, but how many of non-Asian Americans would want to watch an Asian American "mood memory" play? Despite these concerns, however, the production, which featured Sab Shimono and Lauren Tom, was generally well-received by the Public Theater audience.

Unlike Yamauchi's play, which asks the audience to participate in remembering a forgotten history in a serious and even sad way, *FOB* allows the audience to laugh at the cultural clash between the Chinese and Chinese American characters. Hwang knew how to let mainstream audiences laugh at Asian American topics: "One of the things I found very early on at the [Public Theater] was that with predominantly non-Asian audience, you had to give them the permission to laugh because they weren't sure whether or not they were being offensive by laughing, and so after *The New York Times* came out and said that it was funny, then everyone thought it was OK to laugh." Moreover, it deals with contemporary characters and is set in a Chinese restaurant, a familiar location in America. Such details helped the mainstream audiences to care about the characters and the plot. Another element that allowed the mainstream audience to sympathize with the play was the use of language. Whereas Yamauchi's characters speak the awkward language of English that is supposed to be Japanese (in other words, the characters live in a Japanese language world but all speak English for the sake of audience), Hwang's characters interact as they would in an actual situation. For instance, the assimilated Chinese American, Dale, does not understand Steve's Chinese, which has to be explained to Dale and thereby to the audience. However, a Chinese speaking audience can enjoy the play as much as English speaking audience because linguistic and cultural translations are embedded in the dialogues and therefore easy to follow.

David Henry Hwang's *FOB* also gave the mainstream audience what it preferred and expected from an Asian American play. In New York, as in other major cities, the prevailing image of Chinese American culture came from Chinatown. Like the majority of white New Yorkers, Joseph Papp's impression of Asian America came from his encounter with Chinatown: "My wife and I were at a Chinese dance to celebrate the Chinese New Year, and all of my senses were stimulated by watching a thousand young Chinese Americans dancing and discoing. And I told Gail [Merrifield] that we should look for something that captured some of that beauty and energy, that life."[24] In fact, the earlier draft of *FOB* did not have Chinese

---

[24] Oyama, "Asian-Americans Take Centre Stage," 3.

opera movements. Perhaps expecting the same kind of beauty and energy he saw in Chinatown, Papp supported Mako's decision to include Chinese opera in the revisions of *FOB*.

According to Hwang, "Asian theater is an influence that [he] stumbled upon with *FOB*."[25] Even so, it was a savvy decision because the theatricalized version of Chinese opera in *FOB* apparently played a central role in entertaining the mainstream audience. Basically, the theatricalism of Chinese performance reinforced the New York mainstream audience's (and Joseph Papp's) assumption about "Asian American theatre," which for many New Yorkers was synonymous with "Asian theatre" or some variation of it.[26] The mainstream audience went to Hwang's *FOB* expecting such Asian theatre elements, and they were not disappointed. Frank Rich, in his review of *FOB* at the Public Theater, certainly took notice and described the play's appeal "*FOB* is the first show that has ever attempted to marry the conventional well-made play to Oriental theatre and to mix the sensibilities of Maxine Hong Kingston and Norman Lear."[27]

The "mix" of East and West continued to appear in Hwang's later works, including *M. Butterfly*, *Golden Child*, and *Flower Drum Song*, all of which appeared on Broadway. Some critics like James Moy have accused Hwang of reappropriating Orientalist elements for commercial success while others have praised Hwang for finding a true Asian American voice.[28] Even Hwang himself has questioned why his "oriental" plays have been more successful than those plays without any traditional Chinese costumes and exotic stories. Indeed, two of his "flops," *Rich Relations* and *Face Value*, are not visually Asian (there are, for instance, no "oriental" costumes, in either). Some dismiss the pattern as mere coincidence, but

[25] David Savran, "David Hwang," in David Savran, *In Their Own Words: Contemporary American Playwrights* (New York: Theatre Communication Group, 1988), 121.

[26] For example, in a 1972 article in *The New York Times*, Ralph Blumenthal described the theatre scene in Chinatown by mentioning an acrobatic troupe from Taiwan, a Shanghai-born Chinese American singer, amateur Peking opera troupes, and other imported cultures in Chinatown. He conflates traditional Chinese theatrical forms with Frank Chin's plays and called everything "Chinese theater." See Ralph Blumenthal, "Chinese Theater is on the Rise in City," *The New York Times*, August 10, 1972, 37.

[27] Frank Rich, "*FOB* Rites of Immigrant Passage," *The New York Times*, June 10, 1980, C6.

[28] James Moy has criticized Hwang and other second wave playwrights for writing to "seek validation" from Anglo-American spectators instead of attacking stereotypes. Commenting on David Henry Hwang's *M. Butterfly* and Philip Kan Gotanda's *Yankee Dawg You Die*, Moy states: "[their characters] provide a good evening's entertainment and then float as exotic Oriental fetishes articulating Anglo-American desire, now doubly displaced into the new order of stereotypical representations created by Asian Americans." See James S. Moy, "David Henry, Hwang's *M. Butterfly* and Philip Kan Gotanda's *Yankee Dawg You Die*: Repositioning Chinese American Marginality on the American Stage," *Theatre Journal* 42.1 (March 1990), 55.

others have hypothesized that the "oriental" elements expected by the mainstream audience in an Asian American play are essential to the formula of success for Asian American playwrights.

Without question, the addition of Asian American theatre projects in the Public Theater was affirmative action. When David Oyama negotiated with Joseph Papp to start the group and produce Hwang's play, the Public Theater already had in operation an African American theatre group and Latino American theatre group. Thus, an Asian American theatre project seemed to be a natural addition to the assortment of minority groups supported by Papp. It may have been tokenism but it nevertheless opened doors to Hwang and numerous other Asian American playwrights in the 1980s and the 1990s. Since the late 1990s, there has been a running joke that the Public Theater has a "chink slot" in its season, meaning that only one Asian American play is selected annually. The term is a criticism of tokenism, but at the same time, it is an acknowledgement of the Public Theater's affirmative action program that may in the long run benefit Asian American theatre. David Henry Hwang acknowledges: "I entered the American theatre through an affirmative action program, and I hope I have been a good example of it in terms of taking those opportunities and making something out of it."

The Public Theater production of David Henry Hwang's *FOB* in 1980 was a key moment in Asian American theatre history, one that marked the transition from the first-wave to the second wave. Hwang has become a major writer of mainstream theatre and the only Asian American to have works produced on Broadway.[29] As an individual, Hwang has certainly broken the race barrier in American theatre. He has also been an articulate spokesperson for Asian American theatre. But his career raises a number of questions that deserve further exploration. Is he the "token" Asian American in mainstream theatre? How else do we explain the fact that he continues to be the only Asian American playwright to be produced on Broadway? How effective is affirmative action for a minority ethnic theatre? Who gets the credit for "discovering" minority talents like Hwang?

David Oyama left the Public Theater with a mixed feeling towards Joseph Papp.[30] After the success of Wakako Yamauchi's *The Music Lessons* and David Henry Hwang's *FOB*, Oyama wanted to take advantage of the momentum by either extending the run of *FOB* or moving the production

[29] David Henry Hwang's play *The Golden Child* and his adaptation of *Flower Drum Song* by Rogers and Hammerstein have both been staged on Broadway.
[30] Because Joseph Papp passed away in 1989 I am using the version of the story told by David Oyama. I fully acknowledge that this version is one-sided.

to another theatre. Moreover, Oyama wanted to continue the Asian American theatre program that he had developed at the Public Theater. Joseph Papp agreed to extend the run of *FOB*, but he was not as supportive of the Asian American theatre program. After *FOB* closed, without financial and creative support from Papp, Oyama and his program were "cut off." While Oyama appreciated Papp's support of Asian American theatre, he was "bitter" about the way he was treated: "I appreciate his [Papp's] genius at the time when he fully responded to certain things. And definitely, when he cared about a project, when he wanted to move something forward, he's a very persuasive and a very talented person. At the same time, I felt that he fully understood the needs of the Asian American theatre at that time – he fully understood what role I was playing in it – and he didn't respond." Oyama's name has been virtually erased out in the narratives describing David Henry Hwang's career because most think that Joseph Papp discovered Hwang. Papp indeed gave Hwang the opportunity but did so only after he was embarrassed with a protest (and had his "arm twisted," as Oyama puts it). Perhaps Papp let go of Oyama because of interpersonal conflicts. Perhaps the "discovery" of one talented Asian American writer was a sufficient byproduct of the affirmative action. The actual management or artistic structure of the Public Theater did not change, but at least on the surface, the company can claim the credit for producing Hwang's first play and for adding Asian American theatre to its assortment of multicultural programs. One thing for certain: affirmative action in mainstream theatre can disappear as quickly as it appeared.

Specific authenticity and Philip Kan Gotanda (b. 1951)

In 1979, in his senior year at Stanford University, David Henry Hwang organized an Asian American arts event on campus and sought to include original Asian American music. He invited a musician named Philip Kan Gotanda, who was writing songs and performing in coffeehouses and clubs. But Gotanda at the time was in Los Angeles, busy working on his first musical production, *The Avocado Kid or Zen in the Art of Guacamole*, at the East West Players. Gotanda had a master's degree in music and had tried without success to get a record made of songs with titles such as "Ballad of the Issei" and "All-American Asian Punk." Record companies told him that a collection of Asian American folk-rock songs had no market, but he was well-known among Asian American activists, students, and artists. Without much luck in the music industry, Gotanda studied law and eventually graduated from Hasting College of Law in 1978, partly because of his father's wishes. But on a fateful day, Gotanda injured his leg during a beach volleyball game with his law colleagues. The injury kept him in bed for over a month during which he could not work, and he decided to write a musical to pass the time. Unlike the majority of second wave playwrights, Gotanda did not receive formal training in playwriting. Instead, he approached theatre as a musician and gradually learned the craft he as practiced it. After a year, he completed *The Avocado Kid*, which he submitted to the East West Players. According to Gotanda, he sang the entirety of the two-hour musical to Mako, who after hearing it said, "Let's do it."[31] In 1979, the East West Players produced it as the first original Asian American musical in its production history.

It was around this time that Hwang contacted Gotanda. David Henry Hwang wanted to meet him, so he went home to Los Angeles for Christmas break. The two instantly formed a friendship. With shared passion for music and Asian American issues, they decided to form a band (Gotanda on guitar and Hwang on jazz violin). With two other musicians, they called themselves the Bamboo and performed around the West Coast. Gotanda and Hwang also worked together in theatre. For instance, Hwang directed Gotanda's play *A Song for a Nisei Fisherman* at the Asian American Theater Company in 1980. However, the band did not last long because both Hwang and Gotanda found their callings in playwriting. They went their separate ways, but, before they did, the band tour had allowed them to meet other second wave artists who would change the history and direction of Asian American theatre.[32]

Hwang and Gotanda, who have maintained their friendship, are by far the most well-established Asian American playwrights, and the two are often mentioned simultaneously when describing the growing field of Asian American drama. Their careers have become models of how Asian American playwrights can move towards the center of mainstream theatre. Beyond these obvious similarities, however, the two writers are different not only in their dramaturgical styles but also in their attitude towards

---

[31] Philip Kan Gotanda, Personal interview (July, 12 1999). All uncited quotations by Gatanda are from this interview.
[32] For instance, the band was invited to perform in a Vancouver arts festival, and the two met Rick (R. A.) Shiomi, who was then a community worker and an amateur writer. When they met, Shiomi had written a story, which he showed to Hwang and Gotanda. The two encouraged him to adapt it into a play, and it later became *Yellow Fever*, one of the most successful Asian American/Canadian plays of the period.

mainstream success. Whereas Hwang found his big break at the Public Theater and worked mainly in mainstream venues on the East Coast, Gotanda began and developed his career as a playwright at Asian American theatre companies, especially the Asian American Theater Company in San Francisco. Unlike Hwang, Gotanda has yet to write a play that does not have Asian American characters or one that does not explicitly address Asian American issues. Hwang has written plays with no Asian or Asian American characters (*Rich Relations*, for example), and the protagonist of *M. Butterfly* is white. Gotanda, on the other hand, rarely includes non-Asian characters in his plays, and when he does, they are supporting roles. Gotanda realizes that featuring a white character as the protagonist can make an Asian American play more accessible to non-Asian American audiences: "The non-Asian audience needs that axis point where there's a white character or some familiar motif that allows them to identify with [the play]." He is also aware that the "familiar motif" usually implies something "orientalist" such as exotic costumes. However, for Gotanda, there is no point in writing such a play unless he wants to parody orientalist stereotypes and white-centered worldview. "It's not part of my life," he comments.[33] For over two decades, Gotanda has insisted on dramatizing what he describes as "specific authenticity," one that stems from his experiences in growing up as a Sansei in Stockton, California.

Gotanda's first work, *The Avocado Kid*, already featured the kind of specific authenticity he sought. Michael Omi, in his introduction to a collection of Gotanda's plays, describes *The Avocado Kid* as having captured the "uniqueness and irreducibility of Asian American culture."[34] The musical's main character is based on Momotaro the Peach Boy, a character from from a Japanese children's tale. The Avocado Kid in Gotanda's version pops out of an avocado (a quintessential Californian product abundant in Stockton) instead of a peach. Dressed in a pop-culture style of Kabuki costume, the Avocado Kid holds "a glowing rose-gold mane" and moves to a "pulsating new wave beat."[35] A character named Jagaimo,

---

[33] Gotanda is keeping open the possibility of writing a play without any Asian American characters or producing his plays with an all-white cast. However, as long as Asian Americans are peripheral to the dominant (white) culture, he sees no point in perpetuating the social structure in his works. Only when Asian Americans are at the center of the American culture (and Asian American plays are fully canonized) would Gotanda see the validity in reinterpreting his plays from a different racial perspective.

[34] Omi, "Introduction," xv.

[35] Ken Wong, "*Avocado* Sprouts from a Sansei-tional Range of Gifts," *San Francisco Examiner*, June 11, 1980, C2.

who leads a band of outlaws called the Bandelles, represents the dark force that opposes the Avocado Kid's intention to help social outcasts. In the course of the musical, the Avocado Kid goes on to defeat Jagaimo in a musical contest with songs such as "Asian American Dream." Relaxed and playful (often in sexual ways), the musical uses traditional elements but presents them with ironic and contemporary sensibilities of the Sansei experience and American popular culture.

The Avocado Kid was produced at the Asian American Theater Company during the 1980–81 season. As discussed in Chapter 3, the AATC implemented a number of changes after the resignation of Frank Chin in 1978. Instead of an artistic director, a core group of young, mostly Sansei artists managed the company by forming what they called the artistic committee. Until the 1979–80 season, the artistic committee produced plays by first-wave writers such as Momoko Iko and Wakako Yamauchi. To begin the new decade, however, the committee appropriately included plays by second wave writers. The first season of the 1980s was quite ambitious: it featured twelve shows (almost double the previous season), many of which were by second wave writers. Although some of the shows were workshop productions, second wave writers such as Genny Lim, Bernadette Cha, and Lane Nishikawa were introduced to the audiences of AATC. The most impressive aspect of the season was the fact that three out of twelve shows were written by Gotanda: A Song for a Nisei Fisherman, Bullet Headed Birds, and The Avocado Kid. During the decade of 1980s, Gotanda was the most produced writer at AATC. As Frank Chin had envisioned, AATC continued to function as a playwright's theatre, and Gotanda represented the new voice AATC sought.

Conversely, AATC was artistic home for Gotanda throughout the 1980s and until the early 1990s. At AATC, Gotanda developed strong artistic collaborations with his friends and colleagues, including Lane Nishikawa, Eric Hayashi, Marc Hayashi, David Henry Hwang, Rick A. Shiomi, Judi Nihei, Amy Hill, Dennis Dun, Ken Narasaki, Sharon Omi, and his wife Diane Emiko Takei, who worked as the co-artistic director of the company in the mid-1990s. Gotanda was part of the highly creative, confident, and energetic group of second wave artists who created a new kind of Asian American theatre.

Gotanda's debut in New York City was also at an Asian American theatre site. His second musical, Bullet Headed Birds, opened at Pan Asian Repertory Theatre in November 1981. Mel Gussow, in his review of the musical, described it as "a kind of Japanese-American equivalent of

Figure 9. The 1980 production of Philip Kan Gotanda's musical *The Avocado Kid* at the Asian American Theater Company. Bernadette Cha (Top) plays Jayaime, who leads three Bandelles: Marc Hayesti (left side middle), Lane Nishikawa (left side lower), and William Ellis Hammond (right side lower).

Cowboy Mouth by Mr. [Sam] Shepard and Patti Smith."[36] (Gotanda himself cites Shepard as a major influence for opening up theatrical possibilities.) Gussow also noted that the Pan Asian Repertory Theatre, which had "specialized in naturalistic plays" took a "sidestep into surrealism

[36] Mel Gussow, "Surrealist *Bullet Headed Birds*," *New York Times*, November 25, 1981, C24.

and contemporary musical theater" with Gotanda's work.[37] Both the site and reception of Gotanda's musical in New York City differed diametrical from those of Hwang's *FOB*. Hwang's play debuted at a mainstream theatre and was clearly packaged as an Asian American play produced for a mainstream New York audience. *Bullet Headed Birds*, which featured Jessica Hagedorn and Gedde Watanabe, was contexualized as a new type of Asian American show, one that was cutting edge and experimental. In fact, according to Gotanda, Andy Warhol attended one of the performances. As Gussow correctly observed, Pan Asian Repertory Theatre took a chance with the rock-style musical. Gotanda challenged the naturalistic tendencies in Asian American theatre and demanded space for alternative expression. He represented a new generation within the Asian American theatre community, but because he was not writing for mainstream theatre, only those who knew about its historical significance could fully appreciate his early musical works.

The "surreal" elements also appeared in Gotanda's non-musical pieces including *A Song for a Nisei Fisherman* (1980) and *The Dream of Kitamura* (1982), both of which premiered at the AATC.[38] With each subsequent work, Gotanda wrote more dialogue and less music, and the more dialogue he wrote, the more his writing style moved towards naturalism and narrative storytelling. Not surprisingly, his audience base widened as he wrote more in the style of naturalism. *The Wash*, for instance, was the first of Gotanda's works to receive significant mainstream attention. In fact, it was Gotanda's first play to not premiere at an Asian American theatre company. The play received a workshop production at the Mark Taper Forum in Los Angeles in 1985; a world premiere production at the Eureka Theater in 1987; full productions at the Manhattan Theatre Club and the Northwest Asian American Theater in 1990 and at Mark Taper Forum in 1991. Gotanda also wrote the film version of *The Wash*, which was produced in 1988.

The Wash dramatizes the separation of an older Nisei couple. Against cultural expectations, the wife leaves her husband to seek happiness, independence, and new love. The husband must come to terms with the challenges that shake the very foundation of his manhood. The play addresses deeply personal and private issues that the Japanese American community would rather ignore. For instance, the wife is portrayed as a

---

[37] Ibid.
[38] For a list of Gotanda's plays and their production histories, see Randy Barbara Kaplan's entry in *Asian American Playwright: A Bio-Bibliographical Critical Sourcebook*, edited by Miles Xian Liu (Westport, CT: Greenwood, 2002).

sexual person who can appreciate her new lover, and the husband is forced to accept a mixed-race grandchild whose father is black. For the first time, mainstream audiences got a glimpse of the inner world of the Japanese American community. Some in the community disliked the exposure, but the play opened doors for Gotanda to write for audiences beyond the community.

After the mainstream success of *The Wash*, Gotanda found more opportunities in regional theatres. Berkeley Repertory Theatre was especially supportive of his work and commissioned him throughout the late 1980s and 1990s. According to Gotanda, as his plays received more mainstream attention, his audience changed from "mainly young 'politically correct' and hip Asian American[s]" to a "more diverse one of Asians and non-Asians."[39] Although Gotanda was keenly aware of the mainstream audience expectation of an "Asian American" play, he did not change his style. He claimed: "Even though my work was being presented at these larger venues, I refused to compromise the material or try to make it more accessible to a particular audience. The audience should come to you. This may seem arrogant, but what it amounts to is a leap of faith."[40] As a Sansei playwright from Stockton, he knew that he could not reach all audiences in the same way: "If you are Japanese American, you really get the work on some unspoken level. If you are Japanese American from Stockton, I mean literally, you will really get it." Gotanda does not consciously imagine an ideal audience, but rather, he tries to tell stories of the world as he sees it. And since his world is full of Asian American characters, an Asian American audience emerges in his mind during the writing process: "Ultimately, I'm just trying to tell the story, and as I'm trying to tell the story, in the back of my mind, I think I see Asian American faces out there."[41]

Nevertheless, he has invited the mainstream audience to gain a more expansive understanding of America through the world of his plays. In an interview with Misha Berson, he stated "I'm coming from a specific place as a Japanese American, but I want to make sure audiences can meet me halfway. When you want to reach a lot of people, your work should be inclusive enough for everyone to find its center."[42] Gotanda has invited

---

[39] Michael Omi, "Introduction," in Philip Kan Gotanda, *Fish Head Soup and Other Plays* (Seattle: University of Washington Press, 1991), xvi.

[40] Ibid.

[41] Robert B. Ito, "Philip Kan Gotanda," *Words Matter: Conversations with Asian American Writers*, edited by King-Kok Cheung (Honolulu: University of Hawai'i Press, 2000), 178.

[42] Misha Berson, "Role Model on a Role," D1.

non-Asian American audiences to the specific world of his plays not only through his writing but also by forming relationships with regional theatre companies. When a mainstream theatre company decides to produce one of his plays, Gotanda tries to make sure that "it is not just used to get their numbers up, to go after monies."[43] He feels that it is his responsibility as a writer to be aware of how the theatre is willing to "transform" by producing an Asian American play. The company should not think of the production as a "one shot deal"; instead, it should do audience outreach (especially to Asian Americans) and include programs such as panel discussions for educational purposes. Most importantly, the production should reflect the company's commitment to produce other Asian American plays in future seasons.

Gotanda has also encouraged Asian American theatre companies to forge "equitable relationships" with larger regional theatre companies. For him, such relationships are the only way smaller ethnic theatres can survive the competition. He has encouraged co-productions of his works by both Asian American and mainstream theater companies. For example, *Day Standing on Its Head* was co-produced by the Asian American Theater Company and Berkeley Repertory in 1994, and in 1999 *Yohen* was co-produced by the East West Players and Robey Theater, an African American theatre company in Los Angeles (and featured Nobu McCarthy and Danny Glover). According to Gotanda, such collaborations not only validate smaller companies' existence, but also allow larger companies to understand the "language" of Asian American theatre. Only by forging these relationships would both institutions be able to "present a more expansive presentation of Asian America and America."

Gotanda has chosen to work with mainstream companies because he feels a responsibility towards his plays, which deserve, in his opinion, the best possible production. Larger venues present him with advantages that cannot be found in Asian American companies. For instance, Asian American companies tend to cast from the same core group of actors from the community, but mainstream regional companies can draw from a national pool. Also, by staging his plays in larger venues, his plays can benefit from those production details that are possible only with a larger budget and higher level of professionalism. Gotanda, however, did not leave Asian American theatre permanently, mainly because he has always preferred an Asian American audience. Moreover, he describes the

[43] Gotanda is referring to those companies that include ethnic plays in order to receive grants for "multicultural" theatre.

productions of his plays at Asian American theatre companies as "deeper." He explains: "Working with an Asian American theater company is like working with family, where everybody has shorthand. Everybody has gone to some degree through the same experience. So you have a common vocabulary, history. As a consequence, they may not have the production values and all the bells and whistles. But you can sometimes go deeper and present something that is deeper as a theatre piece and a theatre experience than [. . .] if you had all the bells and whistles."

Gotanda admits that he has had more success on the West Coast than he had on the East Coast because he writes from a worldview that comes from a strong sense of a big Asian American community. West Coast regional theatres such as the Eureka Theater, the Berkeley Repertory Theatre, the South Coast Repertory, and the San Jose Repertory Theatre have more than once commissioned and produced Gotanda's plays. East Coast theatres responded only after the plays had already received successful productions at West Coast companies. *Sisters Matsumoto* (1998), for instance, opened at the Huntington Theatre Company in Boston in 2000, giving the play a new kind of audience (which consisted mainly of East Coast, white, older patrons). The Boston production demonstrated the expansion of Gotanda's audience base, but his version of mainstream success has remained mostly a West Coast phenomenon and he has yet to reach the ultimate mainstream venue, Broadway.

While Hwang and Gotanda began their careers around the same time, their career paths have consistently grown wider. Besides the geographical differences (Hwang has lived in New York City since the early 1980s), the two have differed on their views of what it means to be an Asian American playwright. Hwang has, for instance, resisted the label "Asian American playwright" because of the limitations it can imply. "America, however, must not restrict its 'ethnic' writers to 'ethnic' material, while assuming that white males can master any topic they so desire."[44] Unlike Hwang and a number of other Asian American playwrights, Philip Kan Gotanda has not objected to the label and found it not limiting but politically empowering: "I'm happy to be working more in the mainstream regional theatres and in the entertainment industry, but I still believe there is an Asian-American theatre and an Asian-American literature. 'Asian-America' is, in itself, a political term."[45]

[44] David Henry Hwang, "Introduction," *FOB and Other Plays* (New York: Plume, 1990), xiii.
[45] Berson, *Between Worlds*, 33.

Gotanda emphasizes that "Asian America" is a socially constructed term that was created to serve a specific purpose. As long as the purpose needs to be addressed, he feels the responsibility to present himself as an Asian American writer. In his mind, he has always known he is "just a writer, just an American writer." He also questions whether the term is limiting or the work created by an Asian American playwright is limiting:

> I still feel this: on the one hand, if you want to throw off the term [Asian American] now, that's fine because I think it's served [a] purpose, and other things will come up that are more in keeping with what's going on. But at the same time, [I think] the idea is to keep the term evolving and [to keep] making sure it's contemporary. You don't have to write plays forever about the [internment] camps, or immigration. Write whatever you'd like, write about the things that are important now: mixed race issues, all the issues that seem to be about why we shouldn't use the term can be included in the term.

As I discuss in Chapter 8, the term Asian American has been challenged by a new generation of writers since the 1990s, and Gotanda himself has evolved with the changing landscape of American theatre. However, his main goal, to find and dramatize the "specific authenticity" of the world he has experienced, has remained a constant.

Feminism and Velina Hasu Houston (b. 1957)

While David Henry Hwang and Philip Kan Gotanda have often described the Asian American theatre community as "family," the playwright Velina Hasu Houston's experience has been different, to say the least. Her career explicitly highlights the complicated cultural landscape that second wave artists have had to navigate. As an Amerasian, whose mother is Japanese and father African American and Blackfoot Pikuni, Houston has often traversed around and across the boundaries that demarcated Asian American theatre.[46] Her mixed race background has challenged the assumptions of ethnic theatres in the USA. At the same time, she has been one of the most produced second wave playwrights in mainstream theatre. She has also edited two anthologies of Asian American plays and has taught playwriting at the University of Southern California since 1990. She has indeed played

---

[46] Velina Hasu Houston explains "An *Amerasian*, a term coined by Pearl S. Buck, is someone who is half Asian (usually native Asian) and half American. The American half can be of any extraction" (Houston, *Politics of Life*, 9). Original emphasis.

many crucial roles in moving Asian American theatre towards American mainstream culture in terms of both theatre and academia.

Houston made a stellar debut in the profession of playwriting in 1982 when her play *Asa Ga Kimashita* (*Morning Has Broken*) won two prestigious awards at the American College Theater Festival. The two awards were the David Library Playwriting Award for American Freedom and the Lorraine Hansberry Playwriting Award. *Asa Ga Kimashita* tells the story of her parents who fell in love during the 1940s when her father was an American GI stationed in Japan. They decided to get married and leave for the United States, defying her mother's family's wishes and cultural expectations. According to Houston, the play "looked at [the] interconnectivity between two different ethnic cultures."[47] She wrote the play as a thesis for a MFA degree in playwriting at the University of California, Los Angeles. The writing of the play was an act of defiance against one of her professors who advised her to write for a "wider" audience and to avoid "ethnic" topics in order to be produced in mainstream theatre. Houston writes in the Introduction to her anthology, *Politics of Life*, "I was not certain if the professor said 'wider' or 'whiter,' because the fan in his office diminished the sound quality, but there was no need to ask. In this case, the words were synonymous."[48] The play's success in 1982 led her to realize that "apparently, American theater audiences do have an appetite for more than just meat loaf and apple pie."[49]

The play's success may have refuted the professor's concerns, but it also attracted another kind of disapproval. According to Houston, a group of black students complained about her receiving the Lorraine Hansberry Award (which awards the best African American dramatic work) because they did not consider her play "African American." She realized early on that as a professional playwright in the USA, she would not only hear variations of her professor's advice (to write for a "wider" audience) but also encounter friction in ethnic theatres. She was never "black enough" or "Asian enough." After graduating from UCLA, she found production opportunities at both the East West Players and the Negro Ensemble Theater (New York City). According to Houston, those in the leadership positions at both companies supported her: "These were the people who understood that Asian diaspora and African diaspora would begin to include part of each other because that is just the natural evolution of

---

[47] Velina Hasu Houston, Personal interview (February 2, 2005). All uncited quotations by Houston are from this interview.
[48] Houston, *Politics of Life*, 2.
[49] Ibid.

humanity." However, other staff members resisted and sometimes blatantly discriminated against her. For instance, in the lobby of the East West Players, Houston encountered "one of the leading artistic members" who told her, "So you are what somebody who is Japanese and black looks like. You get the worst of both races." As a young writer, Houston learned quickly that the way she looks, as much as her work, was a direct challenge to the established ethnic theatres. Houston remembers: "My own presence as an Afro-Asian individual in either a purely Asian American setting or purely African American setting seemed to be jarring to the monoracial artists who worked in those environments."

Houston wrote *Tea*, her most produced and studied play in 1983, as the third part of a family trilogy she had begun with *Asa Ga Kimashita* (the second in the trilogy is *American Dreams*). The play won the first prize in a multicultural play competition hosted by the Group Theater in Seattle. Contrary to her expectation, the Group Theater did not move forward to produce the play for three years, so she accepted Mako's proposal to give the play a world premiere at the East West Players (EWP) in 1986. Her first play, *Asa Ga Kimashita*, had received a successful run at the EWP in 1983.[50] *Tea* had all the indications of being another popular production because the subscribers of the EWP were predominantly Japanese Americans who welcomed Mako's decision to focus the EWP's seasons on Japanese American plays. The play is based on interviews Houston conducted with the Japanese war brides in an army base in Junction City, Kansas, where she grew up. The play features five Japanese women with unique and untold stories. With one of the characters, Setsuko, based on her mother, Houston had written about the world she intimately knew. Such a world was unknown to the American public, and the play gave it an exposure that both surprised and educated readers and audiences.

Unquestionably, the play was more than suitable to premiere at the EWP. However, the play was never staged at the EWP. Instead, it premiered at the Manhattan Theatre Club in New York City and became one of the most revived Asian American plays in regional theatres. In addition to the EWP, the Asian American Theater Company has never staged the play. In fact, Kumu Kahua in Hawaii was the first Asian American theatre company to do so in 1990. The only other has been the Asian American Repertory Theatre in San Diego in 1997. Indeed,

---

[50] See Kurahashi, *Asian American Culture*, 157–162, for a description of the East West Players' production of *Asa Ga Kimashita*. The production was directed by Shizuko Hoshi and won five *Drama-Logue* awards.

Houston has been the most visible and outspoken Asian American playwright in mainstream theatre, but Asian American theatre companies have not been her primary venue.[51]

At the EWP, Houston faced an obstacle that forced her to make one of the most important decisions of her career. The obstacle may have stemmed from intraracial and gender discrimination, but it was more of a reflection of the style of management (or mismanagement) that plagued the EWP during the 1980s and eventually led to the forced resignation of Mako. When *Tea* went into preproduction at the EWP, Mako told her that the cast had already been selected. Because the EWP was an actors' ensemble company, the auditions were often closed to the public, and the core actors appeared in almost all of the productions. Mako would later be accused of nepotism for almost always casting his wife and daughters. Mako emphatically defends his casting choice, stating that he would rather work with actors who he knows and trusts.[52] Houston liked the entire cast with the exception of one. Mako had chosen his wife Shizuko Hoshi for the role of Himiko, the lead character, and Houston thought she would be better for another role. When Houston objected, she was told that if she did not allow the EWP to produce the play with the cast, she would never be able to work at the company again. After consulting with her agent, she decided to pull out. According to Houston, the decision was a big step for a young playwright, especially when it involved the most established Asian American theatre company in the country: "But I felt that it was wrong, what they were asking. I thought it was based on nepotism. And it wasn't healthy for the artists and certainly not for the

---

[51] One reason that might explain this discrepancy is discrimination within Asian American theatre. For instance, the discrimination against her was obvious when she worked with the Asian American Theater Company during the mid-1980s. Although the AATC had produced her play, *Thirst* in 1986, it never paid her royalty fees. She repeatedly wrote letters asking to be paid. (These letters are included in the AATC archive at the University of California, Santa Barbara.) She eventually learned that the pay system at the AATC functioned on a hierarchy. Although the hierarchy may have not been a formal or even conscious policy, Houston noticed that she was the "last person in the totem pole": "[the producers of the AATC] paid Asian American men first, and then Asian American women, and then I never got paid." Although she understands that the financial situation of the AATC was at its worst at the time, she found it "very odd" that mixed race artists were the last to be paid if at all. Because many of the people involved in the management of the AATC in 1986 refuse to fully explain what they did or did not do, I was not able to verify Houston's claim. As discussed in Chapter 3, 1986 was a stressful year at the AATC, and the management was in transition.

[52] In an interview with me, Mako stated that because both he and his wife were born in Japan, they had a similar style in approaching the practice of theatre. He rhetorically asked "Who can I trust?"

play." Houston believes that she has been "blacklisted" at the EWP since then. After Mako's resignation in 1989, the EWP has undergone a number of changes under the leadership of Tim Dang, but it has yet to produce another play by Houston.

Houston did not know what would happen to *Tea* and her career when she made the decision to sever ties with the EWP. But Houston has never regretted her decision, especially because shortly afterwards, *Tea* received a world premiere at the Manhattan Theatre Club (MTC), a major Off Broadway theatre in New York City. After the MTC production of *Tea*, the play gained a "life of its own," and Houston's career would never be the same. Her work began to receive productions almost solely in mainstream theatres, and she no longer had to depend on ethnic theatres for opportunities. According to Houston, the play tells a story that comes from the personal but that has the power to "resonate into the universal." And it has resonated with audiences of all backgrounds because it tells an immigrant story about "survival of the outsider in a new and strange environment."

The reasons for the play's success should be found in the excellent ways in which the plot and the five female characters have been crafted. The play also exposes a fascinating aspect of American history in a non-threatening, poetic way. But another reason for its success may be found outside the text, in the minds of mainstream audiences. As I have discussed with David Henry Hwang's plays, the success of *Tea* is indicative of what mainstream audiences expect of an Asian American play. Moreover, because Houston is a female playwright, the mainstream expectation is more particular. It seems to be more than a coincidence that the most popular novel by an Asian American female writer is Amy Tan's *Joy Luck Club* (1990), which also involves four Asian women's survival stories in the USA. Also, the film version, directed by Wayne Wang in 1993, has reached more audiences than any other film about Asian Americans. In fact, when Houston submitted a film script of *Tea*, a major film producer commented, "Why this is nothing but a Japanese *Joy Luck Club*," implying that the film version would be redundant. In actual fact *Tea* predates *Joy Luck Club* and there are more differences than similarities, as Houston notes, "The sad thing is the two stories have nothing to do with each other. They are two very different stories. What it boils down to is how mainstream America sees Asian femininity, that anytime you pull together three or four [Asian] women, it's the same old story." *Tea* and *Joy Luck Club* tell completely different stories, but the surface premise that involves the struggle and survival of Asian women in the USA may be the formula that works for the mainstream American public.

Another reason for the popularity of *Tea* is the sharp feminist perspective that Houston articulates. In fact, almost all of her plays feature women and their issues: "I have remained very interested in exploring the way that women face challenges, special challenges that maneuvering in our society causes them to be confronted with." The artistic director of the Manhattan Theatre Club was (and still is) Lynne Meadow, one of the few female leaders of Off Broadway theatre. Houston has maintained a number of productive relationships with female producers and directors. She has also had close friendships with a number of Asian American female theatre artists, especially Japanese Americans. When she met Roberta Uno, for instance, the two instantly found a number of commonalities, including the fact that they have children who are "Afro-Asian" with Japanese background. They also had discussions about creating anthologies of plays by Asian American female writers. Uno, whom Houston considers an "older sister," included *Tea* in her anthology *Unbroken Thread*. Around the same time, with the support of Sucheng Chan, a historian, Houston edited *Politics of Life*. Thus, two anthologies of plays by Asian American female writers were published in the same year, 1993. Uno and Houston have been instrumental in creating a strong network of Asian American female theatre artists, both of the first and second waves.

Houston admits that while her plays deal with women's issues in general and minority women's issues in particular, she has had more interest in the Asian female perspective. She attributes this interest to the way she was raised: by a Japanese mother who taught her the Japanese language, customs, and folklores. The majority of Asian American playwrights of the second wave grew up on the West Coast, but Houston grew up on an army base in Kansas where she was surrounded with Asian women who were secluded like her mother. She did not have a typical American childhood, to say the least. (She jokes that she didn't even know who Mother Goose was.) Her sensibility is thus of the Asian female immigrant. Needless to say, she was not aware of the Asian American Movement or ethnic arts while growing up. When she moved to California to study playwriting at UCLA, she didn't "even have a sense that there was something called Asian American theatre or African American theatre; I had no idea of the strength and history of ethnic theatres in America." When asked to compare herself to other second wave playwrights, Houston notes that when she started to get to know other writers (such as David Henry Hwang and Philip Kan Gotanda), they seemed "culturally distanced" to her: "I felt that the way they behaved and communicated was very much American rather than Asian, relative to how I had grown up."

The irony was not lost on Houston. She, as a mixed race person, was seen as someone who might "dilute" Asian American culture, but in actuality, she was more "Asian" than other second wave writers. Houston adds, "My native Asian identity was so strong that for me, it superceded everything else." The seemingly self-contradictory image Houston embodied may have led ethnic theatre companies to resist her and her plays. On the other hand, the same image may have been perceived by mainstream theatre as "multicultural" in the fullest sense, one that included domestic, international, and diasporic elements. For example, when regional theatre companies choose plays, they have to consider the stark reality that allows only one "multicultural" or "ethnic" play per season if at all. For such "token" selection, Houston's *Tea* would be an excellent choice because it addresses not only an ethnic group and domestic exclusion, but also women's issues and global matters. Houston's mixed-race identity would also benefit the company because it would be able to claim that it is including a play by Asian, African, Native American, female writer. The more boxes it could check, the more "multicultural" the perception.[53]

While these political and financial factors may have affected Houston's career in both positive and negative ways, producers of her plays have maintained that the quality of writing is the reason for the selection. Jack O'Brien, the artistic director of Old Globe Theater, produced a number of Houston's plays, including *Tea* and *Basic Necessities*. In explaining why he chose her plays, he states: "The obvious thing is that here is also a woman of remarkable history and parentage. It begs the question, 'Did you take this playwright because of the area she covers?' No. It's a popular subject right now. We're up to our hip boots in sensitive issues. But that's not why we selected [her play]. It's elegant, stunning writing."[54] Most producers of mainstream theatre would agree with O'Brien that the selection of Houston's or other minority writer's play hinges on quality rather than politics. However, during the 1980s and the early 1990s when second wave writers were beginning to find opportunities in mainstream theatre,

---

[53] I don't intend to sound cynical with this analysis or to take away anything from the excellence of *Tea* as a play. I am pointing out the actual business of running a regional theatre in the USA. Most leaders of regional theatres would prefer to produce more plays by ethnic minorities and women, but they are rarely given the luxury. Instead, they are forced (by the board of directors or because of audience demands and financial incentives) to choose one such play per year or every other year. And, of course, some companies practice tokenism in truly mercenary sense by including "multicultural" plays in order to receive grants.

[54] Jan Breslauer, "Playwright. Amerasian. Single Mother. The Artistry of an Activist," *Los Angeles Times*, July 7, 1991, 3.

quality and politics were inseparable. Both were absolutely necessary for an Asian American writer to be produced, and Houston was an ideal candidate.

Moreover, Houston has willingly played the role of the political minority writer. Houston titled her first anthology *Politics of Life*, explaining:

> It is not enough, then, simply to write about ordinary life in ordinary ways because life can never be ordinary for the female of color. Asian American women playwrights are faced with the task of creating meaningful theater and expressing themselves artistically while sustaining a sensitivity toward culture and gender... The politics of living as women of color in this society and in the global village must continue to be examined.[55]

With the publication of her second anthology, *But Still, Like Air, I'll Rise: New Asian American Plays* (1997), Houston continued her mission to give voice to Asian American playwrights and to educate the academia and the general public. In her introduction, she protested at the enduring racism in American mainstream theatre, which continues to exclude and marginalize Asian American plays.

Laurie Winer of *Los Angeles Times*, in reviewing the anthology, could not disagree more. She criticized the quality of some of the plays in the collection, but her main argument was about Houston's political stance. In response to Houston's claim that American theatre omits minority groups' experiences, Winer retorted: "At this late in the culture wars, could any argument be more tired? [. . . Houston] writes as if the past two decades never occurred."[56] Winer pointed to the successes of bestselling writers Maxine Hong Kingston and Amy Tan and playwrights David Henry Hwang and Philip Gotanda. Houston was surprised to read the review not because of its negativity because it appeared prominently in a Sunday's Calendar section of *Los Angeles Times*. The paper had never before reviewed a collection of Asian American plays, but Winer's review appeared in one of the most popular and visible sections. Houston could not help but wonder what the motive was for giving her anthology such attention. She responded by writing to *Los Angeles Times*, stating essentially that a few Asian American playwrights' success (namely, those of Hwang, Gotanda, and Houston) does not signify the accomplishment of

---

[55] Houston, *Politics of Life*, 29.
[56] Laurie Winer, "A Collection with Much Missing," *Los Angeles Times*, August 31, 1997, 42.

equal access and representation for the entire group. Also, she criticized
Winer's conflation of Asian American prose with plays.

Winer's critique echoed the arguments of those who believed that the
goals of multiculturalism had been reached by the 1990s. As Houston
writes in her response, funding for multicultural theatre was dwindling
during the mid-1990s, and mainstream theatres were losing interest in
"those kinds" of plays.[57] Affirmative action, which for instance benefited
Hwang during the early 1980s, was seen as no longer necessary, and the
rhetoric of Houston's introduction was heard as whining. Moreover,
unlike the early 1980s, Asian American plays were occasionally produced
in mainstream theatre by the mid-1990s. As Winer points out, in 1996,
three full productions of Asian American plays were presented by mainstream regional theatres: Diana Son's *Boy* at the La Jolla Playhouse, Philip
Kan Gotanda's *Ballad of Yachiyo* at the South Coast Repertory, and David
Henry Hwang's *Golden Child* also at the South Coast Repertory. However,
for Houston, American theatre was not even close to truly reflecting all of
America. In 1996, for instance, the three Asian American plays mentioned
by Winer were among over 150 full productions at regional theatres. For
some, a few writers were enough to represent the entire community of
Asian American theatre, but for others, including Houston, it was only the
beginning. The first-wave playwrights created and opened the door of
opportunity for Asian American writers, and the second wave blazed
through it, paving the trail for the next wave.

---

[57] Velina Hasu Houston, "Uphill Fight for Asian American Plays," *Los Angeles Times*, September
15, 1997, 3. The phrase, "those kinds" is from the following passage in the article: "A Southern
California theater's artistic director" told one of her associates that "since nobody was paying
him anymore to produce 'those kinds' of plays, he was free to ignore them" (3).

6

Solo performance

Telling one's story on one's own terms is an act of self-empowerment and validation, as an individual and as a member of a group. It says, "I am here and my experience, our experience in this culture, matters."

Dan Kwong[1]

IN 1994, SOLO PERFORMER DAN KWONG LED THIRTY ASIAN American men in a workshop presentation titled *Everything You Wanted to Know About Asian Men (but didn't give enough of a $#*@! to ask)* at the Japanese American National Museum in Los Angeles and the Highways Performance Space in Santa Monica, CA. The shows were mostly soldout, and more people wanted to participate in Kwong's solo performance workshop, which he continued to offer. Despite the apparent success, Scott Collins of the *Los Angeles Times* wrote a scathing review of the production and criticized the show as "much ado about nothing": "A series of inchoate and painfully long-winded monologues, interspersed with forgettable video segments, 'Asian Men' almost played like a parody of politically correct performance art."[2] A week after the review appeared, the *Los Angeles Times* published Dan Kwong's response, which summed up his philosophy of solo performance:

Telling one's story on one's own terms is an act of self-empowerment and validation, as an individual and as a member of a group. It says, "I am here and my experience, our experience in this culture, matters." To do so takes a stand against everything an oppressive society attempts to

---

[1] Dan Kwong, "Counterpunch: Ethnic Images, Issues and *Asian Men*," *Los Angeles Times*, September 11, 1995, F3.

[2] Scott Collins, "*Asian Men* Closes After Much Ado About Nothing," *Los Angeles Times*, September 4, 1995, calendar section, 4.

shove down our throats – exemplified by those voices that say, "You and your issues are of no concern to us." Collins' dismissal of the group as "having nothing of consequence to say" and his belittlement of "ethnic consciousness-raising" comes from the classic position of privilege in a society that has systematically silenced those not of the dominant group.[3]

Kwong's statement echoes the artistic goals of Asian American solo performers who have struggled to tell their stories on their own terms. At least since the 1970s, Asian American solo performers have increasingly gained in popularity and have become an indispensable part of Asian American culture. Often written, directed, and produced by performers themselves, Asian American solo performances have brought a heightened sense of truth. It has also let artists work beyond and against the conventional styles of established theatre companies by incorporating multimedia techniques, autobiography, storytelling, ethnic specificity, and gender and sexuality in their works. They've also toured nationally and internationally, often as incidental diplomats of Asian America. Some performers have focused more on political issues, and others have been concerned with aesthetic aspects, but all of them have addressed their identities (which include more than race and ethnicity) in the style of what Tom Couser has described as "auto-ethnography."[4] Asian American performers went on stage to tell stories both unique and shared by others, both personal and universal. Together, they have transformed their singular experiences and identities into a collective identity and created a new genre in Asian American theatre.[5]

This chapter surveys the history of Asian American solo performance from the 1970s to the 1990s by examining the approaches, goals, and styles of five representative artists as case studies: Winston Tong, Lane Nishikawa, Jude Narita, Dan Kwong, and Denise Uyehara. As Kwong articulates, one's story has to be told in "one's own terms," and I am interested in analyzing how the stories are told through solo performance,

---

[3] Kwong, "Counterpunch," F3.

[4] Quoted in David T. Mitchell, "Body Solitaire: The Singular Subject of Disability Autobiography," *American Quarterly* 52.2 (2000), 311.

[5] Asian American solo performers began to emerge in large numbers in the late 1980s, but the tradition of solo acts and one-person shows in theatre history is extensive. Indeed, the tradition of one person telling a story to an audience is arguably the oldest form of theatre in both Western and Eastern cultures. As John S. Gentile writes in *Cast of One: One-Person Shows from the Chautauqua Platform to the Broadway Stage* (Urbana and Chicago: University of Illinois Press, 1989), "the one-person show is as old as humankind, dating back to the ancient oral poets and storytellers."

as much as what the stories are. Using a broadly chronological trajectory, I explore four major modes of theatrical representation that have shaped Asian American solo performance. In discussing Winston Tong, I highlight his avant-garde approach to solo performance in the 1970s. I then examine works by Lane Nishikawa and Jude Narita in the 1980s as examples of using conventional acting as a mode of solo performance. The 1990s saw a great increase in the number and diversity of solo performances, and I focus on Dan Kwong to discuss the dominance of autobiography during the decade. Finally, I conclude the chapter with a study of Denise Uyehara's solo performance that purports to represent authenticity by using the concept of "borderless identity," one that both transcends and embodies all labeled identities.

Avant-garde solo performance

In the 1970s, solo performances were usually performed in Off-Off Broadway spaces such as The Kitchen, Franklin Furnace, Performance Space 122, The Performing Garage, and even in nightclubs, storefronts, and loft apartments in New York City. Solo performance, as an alternative theatre, was rarely reviewed by the mainstream press. Needless to say, its audiences were mostly other artists, and the majority of them never made a living with their solo works.[6] Winston Tong was among a number of Asian American avant-garde artists in the 1970s, a group that included Jessica Hagedorn and Ping Chong. Many, like Hagedorn, were known for their multimedia works and experimental art, but Winton Tong was recognized mostly for his originality in solo performance.

Born in San Francisco to immigrant parents, Winston Tong received a BFA degree in music at the California Institute of the Arts and moved to New York City after graduation. Between 1976 and 1979, Tong created more than half a dozen solo shows that are now recognized as the first solo performances by an Asian American artist. He began to work on solo performance because he realized early in his career that going solo was the best way to achieve his artistic goal. Indeed, Tong's style was fiercely independent and original. Eileen Blumenthal, in an article on Tong, describes his work as a melding of "widely divergent forms and sensibilities": "his extreme economy of means is akin to types of traditional Chinese theatre; his use of puppets, dolls, and silhouettes recalls elements

---

[6] Jo Bonney, ed., *Extreme Exposure: An Anthology of Solo Performance Texts from the Twentieth Century* (New York: Theatre Communications Group, 2000), xi.

of Japanese Bunraku and Javanese shadow puppets; and his startling, pervasive eroticism has roots in nineteenth century French Symbolism."[7] Tong's surprisingly unique intercultural and avant-garde sensibility made a powerful impact on the New York audience, and his solo performances earned him an Obie award in 1978.

Of Winston Tong's solo shows in the 1970s, the most well known are the "Three Solo Pieces" performed at La MaMa Experimental Theatre Club in April and May of 1978. The three pieces were *The Wild Boys*, *Bound Feet*, and *A Rimbaud*. Both Daryl Chin and Eileen Blumenthal provide descriptions of each piece in their reviews and give valuable information on the details of the performance. According to Chin, each piece lasted from twenty to thirty minutes with texts as central elements: William Burroughs for *The Wild Boys*, a self-written text in Cantonese for *Bound Feet*, and selections from Arthur Rimbaud's *Illuminations* for *A Rimbaud*.[8] Music was also crucial to the pieces: punk rock in the first, Satie in the second, and Ravel in the last. Stage techniques included slide projection, silhouettes, and a doll, which he used as a character representing both himself and another person.[9]

In *Bound Feet*, two dolls were used to portray the ancient Chinese practice of binding women's feet. The following description by Eileen Blumenthal is long, but I am including it here because it provides a rare detailed description of the performance:

> Tong walks on stage dressed in black, his face [powdered] female-theatre-mask white, and explains earnestly that "In China the Empress is Chinese, and so are all of her subjects." He sits on a small stool, then, and begins to wash, powder, and bind his feet; meanwhile, we hear a recorded dialog in Cantonese between a mother and child – at first lighthearted, then with the child increasingly troubled and finally ago-nized, the mother cajoling and comforting. Partway through binding

[7] Eileen Blumenthal, "The Solo Performances of Winston Tong," *The Drama Review* 23.1 (March 1979), 87. The article includes two photos of Tong in performance. Another photo of his work is included in Eileen Blumenthal, *Puppetry: A World History* (New York: Harry N. Abrams, Inc., 2005), 137. Taken by the photographer Sylvia Plachy, the photos are valuable glimpses of Tong's visual imagination.

[8] Daryl Chin, "Winston Tong: Three Solo Pieces," *Bridge: An Asian American Perspective* (summer 1978), 54.

[9] The opening piece, *The Wild Boys*, was the most jarring of the three with noisy electronic sounds and images of youth rebellion. Mel Gussow of *The New York Times* described the piece as a "brutally and harshly contemporary" tale of a "wild boy." Tong enacted "Johnny," a kid who leaves his home to join the wild boys and experiences rejection, vulnerability, and meaningless sexual (implicitly homosexual) encounters. See Mel Gussow, "*Three Solo Pieces* by Winston Tong," *New York Times*, May 10, 1978, 22.

his first foot, Tong suddenly looks up, registers the intrusion of the audience's curious eyes, and places a small, black screen to hide his preparation. His feet finally bound, he stuffs them into tiny red satin slippers, and limps about the stage a bit – again noticing at one point the distressing witnesses to his very personal toilet. Now the music of Eric Satie's *Gymnopédies* begins, and Tong unfolds a black cloth on the stage, revealing two nude dolls, a male and female, made of white muslin with white plastic faces and black hair. The man has a penis, the woman no visible breasts or genitals - but tiny, red satin slippers on her bound feet. Quietly, almost ceremonially, Tong dons white, satin funeral clothes and, arranging the dolls on the cloth, he kneels facing the audience to manipulate them. He carefully places the woman on her side, head thrown back, one knee bent. The male doll now moves to her, puts a hand to his crotch, then on her feet, removes a slipper, and leans down and kisses the stunted foot. Tong squeezes the woman's waist and her body contracts in an orgasm of pleasure/pain. Suddenly, as if overcome with anguish, passion, and the violation of prying eyes, Tong covers the dolls and hobbles off.[10]

Tong's manipulation of the dolls impressed the spectators and made them feel like voyeurs of a world in which he was playing god. Similar intimacy and eroticism were staged in the third piece, *A Rimbaud*, which featured four dolls: a sultry mermaid, a skeletal death-as-woman, an elegant young man (who looked like a miniature version of Tong), and what Mel Gussow calls "a mysterious catlike female predator" or what Daryl Chin calls "a leopard with a human face." All dolls were animated by Tong himself with much accuracy and realism. He preferred dolls to puppets because for him, "dolls live by themselves, and puppets have to be brought to life."[11] Tong saw himself as androgynous and a "free spirit," and used the dolls as his created actors to represent various facets of himself.

Tong did not explicitly use his Chinese American ethnic identity as a theme in his work and preferred to include it subtly. As Daryl Chin observes, for instance, *The Wild Boys* ends with a popular song "Limehouse Blues" from the 1930s that makes reference to "chinks."[12] Tong also used his Chinese background to tell a universal story of love and pain as he did with *Bound Feet*. But experiences of racism never deterred Tong from exploring the avant-garde art movement. In fact, for Tong, reacting to racism was secondary to developing his performative techniques and

[10] Blumenthal, "The Solo Performances," 88.
[11] Blumenthal, "The Solo Performances," 91.
[12] Chin, "Winston Tong," 56.

artistry, as reflected in the following comment Tong made in an interview: "I started singing with Tuxedo Moon [in San Francisco in the 1970s]. I remember one of the first nights someone said 'Get that screaming chinaman off the stage.' Some punk said, 'He can't even sing, he's just screaming.' They said that in France too, but I was proud of it. We developed that technique. You have to shout a certain way to get it right."[13] Tong continued to focus on his art and performed as a singer, poet, visual artist, and solo performer in the USA and Europe throughout the 1980s. Tong rarely collaborated with other Asian American theatre artists, but in 1992, he participated in Tsunami, a festival of Asian American performance art at the Asian American Theater Company in San Francisco. He performed *1st Generation Stigmas* which had text, music, puppetry, and video and addressed the experience of growing up as the first-born son of immigrant parents in America.[14]

Winston Tong's work from the 1970s remains historically isolated from other Asian American solo pieces, mainly because he was the first and because he did not address the so-called Asian American consciousness that became the foundation of Asian American theatre. Moreover, most Asian American performers outside of the New York City avant-garde theatre circle never got to see Tong's work, and when they did, it was judged apolitical and thus not "Asian American." Indeed, most Asian American solo performances throughout the 1980s bore no resemblances to the sensual style of Winton Tong but instead emphasized Asian American history, experience, and identity.

Solo performance as actors' craft

By the early 1980s, solo performance was no longer limited to Off-Off Broadway theatre, and Asian American performers joined the fast growing number of solo performers around the country. Asian Americans, like other groups, were influenced by feminist solo performers who had

[13] Gina Hall, "The Winston Tong Interview" (November 4, 1996), http://web.archive.org/web/20040506100043/http://www.fadmag.com/items/tong/tong.html.
[14] The show receive an extremely negative review from Steven Winn of *The San Francisco Chronicle*, who echoed other reviewers' description of Tong's later work as self-indulgent and pretentious and concluded that the show was a "mystery" to him. For reviews of Winston Tong's work post-1970s, see: Mel Gussow, "Stage: Puppeteer As *Frankie and Johnnie*," *New York Times*, January 7, 1982, C3; Sylvie Drake, "Stage Review: *Rasputin* Falls Short of the Mark," *Los Angeles Times*, April 15, 1987, Calendar Section, 3; Bernard Weiner, "Acrobatic Actors Work Around a Wall," *San Francisco Chronicle*, November 18, 1989, C8; Steven Winn, "Winston Tong's Solo Show is a Mystery," *San Francisco Chronicle*, January 17, 1992, D13.

developed a particular form of the genre since the 1960s. For feminist performers solo performance provided a powerful mode of representation to expose personal material in public.[15] Preconceived notions of women and womanhood were not enacted or portrayed, but rather, women were themselves on stage. By being themselves on stage, the performers broke taboos and silences repressing women and used the theme "personal is political" in their performances. They took control over their bodies and gained the right to write about themselves, thereby gaining the right to rewrite history and reveal truths about womanhood. Audiences were witnesses to the performers' detailed confession and the revelation of their private lives, and the sharing of the "unspeakable" empowered all those involved by giving them voice. According to Jeanie Forte, "the intimate nature of the work, the emphasis on personal experience and emotional material, not 'acted' or distanced from artist or audience, is what most characterizes this alternative, heterogeneous voice."[16]

Asian American performers also addressed the issues of identity and self-representation. In many ways, Asian American performers had more explaining to do on stage than feminist and other ethnic minority artists. Asian faces and bodies, along with the stereotype of Asian Americans as the perpetual foreigner and stranger, demanded explanation of the obvious: where they were from and what they were doing in America. Similar to disabled performance artists, the body-in-view generated stares and mandated a story. Rosemarie Garland Thomson's explanation of disabled performance artists applies readily to Asian American solo performers:

> The meaning of the body, thus the meaning of self, emerges through social relations. We learn who we are by the responses we elicit from others. In social relations, disabled bodies prompt the question, 'What happened to you?' The disabled body demands a narrative, requires an apologia that accounts for its difference from unexceptional bodies. In this sense, disability identity is constituted by the story of why my body is different from your body.[17]

The Asian American body also demands a narrative and an explanation of why it is different and strange. Asian American solo performers have,

---

[15] See Lenora Champagne, "Introduction," in *Out from Under: Texts by Women Performance Artists*, edited by Lenora Champagne (New York City: Theatre Communications Group, 1990), xi.

[16] Jeanie Forte, "Women's Performance Art: Feminism and Postmodernism," *Theatre Journal* 40 (1988), 221.

[17] Rosemarie Garland Thompson, "Staring Back: Self-Representations of Disabled Performance Artists," *American Quarterly* 52.2 (2000), 334.

thus, been more dedicated to educating the audiences about how Asian Americans have been imagined and actualized in history.

The first people to take on the role of performer/educator were actors. In some ways, they had no choice. Racial discrimination on top of the general low employment rate in the acting industry gave them no option but to create their own roles. For actors Lane Nishikawa and Jude Narita, solo performance became the most (and often the only) viable form of theatrical expression. With solo performance, they found a venue to write their own material, tell stories, enact multiple characters, and teach the audiences about the issues related to the Asian American identity. But most importantly, solo performance gave them the opportunity to create roles for themselves and a way to make a living as actors.

A Sansei, Lane Nishikawa was born in Hawaii and grew up in Southern California. While attending San Francisco State University in the mid-1970s, he met Eric Hayashi and Marc Hayashi, brothers who were active members of the Asian American Theater Workshop (AATW). Nishikawa began his participation in the workshop by appearing in Lonny Kaneko's *Lady Is Dying* (1977) directed by Frank Chin. Nishikawa was an ambitious actor, but he, like others, learned quickly of the casting discrimination of the entertainment industry against Asian American actors. Opportunities in the industry were virtually nonexistent or unacceptable to him. Moreover, Nishikawa did not find characters in Asian American plays satisfying; available characters being the angry Chinaman, the disillusioned Nisei farmer, and even benign versions of popular Asian stereotypes. As a young Sansei living in San Francisco, Nishikawa could not sympathize with such characters and wanted to see characters that he could identify with. Thus, he created his own characters.

Using previous experience as writer, actor, and director, Nishikawa put together a collection of nine monologues about the Asian American experience and created his first one-man show, *Life in the Fast Lane*. The show begins with Nishikawa addressing the audience as if he is talking to an imaginary casting director sitting in the house. It is immediately obvious that the casting director knows nothing about Nishikawa's Japanese American background. Nishikawa tries to explain to the "casting director" who he is. With successive attempts, he finds his voice, which Randy Barbara Kaplan calls "quintessentially Asian American":

> Thus, after responding to imaginary questions about his background, Nishikawa performs a loving tribute to his Oba-chang, the Issei grandmother who nurtured both his spirit and his stomach as a boy. The

succeeding monologue grows out of Nishikawa's delineation of Asian media stereotypes as enemies to be killed or houseboys to be dominated: he portrays a Texas redneck whose children are driving him to racial distraction with their romantic entanglement with Asian Americans. As a sly twist, at the end of the monologue, Nishikawa turns the tables on the audience, transforming himself into a Japanese father who is outraged to learn that his son is marrying a *hakujin* (Caucasian), demonstrating that the door of prejudice swings both ways.[18]

Nishikawa is himself on stage but also acts a number of characters both Asian and non-Asian for the purpose of storytelling. The primary purpose of the monologues is to teach the audience of Asian American history that has been excluded from American education. For instance, in the monologue "They Was Close, Those Brothers," Nishikawa tells the story of Uncle Blackie who fought with the all-Nisei 442nd Regiment during World War II. What Nishikawa reveals is not necessarily his personal life but rather, pieces of forgotten history close to his heart. In other words, Nishikawa's solo performances may not tell much about the intimate details of his own thoughts, but they educate the audience of "the impact of major events in Asian American history on the current stage of Asian America."[19]

The focus on cultural education made Nishikawa's solo shows appealing to many, especially those interested in the contemporary issues of multicultural education. As soon as *Life in the Fast Lane* premiered at the Asian American Theater Company, it was revived the following season and began to tour. For the next four years Nishikawa performed in front of numerous sold-out audiences in theatres and universities around the United States, Canada, and Europe. The success of *Life in the Fast Lane* led Nishikawa to develop more solo performances, which have included *I'm on a Mission From Buddha* (1990) and *Mifune and Me* (1993). In *I'm on a Mission From Buddha*, Nishikawa again plays multiple characters in order to tell stories from Asian America. According to Steven Winn of the *San Francisco Chronicle*, Nishikawa's transformation on stage is "as dangerous as it is empowering" because it raises questions of what and who he really is:

In the course of his 80-minute show, Nishikawa leaps easily from a slide rule-packing nerd to a pseudo-stoical spurned lover, an innocent first-time visitor to Japan to a teary Japanese American veteran of World War II. He plays a rapper in a leather jacket, and he plays himself, facing

[18] Randy Barbara Kaplan, "Lane Nishikawa," in *Asian American Playwrights: A Bio-Bibliographical Critical Sourcebook*, edited by Miles Xian Liu (Westport, CT: Greenwood Press, 2002), 255.

[19] Ibid.

the audience straight on, like Spalding Gray, with nothing more than a table and a beaker of water to mute the autobiographical frankness of his monologues.[20]

The most empowering aspect of the show is Nishikawa's redefinition of Asian American manhood. The characters, all male, range from the stereotypical nerdy Asian man to an honorable war veteran. As Nishikawa subverts undesirable stereotypes of Asian men, he replaces them with confident, sexy, fun, and, most importantly, real characters as a tribute to actual Asian American men he has known.[21]

Jude Narita's career is similar in many ways to Lane Nishikawa's: she is a Sansei, based in California, and turned to solo performance after experiencing disappointments as a struggling actor. Born in Long Beach, California, Narita was a serious student of acting, studying with Stella Adler in New York and Lee Strasberg in Los Angeles. However, such solid training did not give her the opportunity she wanted. Tired of passively waiting, she created her first and the best-known solo show, *Coming into Passion/Song for a Sansei* (1985). Like Nishikawa, she played multiple characters in order to reveal unknown details of Asian American history, especially of the gender roles and expectations. Just as Nishikawa focused on Asian American manhood, Narita addressed the experiences of Asian American women. But unlike Nishikawa, Narita included Asian women outside of the United States in her exploration of Asian American identity. As Melinda L. de Jesús assesses, Narita's work "manifests a distinct Asian American feminist and third-world feminist consciousness."[22]

Coming into Passion begins with the narrator, a Japanese American newscaster, emphatically rejecting her "Asianness" and wanting to be "American." But the assimilated newscaster gradually discovers through her dreams the commonalities she shares with women in other countries: "the Filipino mail-order bride, the Vietnamese bar girl, the nisei woman interned as a child, the Cambodian refugee, and troubled sansei teenager,

---

[20] Steven Winn, "The Many Faces of Asian Actor on a *Mission*," *San Francisco Chronicle*, March 9, 1990, E10.

[21] In the mid-1990s, Nishikawa became increasingly interested in the history of Japanese American soldiers of World War II and developed a semi-fictional two-man show with Victor Talmadge based on a fifty-year friendship between a Japanese American soldier and Jewish American man. Written by Nishikawa and Talmadge, *The Gate of Heaven* chronicles the lives of two men from the time the soldier rescues the Jewish man from the Dachau concentration camp during the war. The full script is published in Brian Nelson, ed., *Asian American Drama* (New York: Applause, 1997).

[22] Melinda L. de Jesús, "Jude Narita," in *Asian American Playwrights: A Bio-Bibliographical Critical Sourcebook*, edited by Miles Xian Liu (Westport, CT: Greenwood Press, 2002), 246.

and the storyteller who weaves the tale of a little girl caught in the bombing of Hiroshima."[23] Each character experiences abuse, loneliness, and suffering, much of which is caused by actions of Western men both abroad and domestically. By empathizing with these women, the narrator experiences what feminists would call "consciousness raising" that allows her to embrace her Asian American female identity.

As other feminist theatre artists have done for many decades, Narita empowers herself and the audience with her message, and she does so not only by preaching but also with her life and artistry. The fact that she writes, acts, and produces the show itself demonstrates her determination and fearlessness, and for Narita, the process of creating is part of the message. "Every woman knows about standing up for herself. But the perception of Asians is that they don't like to rock the boat, be trouble-makers: 'That's past, let's get on with life' – never dealing with the pain, the loss, the injustice. So this is my view of Asian life. And sure, there's some outrage, some things that need to be said, in an artistic way."[24] Moreover, as de Jesús describes, Jude Narita has created solo performances about the "contemporary Asian and Asian American 'Everywoman'" and made a great contribution to Asian American theatre.[25] Her later solo works such as *Stories Waiting to be Told* (1992), *The Wilderness Within* (1993), *Celebrate Me Home* (1996), and *Walk the Mountain* (1997) also address the lives of Asian and Asian American women, including her own. Narita's commitment to the Asian American and third-world feminist consciousness has led her to perform her shows around the United States and Asia in various venues.[26] Moreover, as one of the first Asian American female solo performers, Jude Narita has inspired other artists such as Lauren Tom, Patty Toy, Szu Wang, and Michelle Emoto (aka Darling Narita) to empower themselves by telling stories of Asian and Asian American women on stage.

Lane Nishikawa and Jude Narita were among the first Asian American solo performers to emerge in the first half of the 1980s. Their shows received national and international recognition as having educational values, and they often performed for non-Asian Americans as cultural

---

[23] Ibid.

[24] Janice Arkatov, "Narita's *Song* Looks at Roles of Asian Women," *Los Angeles Times*, August 1987, sec. 6, 3.

[25] de Jesús, "Jude Narita," 248.

[26] For instance in 1992, she traveled to Asia as a member of the Women's Delegation to Vietnam and Cambodia under the sponsorship of the Women's Union of Vietnam and the Asia Resource Center in the United States.

ambassadors. By playing multiple characters, they displayed their acting talents and portrayed a wide range of Asian and Asian American identities that would otherwise never have been seen on stage. Another important factor for their appeal was the low production cost. Because the performer wrote, produced, performed, and sometimes designed the show, the cost was much less than producing or inviting a play production or group performance. The low production cost also meant versatility to perform in all kinds of venues, from school auditoriums to assembly halls. More-over, the multicultural messages of these solo performances touched a chord in the 1980s when schools looked to the arts to teach multicultur-alism and pluralism. In the 1980s, a new flow of money from city, state, and federal agencies gave incentives to schools to promote multicultural edu-cation. With such encouragement and support, Asian American solo performers were able to take Asian American theatre to all parts of the country by performing in colleges, universities, and high schools even in the remotest areas. This combination of multicultural education, low cost, grant incentives, and novelty made Asian American solo performance popular in theatre touring circuits and educational systems.

Starting in the second half of the 1980s, other solo performers such as Brenda Wong Aoki and Sandra Tsing Loh began to create their own shows and joined the group of solo performers who were increasingly being sought after. Moreover, veteran Asian American performers such as Nobuko Miyamoto added solo performance to their repertory. Most of these new solo performers began their careers as actors like Nishikawa and Narita, and by the 1990s, it became almost expected that every actor have a solo piece in his or her back pocket readily available for performance. Amy Hill and Dennis Dun have been particularly successful with their solo shows. A number of other artists emerged from directions other than acting, including visual arts and performance arts. This trend continued through the 1990s, during which the number and diversity of Asian American solo performance grew exponentially. More performers chose solo performance not as an alternative to (or a form of) acting but as a way to develop new modes of artistic representation and storytelling. And a dominant form in the 1990s was autobiographical solo performance.

Autobiographical storytelling

In Asian American theatre, expression of selfhood has been central, as exemplified by artists such as Winston Tong, Lane Nishikawa, and Jude Narita. But since the late 1980s, solo performances have evolved into a more direct form of autobiography in which performers would speak in the first person as themselves during the most of show. Meiling Cheng, in her study of autobiographical solo performance, describes this voice as "halfway between a public presentation of the self and a theatrical construction of this self's multiple personas."[27] Cheng adds that such performances often concern the "artist's auto-projection as a subaltern individual who has been turned into an 'other' – being named as 'multicultural,' 'ethnic,' 'feminist,' 'queer,' 'poor,' 'old,' 'handicap,' or 'foreign' – by her/his acculturation in this country."[28]

As Meiling Cheng's study reveals, a major locale for the new genre was the Highways Performance Space, an alternative live art venue in Los Angeles.[29] Founded in 1989 by writer Linda Frye Burnham and artist Tim Miller, Highways has provided a multifunctional venue for a diverse group of artists who wanted to experiment artistically and explore cultural and social issues. A number of Asian American solo performers have found support and a sense of community at Highways. One of them is Dan Kwong, who is best known as a major autobiographical solo performer in American theatre. Cited by many critics as "a master storyteller," Dan Kwong has been recognized as having created a new form of solo performance. Born in Los Angeles to a Chinese American father and a Japanese American mother, Kwong grew up with a distinct experience of intraracial discrimination. He has received training in dance, baseball, martial arts, and visual arts, all of which are reflected in his performance. He attended the School of the Art Institute of Chicago, where he learned to develop multimedia shows, and in 1989, Kwong presented his first show, *Secrets of the Samurai Centerfielder* at Highways. The show uses baseball as a metaphor for his childhood and family history, which includes immigration of his mother's family, internment of his maternal grandparents during World War II, his parents' divorce, model-minority sisters, and Kwong's inability to fit into either Chinese or Japanese American cliques in school. Kwong resorts to the center, the neutral place where he is farthest from pain and isolation, and most importantly, where he can have the best perspective of his situation.

After the success of *Secrets of the Samurai Centerfielder*, Kwong developed other autobiographical shows, including *Tales from the Fractured Tao*

---

[27] Meiling Cheng, "Highways, L. A.: Multiple Communities in a Heterolocus," *Theatre Journal* 53 (2001), 448.

[28] Ibid.

[29] For an earlier study on Highways, see Linda Frye Burnham, "Getting on the Highways: Taking Responsibility for the Culture in the '90s," *Journal of Dramatic Theory and Criticism* (1990), 265–278.

with Master Nice Guy (1991), *Monkhood in Three Easy Lessons* (1993), *The Dodo Vaccine* (1994), and *The Night the Moon Landed on 39th Street* (1999). While all of his shows are autobiographical in content and multimedia in style, each focuses on a specific theme: *Tales from the Fractured Tao with Master Nice Guy* summarizes Kwong's "dysfunctional family, Asian American style"; *Monkhood in Three Easy Lessons* depicts the experiences of Asian American men; *Dodo Vaccine* examines HIV/AIDS in the Asian American community and homophobia; and *The Night the Moon Landed on 39th Street* asks broader questions of "human existence itself rather than focusing on issues of race, culture, or gender."[30] Kwong would be first to admit that some shows are more didactic than others, and others may be overly personal, but taken together, the body of work reflects the career of a multitalented artist with many stories to tell.

Dan Kwong's contribution to Asian American theatre goes beyond his shows; he has taught and inspired a number of artists to pursue autobiographical solo performance as their career. As mentioned at the beginning of this chapter, he founded the performance workshop Everything You Ever Wanted to Know about Asian Men in Los Angeles. He focused on men because previous performance festivals attracted more Asian American women than men, and he wanted to encourage more men to participate in the arts. In the first workshop, Kwong led about thirty Asian American men to write autobiographical performance pieces for twelve weeks. Gary San Angel (who participated in the workshop and a year later formed his own group, Peeling the Banana in New York City) describes how the workshop let Asian American men open up:

> The first exercise is the basic one: You write down five things that you love about being an Asian male and five things you hate about being an Asian male. Some real key things about what you struggle with come out – about what you appreciate, what you value. At the time I thought, "These would be the kind of questions you'd get from a self-help book." But he just did it in such a way that you felt safe and open enough that these questions allowed me and the rest of the guys to open up in a way that we never did in our lives. For me, it was like putting a mirror to yourself. You get to see all the great things, but you get to see all the ugly things too.[31]

---

[30] SanSan Kwan, "Dan Kwong," in *Asian American Playwrights: A Bio-Bibliographical Critical Sourcebook*, edited by Miles Xian Liu (Westport, CT: Greenwood Press, 2002), 164.

[31] Jana J. Monji, "All *Roads* Lead Home: Gary San Angel and Fellow Performance Artists Ponder Asian American Identity," *Los Angeles Times*, July 6, 2000, sec. calendar, 38.

Figure 10. Performance artist Dan Kwong describes the Khmer Rouge reign of terror in Cambodia, 1975–1979 in his solo performance show, *The Soul of a Country* at the Highways Performance Space, Santa Monica, California, June 2005.

The workshop ended with the presentation of works by nine of the participants (Gary San Angel, Radmar Agana Jao, Hao Chorr, Royd Hatta, Mark Jue, Darrell Kunitomi, Alex Luu, Yoshio Moriwaki, and Hwang Pham). Tying the performances together were the participants' memories of growing up as Asian American boys, experiences of racism, and reconciliation of broken relationships.[32] Dan Kwong empowers the Asian American identity and challenges American identity by telling stories of his life. And he has inspired others to use his workshop techniques to continue breaking the cycle of silence of Asian American men and women. For example, Gary San Angel's group Peeling the Banana has grown since 1995 to include women members and has performed regularly in New York City.[33]

Dan Kwong sometimes enacts other characters, but he makes it obvious that the purpose of such "acting" is to further his autobiographical story. He never becomes other characters (by, for example, changing costume), but instead imitates them as he remembers them from his past. For instance, when Kwong tells a story of his grandfather with a Chinese accent, he imitates the old man's behavior as he saw it as a child. In other words, Kwong does not release his characters from his memory because his purpose is not acting but storytelling. Whereas Lane Nishikawa and Jude Narita do their best to become different characters as authentically as possible by acting them, Kwong shows us what he remembers of the people in his lives by indicating and imitating them.

Interdisciplinary solo performance

In some ways, the 1990s brought Asian American solo performance to a full circle, back to the style of Winston Tong. During the decade, a

[32] T. H. McCulloh, writing for *Los Angeles Times*, describes the show as "decidedly early-'70s in tone, with ritual lighting of candles" and "as varied as the intentions and personalities of each of the members." T. H. McCulloh, "Grief in *Asian Men* Occurs by Occident," *Los Angeles Times*, March 13, 1995, sec. calendar, 2. Also see Robert H. Vorlicky, who has done extensive studies on Kwong's solo performance: Robert H. Vorlicky, "Marking Change, Marking America: Contemporary Performance and Men's Autobiographical Selves," in Jeffrey D. Mason and Ellen Gainor (eds.), *Performing America: Cultural Nationalism in American Theater* (Ann Arbor: University of Michigan Press, 1999), 193–209. Vorlicky also edited an anthology of Kwong's works: Robert H. Vorlicky, ed., *From Inner Worlds to Outer Space* (Ann Arbor: The University of Michigan Press, 2004).

[33] The members of Peeling the Banana specialize in autobiographical writing and performance and have included many talented artists, including Dan Bacalzo, Ed Lin, Aileen Cho, Calvin Lom, Michel Ng, Margarita Alcantara-Tan, Gita Reddy, Bertrand Wang, Ching-Ching Ni, and numerous others. San Angel also formed workshop groups in Philadelphia: Gener-Asian Next for teens and Something to Say for Asian American men and women. Alex Luu, an original member of Dan Kwong's workshop, also formed his own workshop in Boston, where he taught Asian American teenagers to voice their thoughts and feelings through autobiographical writing and performance. For an article on Alex Luu's workshop, see Sandy Coleman, "Theater Class Acts Out Against Stereotypes," *The Boston Globe*, March 5, 2002, B11.

number of artists trained in visual art, modern dance, and performance art intentionally attempted to experiment, subvert, blur, and ultimately expand the definition of solo performance. Focusing on universal sensuality and visual aesthetics, they seemed to continue from where Tong had left off. On the other hand, they also incorporated acting and autobiography in their performance and storytelling. The Asian American solo performers of the 1990s were indeed a truly diverse group of artists, and many of their works successfully integrated various styles taken from both the past and the present.[34] And they did so with a new edge.

Denise Uyehara, in particular, used her body to redefine the notion of authenticity in the context of Asian American history and culture. All Asian American performers, including the four I have discussed thus far, have chosen solo performance in order to realize some form of the authentic self. Winston Tong did so by using dolls as extensions of himself, while Lane Nishikawa and Jude Narita attempted to portray an authentic Asian American experience with acting. For Dan Kwong, there was nothing more authentic than being himself and telling his life stories on stage. For all of these performers, their physical presence on stage was a statement on its own; no one could dispute the authenticity and realness of their bodies and personal histories. Denise Uyehara's shows acknowledged this tradition, but with her later works, she moved beyond the accepted definition of the "authentic" Asian American experience. She presented her body not only to represent herself or her Asian Americanness (or femaleness for that matter) but also to be a signifier of what she calls "borderless identity," one that embraces her existence in the grand history of the humanity.

A fourth-generation Japanese American born and raised in Southern California, Denise Uyehara had some opportunity to explore her Asian American identity in school theatre groups, including the Asian American

---

[34] The originality and creativity of these solo performers is extensive, and an accurate examination of their works would require a truly interdisciplinary study. Dan Bacalzo's study of Muna Tseng in "Portraits of Self and Other: *SlutForArt* and the Photographs of Tseng Kwong Chi" is an example of such a study. It examines the complex autobiographical elements in Muna Tseng's solo performance, as well as her collaboration with Ping Chong and memories of her deceased brother Tseng Kwong Chi and his photographs. We can imagine and anticipate similar studies on, for example, Marcus Quiniones and Hawaiian dance; Maura Nguyen Donohue and modern dance and choreography; lê thi diem thúy and poetry; and other solo performers too many to mention. As a group, these artists seem to be taking Asian American theatre and performance to another level in terms of creativity, diversity, and quality. See Dan Bacalzo, "Portraits of Self and Other: *SlutForArt* and the Photographs of Tseng Kwong Chi," *Theatre Journal* 53 (2001), 73–94.

Theater Projects led by Dom Magwili. Not surprisingly, her early shows more or less reflected the performative tradition set by previous Asian American artists. Her first solo performance piece, *Headless Turtleneck Relatives: A Tale of a Family and a Grandmother's Suicide by Fire*, is about her grandmother who committed suicide by setting herself on fire. A collection of family oral stories, the autobiographical piece helped her make sense of "death, life, and family legacy" and "honor [her] past."[35] Uyehara describes the show as a show she *"had* to create." Her break with the conventional Asian American theatre came with her second and the most well known solo performance piece, *Hello (Sex) Kitty: Mad Asian Bitch on Wheels*. It was one she *"wanted* to create": "I knew it was the right time for me to talk about sex, sexuality, lust, love, all that stuff. If I had written *Hello (Sex) Kitty* as my first solo piece, it probably would have been more difficult to have fun with and less deeply rooted in truth."[36]

Uyehara's new voice and style struck a chord in the 1990s, a decade during which theatre artists of all background celebrated hybridity and multiplicity, especially in terms of sexual identity. Moreover, a new generation of Asian Americans welcomed the complicated and sexualized definitions of race and rejected the "static cultural nationalist conception of racial identity."[37] In 1993, the year before the premiere of *Hello (Sex) Kitty*, she co-founded the Sacred Naked Nature Girls ensemble, a "culturally diverse experimental performative collective," with Danielle Brazell, Laura Meyers, and Akilah Oliver. The four women were of diverse ethnic backgrounds and sexual orientations, but they shared an artistic vision to explore "issues from the specifically feminist to the universal."[38] Their first show was performed entirely nude in the Highways Performance Space in Santa Monica, California as part of its annual "ecce lesbo/ecce homo"

[35] Denise Uyehara, "Hello (Sex) Kitty: Mad Asian Bitch on Wheels," in *O Solo Homo: The New Queer Performance*, edited by Holly Hughes and David Román (New York: Grove Press, 1998), 377.
[36] Ibid.
[37] David Eng and Alice Hom note that this traditional conception of race assumed the Asian American subject as "male, heterosexual, working class, American born, and English speaking." They also describe the decade of the 1990s as "a fertile historical moment to witness the emergence of a distinct and visible queer Asian American identity. We are queer, lesbian, gay, bisexual, and transgendered Asian Americans who are willing to engage actively in the discourses of both Asian American and queer politics but unwilling to bifurcate our identities into the racial and the sexual." See David L. Eng and Alice Y. Hom, "Introduction," in *Q & A: Queer in Asian America*, edited by David L. Eng and Alice Y. Hom (Philadelphia: Temple University Press, 1998), 3–4.
[38] F. Kathleen Foley, "Sacred Naked Nature Girls Offer a Quest for *Home*," *Los Angeles Times*, August 31, 1996, sec. calendar, 3.

festival of lesbian and gay performance art. For Uyehara, stage nudity was used to express the most honest truths of her experience as a woman, a human being, and an Asian American. And her identity as an Asian American was not defined separately from her bisexuality and the celebration of her "natural" female body.

However, some Asian Americans (whom Uyehara calls "older-minded") objected to her approach and criticized her nude performances as not reflecting the ways in which Asians discuss sexuality. Uyehara has responded to such criticism by emphasizing that she never stopped writing about the "Asian American experience" – what she is and the life she has lived. The decision to perform nude, she claims, came "very naturally": "[The Sacred Naked Nature Girls is] a piece about women, womanhood and the intersection of being lesbian, straight, bisexual, African American, Asian American and European American."[39] Denise Uyehara also explores these broader issues of identity in *Hello (Sex) Kitty*, which for her is not just about the Asian American experience.

In *Hello (Sex) Kitty*, Uyehara addresses issues of sexuality, dating, domestic violence, and the AIDS epidemic by portraying several vastly different caricatures of Asian women and men. The characters range from "Asian Chic" to "Mad Kabuki Woman" and from "Dyke Asia" to "Vegetable Girl" who talks to her Hello Kitty doll. The characters represent the wide-ranging experiences of Asian women, and they are certainly meant to contradict each other. While Uyehara's use of multiple characters is similar to the methods of Lane Nishikawa and Jude Narita, she adds a sense of irony and self-consciousness in portraying the characters. In other words, she does not become "Vegetable Girl" or "Asian Chic" and enact these characters as real people but rather parodies them in order to reveal the absurd social constructions of Asian female identity.

Uyehara delivers a more universal message, especially with the ending of the show. This last scene begins with a character named "Woman" examining her naked body in a mirror as if she is alone in a bedroom. She carefully examines her "back, front, breasts, stomach, muscles, and finally between her legs."[40] She then picks up a letter and reads:

Dear Miss Uyehara,
    I saw your work in progress at the Institute for Contemporary Arts in London and I have some suggestions for you. I wished you would keep your shirt on. Also, fishing about in one's pubic area (I admit I wasn't

[39] Ibid.
[40] Uyehara, "*Hello (Sex) Kitty*," 407.

watching this "part" too closely) and then handling members of the audience, probably contradicts with E.E.C. hygiene regulations. These comments are meant to be helpful and I hope that you will take them as such.

Yours sincerely,

wuhajdfjehelwefhkj (illegible signature)

"Woman" puts the letter back into an envelope, looks back into the mirror, and wraps her arms around herself, covering her body. After a moment, when "she is ready" and "finally sees herself clearly," she pulls out black lingerie and puts it on. The show ends with "Woman," dressed in black lingerie, interacting with the audience by sitting on "various laps, crotches, etc." and inviting an "Asian woman" onto the stage for a dance. With the final image of two Asian women dancing flirtatiously, Uyehara's brings an elegant closure to the questions and issues she raises throughout the show, which – according to her – is about "being an Asian American, a bisexual woman, and a human being, not necessarily in that order."[41]

Symbolically, the character of Woman willingly embodies all of the disparate characters with her nakedness. She sings like the Vegetable Girl, wears black lingerie as wished for by another character, and boldly flirts with another woman as fantasized by yet another character. In other words, Uyehara creates and embodies the generalized (and arguably universalized) Asian woman with nudity, with all particulars stripped away. And in doing so, Uyehara subverts the imposed images of Asian women and presents and celebrates the unaffected and authentic "Woman." Uyehara ends the show by hinting towards an identity that is much more and beyond that of Asian America and closer to the intersections of identities or what she would later call "borderless identities."

Uyehara's use of body to express "universal" and "borderless identities" received closer examination in her third solo performance piece, *Maps of City and Body* (1999). In the piece, she tells stories about people of diverse backgrounds while staying in the style of biographical solo performance. For example, in a scene titled "Blue Marks," Uyehara describes a family in her childhood neighborhood of Westminster, a suburban area in Orange County. The Abrams consists of a Jewish couple and an adopted daughter of Mexican descent. In the story, the daughter runs away with a biker to rebel against her adopted parents' Jewish background. In the actual performance, Uyehara pull out a pen as she describes a visit she paid with her

---

[41] Uyehara, "*Hello (Sex) Kitty*," 377.

mom Mrs. Abrams. The following is her narration with a description of her action:

Then I looked over and notice the blue markings on Mrs. Abrams' arm. (*Pulls out a thick blue pen and begins to draw on her arms: first the inside of one wrist, up the arm across the neck, down the other arm, and back* again.) They were blue like varicose veins, but in the shape of small numbers the size of alphabet soup. I knew they were marks from those camps – not the ones my parents were in, but the same war.[42]

By the end of the scene, Uyehara's arm is decorated with blue marking, not in the form of small numbers but with lines, as if she is drawing a map on her body. She makes the intention of this action obvious in a later scene titled "Mapping the Body." In the scene, she describes a past abusive relationship (of hers or someone else's) while also introducing her desire to draw "a map of her body." She juxtaposes the sharp verbal abuses of a "Man" with her calm, poetic narration: "This body does not lie, it knows where it has been and that tells it where it is going."[43]

Unlike her earlier shows that focus on her own racial identity and life stories, *Maps of City and Body* charts the lives of other people she has encountered throughout her life. Her body becomes a canvas on which the paths, courses, and intersections of many people's memories and life stories get drawn. She literally marks the points and lines of the map on her body. Uyehara's approach to "borderless identity" and the concept of embodying other people's lives and memories echo what Erika Fischer-Lichte describes as the "historically determined body": "Yet the human body never exists as pure nature, apart from history. From the beginning of life, culture starts to shape, restructure, and regulate the body and its physical needs and functions . . . As a result each individual body participates not only in the natural order but also in the symbolic order of culture. The body, like any other cultural phenomenon, is historically determined."[44] Uyehara sees her body not only as Asian American female, bisexual, and fourth-generation Japanese American, but as a byproduct of the history of which she is a part with billions of other people on the globe. And the collective identity is essentially borderless. In doing so, she empowers the Asian body on stage: she can now be anyone and everyone.

---

[42] Denise Uyehara, *Maps of City & Body: Shedding Light on the Performances of Denise Uyehara* (New York: Kaya Press, 2003), 89–90.

[43] Ibid, 100.

[44] Erika Fischer-Lichte, *The Show and the Gaze of Theatre: A European Perspective* (Iowa City: University of Iowa Press, 1997), 27.

Denise Uyehara's later solo shows have many resemblances to Winston Tong's solo performances of the 1970s: both address the universality of human suffering, love, and loss, and both use their bodies and visual metaphors to reveal the most vulnerable aspects of themselves. Both reach for the universal by using the personal. Within this spectrum of the personal and the universal, Asian American solo performance has flourished in the last three decades. Stories from Asian American solo performances are deeply and sometimes disturbingly personal, and audiences become voyeurs to the performer's private thoughts. Without the conventional medium of theatrical representation (e.g. an actor enacting a character written by a playwright) filtering the "truthfulness," solo performers are as "authentic" as they can be on stage. However, as I have described in this chapter, Asian American solo performers have also enacted other characters and embodied other cultural identities. Their live presence on stage has not been used exclusively for telling personal stories, but they relate other stories and other experiences. Some have focused on Asian American experiences, while others found no limit as long as they could empathize. They have shown that an Asian American body on stage is both culturally specific and historically determined. They also have shown that while it is crucial to experiment artistically and to know and educate their culture and history, it is also imperative to acknowledge their "borderless identity" and humanity.

7

The Miss Saigon *controversy*

> The *Miss Saigon* dispute was part of a sociopolitical drama far weightier and broader than any single play.
>
> Frank Rich[1]

IN 1989, THE ACTOR B. D. WONG ATTENDED A DINNER PARTY where some friends described what they had seen in London: white actors performing in yellowface in a musical called *Miss Saigon*. Their eyes were made up using prosthetics to look slanted and their complexion was darkened.[2] The lead role, played by Jonathan Pryce, was Eurasian, but the actor seemed to do all he could to look as "Asian" as possible. Apparently, the British Equity (the actors' union in Britain) did not find this situation problematic. Wong and his friends were embarrassed by it and agreed that such thing could never happen in the United States.[3] Yellowface on the American stage was unimaginable to them. Wong and others were keenly aware of the Western theatrical convention that often justified a white actor playing what is essentially an Asian character by conveniently changing it to Eurasian. Moreover, Wong had received a Tony Award for his role in David Henry Hwang's *M. Butterfly*, a play that criticizes "oriental" stereotypes. And the play was still playing on

---

[1] Frank Rich, "*Miss Saigon* Arrives, From the Old School," *New York Times*, April 12, 1991, C1.

[2] The actor Jonathan Pryce was accused of painting his face "yellow," taping his eyes, and wearing fake bushy eyebrows and a wig. He defended himself by saying that although he did use prosthetics to change the shape of his eyes, fake brows and wigs were never used and that "just a Clinique bronzing lotion" was applied to his face. When the American controversy started, Pryce stopped using prosthetics. See Edward Behr and Mark Steyn, *The Story of Miss Saigon* (London: Jonathan Cape, 1993), 183.

[3] The anecdote appears in Helen Zia, *Asian American Dreams* (New York: Farrar, Straus and Giroux, 2001), 119. Zia was the president of the New York chapter of the Asian American Journalists Association during the controversy.

Broadway at the time. *Miss Saigon*, an unapologetic adaptation of *Madame Butterfly*, did not seem appropriate for the culturally enlightened American audience. The London production seemed all too anachronistic for America. In 1990, they were proven wrong. Controversies over the casting decision and content of the musical blew up when it was announced that the Broadway version would be the same as the London show. The controversies led to one of the most divisive debates over racial representation and affirmative action in American theatre history and mobilized the Asian American theatre community from coast to coast. The event was, as Dorinne Kondo describes, "a historical and political watershed" in Asian American theatre.[4]

The casting controversy shocked the veteran Asian American theatre artists who realized that what they had fought for since the 1960s had made no impact in American mainstream theatre. Former members of the Oriental Actors of America found the controversy eerily similar to the battle they fought against the Lincoln Center in the early 1970s. Twenty years later, they were back to where they had started. Younger artists, including B. D. Wong realized that nothing could be taken for granted and that their naïveté and optimism had to be replaced with renewed activism. However, the controversy was more than about the rights of Asian American actors to play Asian roles; it was also about what is actually accomplished by playing those roles. As I describe in this chapter, all of the Asian characters in *Miss Saigon* were, at best, unexamined stereotypes of Asians and Asian Americans, and the musical presented a deeply racist and problematic construction of post-Vietnam Orientalism. For Asian American actors, the musical provided a rare opportunity to perform in a mega hit Broadway show, and they were willing to compete and protest their way to stardom. But for the Asian American theatre community as a whole, the musical presented a major setback not only in terms of casting and stereotypes but also in terms of how the economic power of mainstream theatre has utterly dictated minority theatres.

The making of *Miss Saigon*

The concept for the musical *Miss Saigon* was born in the minds of French musical theatre writers Alain Boublil and Claude-Michel Schönberg in 1985. (The lyricist-and-composer team had adapted Victor Hugo's

---

[4] Dorinne Kondo, *About Face: Performing Race in Fashion and Theater* (New York: Routledge, 1997), 229.

nineteenth century novel into a hit musical *Les Miserables*.) They saw in the *France-Soir* newspaper a photograph of a Vietnamese woman giving up her child to an American GI in the Ho Chi Min airport in 1985. It showed a biracial female child sobbing and looking at her mother, who stands with her mouth tightly closed.[5] According to Boublil and Schönberg, the picture reminded them of the "ultimate sacrifice" of Cio Cio San in Puccini's opera *Madame Butterfly* and they wanted to tell a modernized story linking the photograph to the opera. In search of the link, they learned that Puccini's three-act opera was based on a one-act American play of the same title by David Belasco, which premiered in New York City in 1900. Furthermore, they discovered that Belasco's play was an adaptation of a novella by John Luther Long and that Long's story was based on an autobiographical account by Pierre Loti titled *Madame Chrysantheme* and published in 1887. Loti, whose real name was Julien Viaud, was a naval officer of France and a prolific recorder of his exotic adventures in the Middle and the Far East. His writing was widely read, and he claimed that *Madame Chrysantheme* was based on his short stay in Japan and his contract marriage in Nagasaki to a Japanese geisha.[6] Boublil and Schönberg found their link. With it, they found much needed authenticity and authority to write about Vietnam. According to Boublil: "[Loti's story] somehow completed the circle. In a curious way the story had been returned to us. It freed us from Puccini and, at the same time, freed us to write a story that begins in the Saigon of 1975 – since it must not be forgotten that Vietnam was a French colony and a French mistake before it became an American one."[7] However, Boublil and Schönberg completely ignored the way that Loti's autobiographical story had evolved into Puccini's famous and much-fictionalized plot.

For instance, in Loti's story, the Japanese geisha does not commit suicide. In fact, the story ends with Loti leaving Japan, and she lets him go with a proper, traditional Japanese goodbye. Nothing is told of what happened to her afterwards. In John Luther Long's fictional adaptation of Loti's novella, the French naval officer becomes the very unlikable

---

[5] The picture is reprinted in Karen Shimakawa, *National Abjection: The Asian American Body Onstage* (Durham: Duke University Press, 2002), 25.

[6] Maria Degabriele, "From *Madame Butterfly* to *Miss Saigon*: One Hundred Years of Popular Orientalism," *Critical Arts* 10.2 (1996), 106.

[7] Alain Boublil, "From Madame Chryssanthemum to Miss Saigon." This article originally appeared at: www.miss-saigon.com/origins/madame.html. After the musical closed on Broadway, the article no longer appeared on the website. A copy of the article appears on the following site: www.towards-esfahan.com/pla16.htm.

American named Pinkerton, and Madame Chrysantheme is renamed "Madame Butterfly." Along with name changes, the characters become instantaneously recognizable as reductive melodramatic characters with absolute moral values: Pinkerton as the embodiment of manipulation and evil and Butterfly as the tragic heroine. Such a combination of characters dominated the world of literature and theatre in nineteenth-century America, and along with them was demanded a tragic ending. John Long fully utilized this melodramatic formula, not only by adding a deadly ending for Butterfly but by focusing on her painful longing for Pinkerton and secretly raising their child. In fact, while most of Loti's novella describes in detail his curious relationship with Chrysantheme, only the first three chapters (out of fifteen) in Long's story are about the actual relationship. The rest of the story details Butterfly's agonizing days of waiting for Pinkerton's return and leads ultimately to her suicide in the last chapter. In David Belasco's dramatic adaptation of John Long's short story, the Butterfly's role as the tragic heroine in melodrama is accentuated even further. The relationship sequence (which took up three chapters in Long's version) is cut entirely in Belasco's adaptation, and the one-act play begins with Butterfly waiting for Pinkerton to return. The play is essentially a waiting play with death at the end. In fact, at its premiere in New York City, the waiting element made the strongest impact on the audience. When Puccini saw a production of Belasco's *Madame Butterfly* in London, he immediate asked for the rights to adapt it into an opera. It's obvious that Puccini was most impressed with the silent waiting and tragic death scene because Puccini's opera goes even further than Belasco in accentuating the plight of the heroine. Indeed, Puccini's opera takes full advantage of the last scene, and the Japanese woman is reduced to the tragic butterfly stereotype and distilled down to her final aria.[8]

Although Boublil and Schönberg admit that the French colonization of Vietnam was a "mistake," they nevertheless claimed the right to resurrect the tragic butterfly stereotype as if it was based on reality and used it to tell

---

[8] Such reduction of female characters to a tragic stereotype was common in nineteenth-century opera. Catherine Clément, *Opera: Or The Undoing of Women*, translated by Betsy Wing (Minneapolis: University of Minnesota Press, 1988), describes nineteenth-century European bourgeois opera as a "delicious dish of men's culture" (5). As Clément articulates, we are discouraged from analyzing the plot of operas: "The music makes one forget the plot, but the plot sets traps for the imaginary" (10). The pleasure of listening to Madame Butterfly's final aria makes us forget about why she is committing suicide and whether her action is coherent with the rest of the story. In essence, the aria (the distilled version of the fictional melodramatic ending) completes the creation process of the tragic butterfly stereotype; it is the blindfold over our eyes and the final touch that gives the stereotype a life of its own.

a story about the American involvement in Vietnam. Thus, the character of Kim was created to carry out the tradition of Cio Cio San's "ultimate sacrifice." A twentieth-century version of Cio Cio San, Kim was to be a young virgin Vietnamese girl who comes to work as a prostitute in a brothel for American men. On the other hand, Boublil and Schönberg radically updated American characters to seem more sympathetic. For example, where as Pinkerton in Puccini's opera is heartless and selfish, the American GI in *Miss Saigon*, Chris, is a gentleman and likable. As Karen Shimakawa observes, the musical "labors to establish Chris as well intentioned and without fault at every stage of the narrative."[9] Other American characters also received moral facelifts: Chris's white wife, Ellen, is an empathetic modern American woman, and Chris's friend, John, redeems himself in the second half of the musical by working on behalf of Bui-Doi (children of Vietnamese women and American soldiers during the war).

Thus, with Asian characters that are unabashed replicas of the nineteenth-century stereotypes and American characters with modernized moral values, the story of the musical goes as follows. Set in Saigon at the end of the Vietnam War (April 1975), the musical begins with the meeting of seventeen-year-old orphan Kim and Chris in a bar: Kim on her first day as a prostitute and Chris as an American GI socializing with his buddies. One of Chris's friends, John "buys" Kim for the reluctant but interested Chris from The Engineer, a half-Vietnamese half-French pimp in the bar. After their first night together, Kim and Chris fall in love and "marry." Chris promises Kim that they will go to America together. But a few days later, Saigon falls, and in the midst of chaos, Chris is pulled by his battalion onto a US Embassy helicopter, and Kim is left behind. Three years later, we learn that Kim has a son named Tam and is resolutely waiting for Chris to return. Kim rejects proposals from Thuy, her cousin and fiancé by family arrangement, despite the fact that he is a high-ranking officer in the North Vietnamese army. When Thuy finds her and threatens to kill her son, she shoots him with a gun. Determined to send Tam to America, Kim flees to Thailand with the help of The Engineer (who calculates to go to America by pretending to be Tam's uncle). With the help of John, Chris discovers that Kim and his son are in Thailand. Chris and his American wife go to Thailand to find them, and when they do, Kim knows what she has to do. She commits suicide in

---

[9] Karen Shimakawa, *National Abjection*, 28.

order to allow Chris to take their son to a "better life" in America. As the
curtain falls Kim sings to Chris about how happy she is to be dying in his
arms: "How in the light of one night have we come so far?"

As the musical was being written, the creative team was joined by
lyricist Richard Maltby Jr., producer Cameron Mackintosh and director
Nicolas Hyther, and *Miss Saigon* went into pre-production. The creative
process is partially documented in the HBO production of *The Making of
Miss Saigon* (1989). The video documentary follows the team from musical
composition to opening night, but the majority of film time is devoted to
the international search for the actress to play the role of Kim. They
traveled to New York, Hollywood, Hawaii, and the Philippines to interview hundreds of Asian actresses and to find the one who had the innocent
charm (as well as sexiness to seduce a young American GI) and could sing
the difficult songs required in the musical. The creative team (four white
men) had a specific image of Kim in mind, and as the documentary shows,
they rejected many Asian performers for looking too mature, or too
model-like, but mostly for not possessing the necessary singing voice.
They finally found their ingénue in the Philippines: 18-year-old Lea
Salonga who had trained her entire life to speak perfect American English
and to perform in Western musical theatre. She was also a light-skinned
Filipina with Western facial features. The creative team knew that they
had found their Kim. Other major Asian characters, including Thuy and
The Engineer were played by white actors in yellowface, which included
taped eyes to create the "slant." The role of The Engineer was cast with
the talented British actor Jonathan Pryce who had won a Tony Award for
best actor in the 1976 Broadway production of *Comedians*. Asian actors
were never auditioned for Pryce's role, mainly because he co-created the
role. While some minor Asian characters (who were either prostitutes or
communists) were played by Asian actors, most were played by white
actors in yellowface.

Miss Saigon opened on September 20, 1989 at the Theater Royal, Drury
Lane in London. With forty-two cast members from ten countries, the
production took four years to make and cost over $5 million. It sold a
record advance of $8 million and sold out for the first six months.
Receiving rave reviews, Lea Salonga became an instant star, and Jonathan
Pryce was singled out as the best performer in the London theatre season
by receiving the Olivier Award. Producer Cameron Mackintosh soon
began the process of exporting the show to Broadway as he had successfully done with blockbuster musicals such as *Cats, Les Miserables,* and
Phantom of the Opera. A few months later, Mackintosh announced a

Broadway production to open in 1991 with the original stars, Jonathan Pryce and Lea Salonga.

Keeping the same cast was not unusual because imported musicals often promoted star actors for maximum ticket sales. But Macintosh's casting choice had to get the final approval from the Actors' Equity Association (AEA), an American actors' union. In the initial stages of Mackintosh's negotiations with the AEA, the only criticism was the absence of African American performers among the American soldiers, despite the exemplary participation of African Americans in the Vietnam War. Mackintosh agreed to recast some roles including the character of John, which would be performed by Hinton Battle (who would later go on to win a Tony Award for best featured actor in a musical). However, when it came to the role of The Engineer, a Eurasian character, Mackintosh was adamant about his choice of Jonathan Pryce and believed that the success of the musical would depend on him. In June 1990, as designers were already redesigning the set for the Broadway production, Asian American theatre artists contacted the AEA to express their objection to the casting of Jonathan Pryce in the Eurasian role.

The casting controversy

On June 6, 1990, producers Tisa Chang and Dominick Balletta wrote a letter to AEA's executive director Alan Eisenberg stating that:

> The insensitivity of this action could only be compared to having the role of Boy Willie in *The Piano Lesson* [by August Wilson] portrayed by a man in blackface. It is a shame that Cameron Mackintosh and the AEA both believe that painting a Caucasian actor yellow is an acceptable action . . . Equity is sending the following message to its minority members: we will support your right to work as long as your role is not central to the play.[10]

B. D. Wong also made formal complaints to the AEA. In response to the complaints, the Committee on Racial Equality of the AEA invited Wong and others to a meeting to discuss the matter. They were joined by more than twenty actors who were mostly Asian American but included African American and Latino. They shared their experience and frustration of being repeatedly denied to play not only white characters but characters of their own racial background. In comparison to white actors

---

[10] Edward Behr and Mark Steyn, *The Story of Miss Saigon*, 182.

who have historically played characters of all colors, it seemed to be assumed that minority actors could not even play themselves. Their frustration quickly led to mobilization. News of Jonathan Pryce's role traveled to the West Coast, and actors from all parts of the country signed on to form a new group, the Asian Pacific Alliance for Creative Equality (APACE).

In mid-June, B. D. Wong and other APACE members wrote letters to the AEA leaders. The main point of the letters was to persuade the Executive Director of the AEA, Alan Eisenberg, to deny Jonathan Pryce's request for a visa (which was required of all foreign actors to perform on American stages). Wong also authored a form letter, which he had other Equity members to sign in support. The letter was addressed to Colleen Dewhurst, the President of the AEA. Dated June 21, the letter read:

> I am writing to demand protection of my rights as an Equity actor of color by calling for rejection of producer Cameron Mackintosh's application which would allow a non-Asian British actor to play a leading, specifically Asian role in the forthcoming American production of *Miss Saigon*. There is no doubt in my mind of the irreparable damage to my rights as an actor that would be wrought if (at the threshold of the 21st century) Asian actors are kept from bringing their unique dignity to the specifically Asian roles in *Miss Saigon* . . . At this time in history, blackface is wrong, yellowface is wrong. Only Equity and her Alien Committee has the power to stop this ridiculous notion, or else it will magnify and multiply itself so fast that it will become an *hourly* issue which Equity simply is not equipped to fight . . . Force Cameron Mackintosh and future producers to cast their productions with racial authenticity.[11]

The letter was accompanied by a more personal note for other actors: "We may *never* be able to do the *real* work we dream to do if a Caucasian actor with taped eyelids hops on the Concorde . . . Chances to nail the big guys like this don't come often. Let's do it."[12]

Both the letter and the note appeared in excerpts in an article by Alex Witchel in the July 25 issue of *The New York Times*. Titled "Union Weighs *Miss Saigon* Casting," the article reported that the AEA failed to decide the previous day whether the union would grant Pryce the permit to perform on Broadway. The timing of this article could not have been more critical. Apparently, Cameron Mackintosh had been on a vacation

---

[11] Ibid.
[12] Ibid., 183.

and did not become aware of the complaints from Asian American artists until the second week of July 1990 when the controversy began to receive publicity.[13] During the month of July, Cameron Mackintosh and Equity executives struggled to come to an agreement over the controversy while the latter postponed its formal decision. Their meetings were filled with argument, diatribe, and insinuation. Dewhurst reasoned that because $25 million-worth of tickets had already been sold, "it made little difference who played The Engineer." The comment made Mackintosh especially "dismayed and infuriated." Adding to Mackintosh's frustration was Equity's announcement that the casting of Pryce would be "especially insensitive and an affront to the Asian Community."[14] *The New York Times* article appeared at the height of everyone's frustration and intense anticipation of what the AEA would decide to do.

The article, however, did more than report the controversy: it added fuel to the fire with quotes from the casting director of *Miss Saigon*, Vincent G. Liff of the Johnson, Liff & Zerman casting agency. He wrote to Mackintosh in response to the complaint that after auditioning hundreds of Asian performers he could not find anyone qualified to play the role of The Engineer. The following excerpts appeared in the article:

> There has been no professional venue for the development of the Asian actor or Asian actor/singer to exercise his talents on the Broadway stage between *Flower Drum Song* and *The World of Suzie Wong* in 1958 and *M. Butterfly* in 1988, a 30-year span. With the exception of the original and revival companies of *Pacific Overtures* and two Broadway revivals of *The King and I*, there was nothing in between. The bottom line is there was just no product to provide Asian actors with successful, financially viable acting careers in the mainstream venues of Broadway, film, and television . . . We have overall auditioned hundreds more Asian performers in the continental United States and Hawaii than we have Caucasian performers . . . We have conducted endless totally open calls in New York City (many), Los Angeles (3 occasions), San Francisco (3 occasions), Hawaii (3 occasions), Manila (3 occasions), San Jose (once), Orange County (once). We are currently on our way to Daly City (California), Vancouver and Toronto continuing our quest for Asian talent in these Asian centers of population. I can say with the greatest assurance that if there were an Asian actor of 45–50 years, with classical stage background and an international stature and reputation, we would

---

[13] Ibid., 181.
[14] Ibid., 184.

surely have sniffed him out by now. Furthermore, if we hadn't found him, he certainly would have found us.[15]

In addition to the letter, Liff presented a lengthy, handwritten letter on a yellow notepad which specified every Asian actor he knew of and why each was unsuitable for the part.[16] Liff's assessment of Asian American actors was a direct insult to the entire Asian American theatre community. He ignored the history of Asian American theatre companies around the country and what David Henry Hwang has described as "our aesthetic legacy."[17] Moreover, Liff did not give any credit to actors like Randall Duk Kim who has had a successful career (both in Asian American theatre and mainstream theatre) as a classically trained actor despite institutional racism. On the other hand, Liff's comments revealed the "casting catch-22." As Karen Shimakawa explains, Asian American actors are "not deemed commercially viable, they cannot get cast in leading roles, and not being cast in such roles renders them commercially unviable."[18]

Liff's comments shocked and infuriated the Asian American theatre community. According to Kim Miyori, who helped organize the Los Angeles protest, the anger led to unity: "For the first time so many Asian Americans – actors and community members – came together to say we're deeply offended and we're mad as hell."[19] They immediately took action and protested the inaccuracies in Liff's assessment and asked *The New York Times* to make two corrections. First, they objected to the ways in which Liff's quotes were presented as if they were factual. The article gave no mention of Asian American theatre and its talent pool. Secondly, there had never been an open audition for the role of The Engineer as the article implied. *The New York Times* never provided correction or explanation and continued to misrepresent the Asian American theatre community. Weeks later, Cameron Mackintosh admitted that the auditions listed by Liff were in fact to find the female lead role and that no auditions were held for The Engineer.

The media, led by *The New York Times*, presented an image of Asian American actors as "less qualified" but who claimed the right to play the Eurasian role only because of their race. In the July 28 editorial, *The New York Times* criticized the Actors' Equity Association and Asian American

---

[15] Alex Witchell, "British Star Talks of Racial Harmony and Disillusionment with Equity," *The New York Times*, August 11, 1990, 12.
[16] Zia, *Asian American Dreams*, 121.
[17] Ibid., 121.
[18] Shimakawa, *National Abjection*, 45.
[19] Zia, *Asian American Dreams*, 120.

actors. It asked why the casting of Pryce would be offensive to Asian Americans if "Britain's substantial Asian community" had no complaints. It also cited the history of AEA's role in protecting its members' jobs from "foreign talent and twisting agreed rules in the process." But the point of the editorial was an accusation of reverse discrimination: "if the race test were applied to American shows, Morgan Freeman couldn't have starred in *The Taming of the Shrew* in Central Park this summer; whites could never portray Othello on an American stage; and who on earth would have played the King of Siam?"[20] As criticism against them grew in the mainstream media and theatre community, Asian American actors became even more determined to fight.

On August 7, they felt victorious. After a long and emotional debate, AEA formally declined Mackintosh's request to have Pryce perform the role of The Engineer. Alan Eisenberg announced in a press conference that the Association was concerned that Mackintosh never made the efforts to recast the role of The Engineer with an Asian American actor. At the same time, the AEA invited Mackintosh to appeal and to meet for arbitration. It was expected that Mackintosh would win in the arbitration and the musical would open on Broadway. That way, the AEA would win morally and Mackintosh could keep Pryce. However, Mackintosh refused arbitration and stated: "The inaccurate and inflammatory statements which Equity had made have served only to create a poisonous atmosphere in which artistic freedom cannot function or survive. Arbitration cannot clear this atmosphere."[21] He announced the next day that he was canceling the show and the day after that (August 9, 1990), he placed an ad in the *New York Times*:

"*Miss Saigon* Cancelled"
    Actors' Equity has refused to approve Jonathan Pryce to play the role of the Engineer in the Broadway production of MISS SAIGON, as they cannot "condone the casting of a Caucasian actor in the role of a Eurasian." The creative team of MISS SAIGON finds this position to be irresponsible, and a disturbing violation of the principles of artistic integrity and freedom. As a result, we are forced to announce the cancellation of next year's Broadway production of MISS SAIGON. The debate is no longer about the casting of MISS SAIGON, but the art of acting itself. Because we feel so strongly about our own artistic position, we understand the depth of feeling within the Asian acting

[20] "Acting Silly About Color," *New York Times*, July 28, 1990, Editorial Section, 20.
[21] Simon Tait, "No Debut for *Miss Saigon*," *The Times*, August 9, 1990, 4.

community and believe we share many of their aims. We passionately disapprove of stereotype casting, which is why we continue to champion freedom of artistic choice. Racial barriers can only undermine the very foundations of our profession. We share the disappointment of the American public who have ordered tickets to see MISS SAIGON, but we look forward to a time when a calmer, more balanced atmosphere prevails. The original British Company is currently running at The Theater Royal, Drury Lane, London. The Asian Company premieres at The Imperial Theater, Tokyo on April 22, 1992 (Japanese language production).[22]

Mackintosh called his announcement "a final decision in the light of Equity's repeated condemnation of our artistic decision on this production."[23]

Many members of the theatre community supported Mackintosh. On the evening of the cancellation announcement, 140 plus members of the AEA signed a petition requesting that the decision be reconsidered.[24] Many used the nontraditional casting policy to support Mackintosh's decision: any actor should be allowed to play any role. Some criticized the AEA for canceling work for many of its members (including thirty-four Asian Americans) and other theatre artists. The musical was to employ 182 people, including 50 actors and stage managers, 26 musicians, and 34 stagehands. Charlton Heston called the AEA's decision "racist," and even Joanna Merlin, the co-chairwoman of the Nontraditional Casting Project (a nonprofit organization that seeks to advance the principles of nondiscriminatory casting) carefully agreed with Mackintosh: "However strongly Equity feels they must condemn the casting of Jonathan Pryce for these reasons, I believe their vote seriously threatens freedom of artistic choice. How can anyone legitimately dictate who will or will not be cast in a show except the creative team?"[25] Moreover, the media (including *The New York Times* and *Variety*) did not hesitate to side with Cameron Mackintosh and to have a "field day," or what Joseph Papp called "the charge of the white brigade."[26] By the end of August, the standoff was

---

[22] "Miss Saigon Cancelled," Advertisement, *New York Times*, August 9, 1990, C18.

[23] Mervyn Rothstein, "Equity Will Reconsider *Miss Saigon* Decision," *New York Times*, August 10, 1990, C3.

[24] According to its bylaws, the Actor's Equity Association is required to heed any petition with 100 or more signatures from its membership.

[25] Mervyn Rothstein, "Producer Cancels *Miss Saigon*; 140 Members Challenge Equity," *New York Times*, August 9, 1990, C15.

[26] Cecilia Pang and Elizabeth Wong, "The *Miss Saigon* Diaries," *American Theatre* (December 1990), 40–43.

between Mackintosh and the AEA while Asian American activists were pushed to the background as the ones who started the controversy but no longer had a decisive voice. The final meetings between Cameron Mackintosh and the AEA were held in private to prevent "further press 'leaks' which might exacerbate matters and cause the 'activists' in AEA to renew their campaign."[27] Asian American "activists" took no part in the final decision, and Asian American actors had to observe – yet again – others choose their destiny.

Some theatre artists were torn between their support for minority casting and for artistic freedom. Joseph Papp articulated this dilemma when he said, "There's something maybe foolish, but brave, about Equity's position. I think in the final analysis their position will mean more employment for Asian American actors. As a producer, I have certain resistance to their position, but as a citizen, and because of my commitment to minority casting, I think they did the proper and heroic thing."[28] But most people took a side, and the theatre community was sharply divided.

The division was never clearly along the racial lines because the cancellation also divided the Asian American theatre community. Over thirty Asian and Asian American actors had been already cast in the show, and some did not want this rare chance to perform on Broadway to dissipate. Moreover, it was never the intention of the AEA and Asian American actors to see the show canceled. David Henry Hwang stated, "It has certainly never been my intention to see a show canceled. I simply felt that an important point had to be made, and this has clearly been achieved." Tisa Chang praised "the courageous decision of Actors' Equity," but nevertheless agreed that canceling the show was not the best solution.

Pressure against the AEA to reconsider its decision grew as days passed and the reality of show's cancellation settled in people's minds. The loss of employment for its members, the record advance ticket sales of $25 million, a petition with 140 signatures, and phone calls from prominent figures in New York City put heavy pressure on the AEA. Mayor David Norman Dinkins, who was the first African American mayor in New York City history, also made calls to AEA. Eventually, the AEA gave in. Or, as Helen Zia puts it, "Cameron Mackintosh had called Equity's bluff, and the union flinched."[29] A week after Mackintosh's announcement, on August 16, 1990, the AEA rescinded its decision and granted Pryce the visa to perform in

[27] Edward Behr and Mark Steyn, *The Story of Miss Saigon*, 188.
[28] Rothstein, "Producer Cancels," C15.
[29] Zia, *Asian American Dreams*, 127.

Miss Saigon. With the decision, the AEA issued a statement to clarify its position. It acknowledged the plight of minority actors in American theatre and noted that it asked Mackintosh to seek Asian actors as replacements or understudies on Broadway. After a month of consideration, on September 20, 1990, Mackintosh decided to reinstate his multi-million dollar production and scheduled it to open in March 1991.

Asian American actors suddenly found themselves in a worse situation than they were at the beginning of the controversy. Many felt further insulted and ignored by the AEA's final decision. However, they continued their labor by taking on a more political tone. They began to educate the public about the history of yellowface and racism in American theatre by writing to newspapers and mobilizing in organized protests. In a *USA Today* column, Tisa Chang argued that the practice of "yellowface" had for many decades caused "pain and humiliation of Asian-Americans": "We support artistic statement, but it cannot be at the expense of denigrating people of color. We are sensitive to the economic impact of a successful Broadway show, but it cannot be at the expense of perpetuating discriminatory practices and images."[30]

Asian Pacific Alliance for Creative Equality also took further action. The members solicited support from other organizations, including the East West Players (headed by actress and artistic director Nobu McCarthy) and the Association of Asian/Pacific American Artists. About twenty organizations signed on. Established actors such as George Takei, Kim Miyori, and Tamlyn Tomida, as well as others of different racial backgrounds, joined in support. Together, they placed a full-page advertisement in *Variety* on August 20, 1990:

> True Equity Now!
>
> We, as artists of Asian/Pacific heritage and highly concerned community members and organizations, are outraged at the insensitive casting by Cameron Mackintosh of a Caucasian actor in what is clearly a minority role in the production, "Miss Saigon". This act has provoked tremendous furor because it perpetuates the gross injustices Asian/ Pacific actors have always faced:
>
> 1. Traditionally, Caucasian actors have the freedom to portray all races, but Asian/Pacific actors have been denied that freedom.
>
> 2. Not only are Asian/Pacific actors restricted to racially specific roles, but they routinely have been denied those roles – especially leading ones.

---

[30] Tisa Chang, "Race is Crucial in Some Stage Roles," *USA Today*, August 17, 1990, A12.

3. Although "blackface" is vehemently condemned, WHY IS "YEL-LOWFACE" STILL ACCEPTABLE?

4. Is "Miss Saigon" another example of the blatant practice of labeling a role "Eurasian" to justify casting a Caucasian in visibly Asian/Pacific leading role?

5. "Non-traditional casting" has been completely distorted to justify casting a Caucasian in a specifically Asian/Pacific role. Non-traditional casting is defined by Actors' Equity Association and agreed to by the League of American Theatres and Producers as "the casting of ethnic, minority and female actors in roles where race, ethnicity or sex is not germane."

6. There are false claims that there is no qualified Asian/Pacific talent. In fact, the few instances where Asian/Pacifics were given their rightful opportunities, they have excelled, and have been awarded for their outstanding performances.

7. We demand that these exclusionary, discriminatory, and extremely insensitive practices be abandoned. We refuse to sacrifice yet another generation of talented Asian/Pacific artists.

WE MUST ALL COMMIT TO ACHIEVE TRUE EQUITY NOW![31]

The advertisement listed all twenty organizations supporting the statements.[32] It should be highlighted that some of the most influential Hispanic American organizations and nonethnic specific groups signed the statement.

The political tone and activism had some effect. A few articles began to appear in major newspapers sympathizing with Asian American theatre artists. For instance, on August 26, 1990, *The New York Times* printed two articles on the difficulties that Asian American actors faced in finding opportunities to act. Written by two guest columnists, Ellen Holly (a black actress) and Shirley Sun (an Asian American director), the articles provided a brief history of white actors playing Asian roles. The articles revealed the history of racism in American theatre and explained what yellowface meant for Asian Americans. Also, in "Letters to the Editor" of

---

[31] "True Equity Now!," Advertisement, *Variety*, August 20, 1990, 82.

[32] Association of Asian Pacific American Artists, Angel Island Theater Company, Asian Pacific American Legal Center of Southern California, East West Players, El Teatro Campesino, Film Arts Foundation, Japanese American Citizens League, League of United Latin American Citizens, Magic Theatre, National Hispanic Media Coalition, Northwest Asian American Theater, Organization of Chinese Americans, Inc., Pan Asian Repertory Theatre, Peter Wang Films, Inc., The Seattle Group Theater, The Los Angeles Center of Asian American Films Studies and Research, The New York Chapter of Asian American Journalists Association, Thick Description, and Visual Communications.

The New York Times, three actors (Robin Barlett, Victor Barber, and Ellen Park) and three playwrights (Craig Lucas, Terrence McNally, and Larry Kramer) expressed their support for Asian American artists: "Actors of color live in a world where almost all roles are denied them because of their race. Jonathan Pryce does not need affirmative action to give him an even break . . . that is why charges of 'reverse discrimination' do not apply"[33] However, other than such editorial letters and somewhat sympathetic articles written mostly by nonstaff writers, major newspapers in New York City paid little attention to Asian American theatre artists' protest. The *Los Angeles Times* gave a more balanced press with a special page on the controversy in the August 13 issue. Contributors included Velina Hasu Houston, Dom Magwili, Jack O'Brien, Jon Lawrence Rivera, and Charlton Heston, providing the full spectrum of views.

The *Miss Saigon* casting controversy erupted as Americans were learning the new keywords of the 1990s such as "political correctness" and "identity politics." Michael Omi and Howard Winant call the phenomenon "a moral panic about the continuing disruptive effects of racial divisions (and polarization around gender and sexuality as well) in American society."[34] The panic soon resulted in a "culture war." Martha Minow compares the *Miss Saigon* controversy with what she experienced at Harvard law school when the faculty was divided over its hiring practices:

> The context of the [*Miss Saigon*] controversy included advance ticket sales of $25 million; the recent election of an African-American mayor concerned about both remedying discrimination and preserving the theater industry; the political attack on controversial art by conservative American officials seeking to control the uses of federal subsidies; an emerging public conflict over attention to 'politically correct' claims about racism, sexism, and homophobia; and the United States Supreme Court's repudiation of most public affirmative action programs.[35]

Similar debates flourished over university faculty tenure processes, college entrance criteria, employment, funding by the National Endowment for the Arts, and many other issues affecting all aspects of American life. In the larger context of American history, the *Miss Saigon* controversy was only one of many battles in the culture war.

---

[33] Pang and Wong, "The *Miss Saigon* Diaries," 42.
[34] Michael Omi and Howard Winant, *Racial Formation in the U.S.: From the 1960s to the 1990s*, (New York: Routledge, 1994), 148.
[35] Martha Minow, "From Class Actions to *Miss Saigon*: The Concept of Representation in the Law," *Representing Women: Law, Literature, and Feminism* (Durham: Duke University Press, 1994), 8–43.

The content controversy

When it was clear to Asian American theatre artists that they were defeated in the casting battle, they realized that it was only the beginning of a bigger war. Some were awakened by the thought that they should have perhaps rejected *Miss Saigon* for the racist stereotypes it reincarnated. In retrospect, the story of the musical was as (if not more) problematic and harmful as the casting of a white actor in a Eurasian role. Created by white (French and British) men, *Miss Saigon* resuscitated the quintessentially Orientalist story of *Madame Butterfly* and presented popular stereotypes of Asians, both old and new. Although Mackintosh disagreed with Asian American actors on the casting controversy, he nevertheless understood why the actors were upset. But he never comprehended why the story of the musical would be offensive; at the height of the casting controversy, he stated, "It is particularly sad and ironic that this controversy should surround a piece of theatre such as *Miss Saigon*, a tragic love story in which a young woman sacrifices her life to ensure that her Amerasian son may find a better life in America."[36] He has maintained this view, and when the musical closed in 2000, he reiterated his pride in having produced the musical.

During the casting controversy, the storyline rarely became an issue or concern. Many viewed the musical as a beautiful story in which thirty-four Asian actors would bring cultural authenticity. But as time passed, Asian Americans voiced their objection to the story. For example, Dorinne Kondo stated in her letter to the *Los Angeles Times*, "Ultimately, the casting controversy is – or should be – a relatively minor aspect of the *Miss Saigon* story, for the striking feature here is the problematic politics of representation. *Miss Saigon* is a 'colored museum of Asian stereotypes.'"[37] The same stereotypes that Asian American theatre artists had been fighting against for decades not only reappeared but also overwhelmed them with a multi-million dollar Broadway production that included helicopters and the glitzy spectacle of a virtual Saigon. Familiar Asian stereotypes decorated the stage in the musical: shy lotus blossom, evil Asian male lover (and therefore competitor to the white man), virgin/prostitute, over-sexualized Asian women in skimpy clothing, simple and victimized peasants, the Red Army, and the "butterfly" that dies for the white man. One of the "improvements" is its inclusion of the problems of Bui-Doi

---

[36] Edward Behr and Mark Steyn, *The Story of Miss Saigon*, 186.
[37] Kondo, *About Face*, 231.

and American guilt over Vietnam. However, there is no sense of "guilt" over the main narrative, which resurrects Puccini's (and Belasco's) Cio-Cio-san as Kim.

The story was even more appalling to the Asian American theatre community because David Henry Hwang's *M. Butterfly* had closed only a few months before the controversy.[38] Hwang's play not only deconstructs *Madame Butterfly* but also directly criticizes America's underestimation of Vietnam and Asia as a whole. (The play is set in China with the Vietnam War as the background.) If *M. Butterfly* was one step forward, *Miss Saigon* was two steps back. Hwang tried to explain this irony in an interview with Kevin Kelly of the *Boston Globe*: "And of course, there's always the fashion aspect. Every 20 years or so, there seems to be a new wave of chinoiserie, japonism."[39] In the Asian American theatre community, there was certainly a sense that the success of both *M. Butterfly* and *Miss Saigon* represented yet another case of America's fascination with Asian subjects. For mainstream theatre audiences, an Asian man in drag as a beautiful Chinese opera singer in *M. Butterfly* may provide a similar type of entertainment as Vietnamese prostitutes in bikinis luring American soldiers. From this perspective, both *M. Butterfly* and *Miss Saigon* were the new Asian "fad" in American theatre. Or, as Josephine Lee points out, both used the "seduction of stereotypes," stereotypes that attracted even Asian American spectators in "contradictory ways."[40]

Frank Chin, who has been critical of Hwang's play for perpetuating the stereotype of Asian men being effeminate, described *Miss Saigon* as a "racist musical" and viewed the casting controversy as Asian American actors fighting to play racist stereotypes. He supported the musical's creative team in its artistic freedom and the right to cast the production as it wished.[41] Hwang never disagreed with Chin on either of his points. On several occasions, including in the interview I conducted with him, Hwang has expressed his regret at not protesting the content of the show first. For Hwang, it was never planned that the casting issue would come first: "it was just so off the wall that they were thinking of doing

[38] *M. Butterfly* closed its Broadway run on January 27, 1990 and went on a national tour in September.

[39] Kevin Kelly, "*M. Butterfly, Miss Saigon* and Mr. Hwang," *Boston Globe*, September 2, 1990, B91.

[40] Josephine Lee, *Performing Asian America: Race and Ethnicity on the Contemporary Stage* (Philadelphia: Temple University Press, 1997), 119.

[41] Bill Wong, "Column: Bill Wong," *Asia Week* (August 24, 1990), 9. Wong's article is reprinted in Bill Wong, *Yellow Journalist: Dispatches from Asian America* (Philadelphia: Temple University Press, 2001), 219–223. Frank Chin's position on the *Miss Saigon* controversy is articulated on page 222.

yellowface, we were shocked."[42] He has even suggested that the ideal way to address the "*Miss Saigon* content debate" would be for "Asian women to refuse to perform in it."[43] Indeed, without the "authentic" and "exotic erotic" Asian women, the show would lose its appeal and audience. Hwang dismissed this thought as "just a fantasy," but it is precisely what Frank Chin has been arguing since the early 1970s.

Hwang's "fantasy" remained just that, but Asian American actors and supporters took their protest to both press and streets. However, their protest seemed anticlimactic after the casting controversy. It did not generate as much publicity until the opening night on April 11, 1991. In the months leading up to the night, several articles appeared in the mainstream media explaining why the musical is so offensive to Asian Americans. For instance, Mary Suh wrote in *Ms. Magazine*, "Artistic integrity? Mackintosh's vision of Asian women is racist and redundant, sexist and simple-minded. The man hasn't conjured up anything new; it's just the same, sick love affair."[44] She also pointed out the show's promotional photographs that feature bikini-clad actresses. She, like many other writers, cited the lyrics from the musical that includes offensive phrases such as "Tonight I will be Miss Saigon/ . . . He'll screw you with your crown still on" and racial slurs such as "chink."

In December of 1990, there was an opportunity to start another casting controversy. Cameron Mackintosh asked the Actors' Equity Association to grant permission to bring Lea Salonga to Broadway to play the role of Kim. He reportedly stated that 1200 Asian American actresses had been auditioned and none had the qualities matching Salonga. Without much complaint or criticism, Salonga came to America and opened the show. This demonstrated that the momentum of the initial protest had weakened and that the Asian Americans were in a more passive position. Or, they were simply exhausted. In fact, a City Hall hearing was requested by Mayor David Norman Dinkins, not Asian Americans, in December. He wrote a letter to Alan Eisenberg to propose sessions with the New York City Commission on Human Rights. Over forty speakers attended the hearing to "record the full range of views on hiring practices in an industry that has not previously been subjected to the scrutiny of civil rights authorities."[45] Asian American speakers raised issues of both casting and

[42] Zia, *Asian American Dream*, 130.
[43] Ibid.
[44] Mary Suh, "The Many Sins of Miss Saigon," *Ms. Magazine* (July 1990), p. 63.
[45] Lisa Yoffee, "Ethnic Casting Issues Get Soapbox Treatment: Beyond *Miss Saigon* at Human Rights Hearings," *American Theatre* (February 1991), 34-35.

content of the musical, and actresses such as Mary Lum pointed out the stereotypical roles for Asian actresses.

As the debate over *Miss Saigon* took on a more subdued and reflective tone, everyone waited for the opening night, some to watch the musical and others to protest it. The protestors included some unexpected supporters: members of the Asian Lesbians of the East Coast (ALOEC) and Gay Asian and Pacific Islander Men of New York (GAPIMNY). The two groups found out months before that the Lambda Legal Defense and Education Fund (LLDEF), a national law organization that champions the rights of gays and lesbians, was using *Miss Saigon* as their annual fundraiser event. They were outraged at the musical's racist and sexist representation of Asians. They demanded Lambda drop the fundraiser, but it refused citing its "fiscal bottom line."[46] The Asian American members scheduled an "anti-*Miss Saigon*" fundraiser for the same night as the Lambda event, a preview of the musical on August 6. Yoko Yoshikawa was one of over 300 protesters who experienced the "heat" of *Miss Saigon* first hand. She writes that fifty-five New York police officers made six arrests and disrupted the demonstration. However, she and Milyoung Cho managed to infiltrate the theatre using two $100 tickets given by two donors who turned away in support of the protest. Yoshikawa describes what happened in the theatre:

> The opening number was dazzling – and loud. The musical opens in a brothel in Saigon, where prostitutes vie for the title *Miss Saigon*. US Soldiers buy raffle tickets; Miss Saigon will be the prize. But I was not following the songs – this lusty dance of glistening legs and dark breasts, of ogling eyes and lathered lips in uniform mesmerized me. It pulled me in, as soft porn will. But I also felt sickened and alienated. The show was designed to seduce, flooding the senses with a 3-D fantasy – specifically targeted at a heterosexual western man's pleasure center. Rumor had it that Jonathan Pryce, a Caucasian British man and leading actor, was close to a nervous breakdown, unnerved by all the controversy and criticism of his role as a Vietnamese pimp. We sat and nervously waited specifically for him. As Pryce entered the set and launched into song, we blasted into ours – deliberate discord, whistling, yelling at the top of our lungs: "This play is racist and sexist, Lambda is racist and sexist!"[47]

---

[46] Yoko Yoshikawa, "The Heat is on *Miss Saigon* Coalition," in Karin Aguilar-San Juan, ed., *The State of Asian American Activism and Resistance in the 1990s* (Boston: South End Press, 1994), 276.

[47] Ibid., 277.

They were thrown out to the streets, but their testimony of what they did inside brought a "roar of sheer power" to the crowd. Unlike the theatrical protest of the preview on April 6, the demonstration on the opening night was less well organized and attended. Some protesters found the second protest anticlimactic compared to the first one, and many failed to show up for the 6:30pm weekday opening. (Many thought that it would begin at 8:00 pm as do most Broadway shows.) Nevertheless, more than 200 people participated in the protest, holding picket signs and chanting their objection to the content of the musical while the police kept them behind barricades. The group leading the protest was "The Heat Is On *Miss Saigon*: Coalition to End Racism and Sexism on Broadway." The protest succeeded in attracting the media. All major networks showed up with cameras and featured the protest as top story on the evening news. Many protesters spoke in front of camera and voiced their criticism of the musical as racist and sexist, emphasizing that the protest was going one step further than the casting controversy. They demanded that Asian Americans be portrayed as "whole human beings, not as prostitutes, pimps, geishas and gangsters – as inhuman."[48]

Figure 11. Protesters picket the opening night of *Miss Saigon* in front of the Broadway Theater in New York City.

[48] The quote was spoken by Veena Cabreros Sud, a spokeswoman for the coalition. See: Karin Lipson, "Over 200 Protest Race Stereotypes in *Miss Saigon*: Firstnighters Pass by Pickets," *Newsday*, April 12, 1991, 4.

The day after the opening night, New York waited for the reviews, which can make or break a show. Most critics agreed that the technology that pushed the limits of theatrical set design was extraordinary. The critics were not enthusiastic about the music, which some found too similar to *Les Miserables*, another musical by Boublil and Schönberg. But virtually all of the critics praised the performances of Lea Salonga and Jonathan Pryce. Frank Rich of *The New York Times* found Salonga "irresistibly moving" and Pryce "electrifying."[49] Some critics went as far as to say that the actors' performances seemed to justify the casting choices. Clive Barnes of the *New York Post* described the musical as "unquestionably a triumph for its cast" and congratulated Cameron Mackintosh for insisting on Pryce and Salonga, a decision that "now seems fully justified."[50]

Ten years later

On December 31, 2000, the musical *Miss Saigon* closed on Broadway after nearly ten years. Since its premiere in London, the musical has grossed more than $1.3 billion internationally at the box office, and the Broadway production alone took more than $266 million and was seen by nearly six million people. Playing 4,063 performances on Broadway, it was the sixth longest running musical in Broadway history. The musical also provided an unprecedented number of employment opportunities and a steady income to actors of all ethnic backgrounds and cultivated a generation of Asian American actors with Broadway credits. Beginning with the Filipino Chinese actor Francis Ruivivar, who stepped into the role of The Engineer in December 1991, the Eurasian role has been successfully played by actors of Asian descent, despite the complaints of Cameron Mackintosh and Vincent G. Liff over the "lack" of qualified Asian American actors. In the long run, Asian American actors won the casting war. And the worldwide publicity of the controversy made Asian American actors visible and recognizable as talented artists. While it is true that shows like *Miss Saigon* (with over thirty Asian parts) don't come along every year, the experiences of the actors have provided a strong base for Asian American theatre. For example, when David Henry Hwang revived *Flower Drum Song* on Broadway in 2002, the producers had a large pool of

---

[49] Frank Rich, "*Miss Saigon* Arrives, From the Old School," *The New York Times*, April 12, 1991, C1.
[50] Quoted in W. J. Weatherby, "A March on Broadway: Protesters and Rave Reviews Greeted Miss Saigon," *The Guardian*, April 13, 1991, 21.

actors (especially Filipino Americans) with both talent and experience to draw from.

Overall, the *Miss Saigon* controversy had a positive effect on the Asian American community. It unified the Asian American theatre community and led to solidarity among artists of all backgrounds. It also educated the mainstream critics, media, and audiences of the history of racism and stereotypical representation of Asians in American theatre. For instance, it has made theatre producers think twice before staging an Orientalist story. And it made yellowface as taboo as blackface. Most importantly, the musical became what *The New York Times* calls a "gold mine" for Asian and Asian American actors.[51] However, below the surface lies a thorny question: at what cost? If the progress came at the expense of luring six million spectators with Asian prostitutes in bikinis, how far have we come? Also, what about the ten-year perpetuation of a century-old stereotype of the virgin/whore killing herself for a Western man? Indeed, "For what kinds of roles are we competing?"[52] Are Asian American actors commodities and destined to be dictated to by the increasing commercialization and capitalization of theatre?

The musical and the controversy revealed how deep and far racism and sexism can run in American theatre, and Asian American actors once again found themselves in the familiar crevice. In the early 1970s, Oriental Actors of America protested against the Lincoln Center without causing any major change in attitude, and in the late 1970s, David Oyama and others protested against the Public Theater, with limited results. In the early 1990s, the scale of the protest was greater, and America as a culture was more sensitive to issues of race, affirmative action, and representation. Perhaps finally, Asian American actors had been heard, and could be certain that the era of yellowface on stage is over. This hesitant promise came at the sacrifice of playing in *Miss Saigon* for ten years. Hopefully, it would be the "ultimate" and the final sacrifice they would need to make.

---

[51] Robin Pogrebin, "For *Miss Saigon*, Light at the End," *New York Times*, August 25, 2000, E1.
[52] Kondo, *About Face*, 231.

8

Asian American theatre in the 1990s

> The earlier generation . . . felt the responsibility to first present images of Asian Americans and say "We are here." And I think it is my generation who's going to say, "We are weird."
>
> Diana Son[1]

IN MAY 1999, A HISTORIC MEETING TOOK PLACE IN SEATTLE. For the first time, Asian American theatre artists convened in a formal way to discuss the state of their profession. Supported by the Ford Foundation and organized by the Northwest Asian American Theater, the meeting was initially intended for artistic directors around the country to gather and share information on funding and other administrative matters. But as the word of the meeting spread, other people wanted to participate, and it eventually grew into a well-attended general conference on Asian American theatre. There were in total five panels. The first panel, "A Retrospective of Asian American Theatre," highlighted the important moments from the histories of the first four theatre companies. Although most original founders, including Mako, Frank Chin, and Tisa Chang, were not present, the panel acknowledged their indispensable contributions and provided a historical context to the conference. The last panel, on the other hand, looked to the future. Participants openly discussed the challenges they anticipated in the new century and agreed that there should be more collaboration and communication between the artists and organizations.

Central to the conference were the three panels scheduled between the first and the last. They focused on issues that have been particularly pertinent to Asian American theatre artists in the 1990s. The second

---

[1] Alvin Eng, ed., *Tokens?: The NYC Asian American Experience on Stage* (Philadelphia: Temple University Press, 1999), 415.

panel, "Writing for Asian American Theatre," addressed who is writing for Asian American theatre and what they are writing about. In the third panel titled, "Merging Traditions/East and West," participants discussed new forms of intercultural theatre. The fourth panel, titled "Asian American Theatre in an Evolving Ethnic Landscape," addressed how Asian American theatre is responding to and participating in the growing diversity of Asians in America. In this chapter, I examine these panel topics as major trajectories of Asian American theatre in the 1990s. The following sections are not necessarily a review of what was discussed in the panels, but rather, I use the topics as headlines to organize a number of wide-ranging issues.

According to the US census reports, the population of Asian Americans in 1990 was 6.9 million, a ninety-nine percent increase since the 1980 census. In 2000, the number grew to 11.9 million or 4.2 percent of the total US population.[2] Much of the growth resulted from new immigration, especially from Southeast Asia and South Asia. Also noticeable in 2000 was the increasing diversity of Asian Americans in terms of ethnic, economic, and educational backgrounds. All of these numbers and variables were consistent with the changes in Asian American theatre. For instance, during the 1990s, the number of Asian American performance groups and theatre companies grew from under ten in the beginning of the decade to over thirty by the end of it. A lot more appeared and disappeared as do many theatre groups, but the overall growth of Asian American theatre in the 1990s indicated an unprecedented increase in organized activities.

Additionally, the changes and new directions in theatre reflected a broader trend in the academic discipline of Asian American studies. Many scholars criticized the ways in which "Asian America" had been constructed in the context of a "nationalist hermeneutic of 'America'" and failed to address its international and transnational links. Sucheta Mazumdar, for instance, describes Asian American Studies as "revisionist" and emphasizes the need to integrate Asian America history to "the global context of capital and labor migration."[3] Mazumdar and others have

---

[2] This figure included 10.2 million people or 3.6 percent who selected to respond as only Asian and 1.7 million people or 0.6 percent who marked Asian and one or more other races in their answers. For more detailed analysis, see Jessica S. Barnes and Claudette E. Bennett, "The Asian Population: 2000" in *Census 2000 Brief* (Washington, DC: US Census Bureau, February 2002).

[3] Sucheta Mazumdar, "Asian American Studies and Asian Studies: Rethinking Roots," in *Asian Americans: Comparative and Global Perspectives*, edited by Shirley Hune, Hyung Chan Kim, Stephen Stugita, and Amy Ling (Pullman: Washington State University Press, 1991), 41.

posited that concepts of panethnicity, cultural nationalism, and strategic coalition that defined the Asian American Movement in the 1960s and 1970s were inefficient to address the complexity of Asian American history and culture. Published in 1991, Lisa Lowe's ground-breaking essay, "Heterogeneity, Hybridity, Multiplicity: Marking Asian American Differences," challenged the notions of "Asian America" – or any culture for that matter – as pure, fixed, and monolithic. According to Lowe, "The making of Asian American culture includes practices that are partly inherited, partly modified, as well as partly invented."[4] Not surprisingly, the recognition of "heterogeneity, hybridity, and multiplicity," also emerged in the works by Asian American theatre artists in the 1990s. Their generation, as Chay Yew states, had a "whole new agenda."[5] For Yew, "race ceases to be the primary focus" and becomes, instead, "the jumping-off point."[6] With the doors wide open, Asian American theatre artists were free to navigate any and every territory of the human experience. Some chose to focus on specific ethnic and cultural themes, and others preferred to revisit the familiar issues with a more self-conscious and self-effacing manner. While some embraced their Asian "roots," others rejected it entirely.

Writing for Asian American theatre

In 1998, the Public Theater's production of Diana Son's *Stop Kiss* surprised everyone – especially the Asian American theatre community – by receiving a number of extended performances and becoming the Off Broadway hit of the season. The Korean American playwright Son wrote a play set in New York City with characters that could be of any racial and ethnic background. The play had no hint of being an Asian American work.[7] Son did insist that one of the main characters, Sarah, be played by the Canadian born Korean American actress, Sandra Oh, not because the character had to be played by an Asian American, but because she felt Oh would be the best actress for the role. Moreover, she wanted to give minority actors the opportunity to play complex characters. Son used the

[4] Lisa Lowe, *Immigrant Acts: On Asian American Cultural Politics* (Durham and London: Duke University Press, 1996), 65.
[5] David Román, "Los Angeles Intersections: Chay Yew," in *The Color of Theater: Race, Culture, and Contemporary Performance* edited by Roberta Uno and Lucy Mae San Pablo Buns (New York: Continuum, 2002), 250.
[6] Ibid.
[7] *Stop Kiss* is about two heterosexual women who find themselves falling in love with each other and having to deal with the assumptions and perceptions of other people, as well as their own.

same reasoning to insist that an African American actor play one of the male characters. The play's success and Son's unconventional attitude towards casting raised and challenged the familiar questions of how "Asian American" an Asian American play has to be. While the previous generation of writers struggled with this question, the "third wave" playwrights such as Diana Son had a simpler answer: Asian Americanness is not required and is only incidental.[8]

It is not that the third wave Asian American playwrights rejected their racial and ethnic identities; rather, they revealed and expressed both the relevance and irrelevance of such labels in their lives. Many first and second wave writers struggled with the dilemma of *either* writing a play about the Asian American experience *or* writing non-Asian American or "universal" (often meaning "white") plays. Usually, the writing of an Asian American play signified political awareness and responsibility of the writer while the "universal" plays reflected the writer's desire to be recognized as a serious and talented writer who could write on any subject. The third wave writers rejected the binary choice and the responsibility of representing their entire group. Instead, they began to tell their individual stories, in which the Asian American identity is only a part of their complex experiences.

Dorinne Kondo articulates the new attitude in her introduction to *Asian American Drama: 9 Plays from Multiethnic Landscape* (1997), a collection of "third wave" Asian American plays edited by Brian Nelson, who served as the literary manager of the East West Players in the early 1990s. According to Kondo, the collection "addresses the contradictions and tensions within any collective identity, including 'Asian America' itself, or even more obviously, within the broader rubric 'people of color.'"[9] In the same collection, David Henry Hwang echoes Kondo's assessment in his preface titled "The Myth of Immutable Cultural Identity":

> Taken together, the plays . . . seriously challenge notions of cultural purity and racial isolationism; indeed, they explode the very myth of an immutable cultural identity. Written largely by younger, or "Third

---

[8] The number of "third wave" Asian American playwrights runs into the hundreds and thus too many to list in this note. Some of the published playwrights have included Robert Chin, Sung Rno, Diana Son, Dwight Okita, Garrett H. Omata, Chay Yew, Han Ong, Huynh Quang Nhuong, Victoria Nalani Kneubuhl, Dmae Roberts, Lucy Wang, Aasif Mandvi, Ralph B. Peña, and Naomi Iizuka.

[9] Dorinne Kondo, "Introduction," in *Asian American Drama: 9 Plays from the Multiethnic Landscape*, edited by Brian Nelson (New York: Applause, 1997), xiii.

Wave" Asian/Pacific playwrights, these works acknowledge the fluidity of culture itself, declaring it a living thing, born of ever-changing experience and therefore subject to continual reinterpretation.[10]

As a second wave writer, Hwang himself has taken up these issues in his more recent works such as *Bondage* and *Trying to Find Chinatown*. For instance, *Bondage* is set in an S&M parlor in which a dominatrix, Terri, and her male customer, Mark, play a game of power by taking on different racial identities. Their faces are covered with full masks and hoods, so the audience does not see their true identities until the very end. The power relations are strangely twisted and reversed throughout the play as the two characters carefully play their game of identity. They continue the competition until the end when they both remove the masks and stand gazing at each other's face. The question raised in the play is not "how to define Asian American identity," but if Asian American identity can be defined. In *Trying to Find Chinatown*, the Caucasian character Benjamin tells the Asian American character Ronnie that he was adopted and raised by Chinese American parents and that he proudly chooses to be Chinese American himself. In both plays, Hwang dramatizes the rejection of what he calls "cultural fundamentalism" and envisions the "coming century" in which race is a matter of choice. A character in *Bondage* expresses Hwang's view: "all labels have to be rewritten, all assumptions re-examined, all associations redefined" in the "coming millennium"[11]

For many third wave playwrights and artists, the rejection of essentialist identity necessitated the questioning of ancestry and history. For instance, the protagonist in Sung Rno's *Cleveland Raining* (1995) says, "We have nothing. Our family was a ghost family. It looked and felt like a family. But it really wasn't there. It was this faded photograph. Black and white. Smudged. Grainy."[12] This sense of feeling detached from ancestry is common in plays by the third generation writers, as opposed to the first and second generation of playwrights whose mission was to claim their history and ancestry in America. Unlike the earlier writers, the new playwrights view their ancestry as remotely relevant, if at all, in explaining who

---

[10] David Henry Hwang, "The Myth of Immutable Cultural Identity," in *Asian American Drama: 9 Plays from the Multiethnic Landscape*, edited by Brian Nelson (New York: Applause, 1997), vii-viii.

[11] David Henry Hwang, *Bondage*, in *But Still Like Air, I'll Rise: New Asian American Plays*, edited by Velina Hasu Houston (Philadelphia: Temple University Press, 1997), 53.

[12] Sung Rno, *Cleveland Raining*, in *But Still Like Air, I'll Rise: New Asian American Plays*, edited by Velina Hasu Houston (Philadelphia: Temple University Press, 1997), 263.

they are. Most characters in the plays confess a sense of not belonging to any particular culture, and such isolation becomes a metaphor for the human condition in all of its multiple forms and heterogeneity.[13]

In *A Language of Their Own* (1997) by Chay Yew, for instance, the main characters, Oscar and Ming, are Asian Americans and lovers, and the two begin the play with the familiar discussion of who is more "Asian" and what that means for their relationship. Oscar tells Ming, "The only thing that truly binds us together is being Chinese," to which Ming replies, "The other thing that truly pits us against each other is being Chinese."[14] The play takes a less familiar turn when it is revealed that Oscar is HIV-positive. As they grow apart, despite both of them wishing to remain together, both realize that their common ethnic background had a less significant role in defining the relationship. What held them together was not their "being Chinese" but the metaphoric language they created together as lovers (not the literal language of Chinese or English). What caused the breakup was the breakdown of the language: "Words gradually lost their meaning and significance / Like drunken dancers, we emphasized wrong accents in words / Sentences led to misinterpretations / Misinterpretations led to misunderstandings / Misunderstandings led to inevitable silence. In the end, we spoke different languages."[15]

The notion of incidental identity has always had more meaning for racially mixed writers and artists. For playwright Naomi Iizuka, whose father is Japanese and mother Latina, the issues of race and ethnicity have been more complicated especially in terms of perception and expectation. She notes that people who look at her "don't know what they're seeing."[16] Iizuka's plays do not address the issues of mixed race directly, but instead explore the fluidity and blurring of all categories, including the physiological and conceptual ones. In *36 Views*, Iizuka tells a story of the power of perception and illusion in art and human relationships. A character says in the play: "I look at you and I don't know what I'm seeing," a line that echoes Iizuka's personal experiences, but one that also signifies a larger

[13] See Karen Shimakawa, "Ghost Families in Sung Rno's *Cleveland Raining*," *Theatre Journal* 52 (2000), 381–396 for a study on Rno's play and the motif of absent family.

[14] Chay Yew, *Porcelain and A Language of Their Own: Two Plays* (New York: Grove Press, 1997), 457.

[15] Ibid., 507. Chay Yew is one of many third wave playwrights who have addressed the gay experience among Asian Americans. Han Ong and Dwight Okita have also written about the multiple landscapes of homosexuality and homoerotic love.

[16] Quoted in Cindy Yoon, "Interview with Naomi Iizuka, Playwright of *36 Views*," *AsiaSource*, (March 29, 2002), www.asiasource.org/arts/36views.cfm.

ontological meaning. Iizuka and others have indicated, quite correctly, that as the number of racially mixed Americans continues to grow, the boundaries of "Asian American" will eventually become ineffective and irrelevant. A character in Iizuka's *17 Reasons (Why)* explains that she is a young lesbian with a long list of ancestry (including Asian, European, Pacific Islander, Latino, and North African) and that "The future is me."[17]

In addition to the third wave playwrights, others joined the growing landscape of Asian American theatre in the 1990s not as playwrights in the traditional sense but as writers of skits and comedies. Most of these writers were performers themselves and often worked with other writer/performers in groups. The performance groups saw the canonized Asian American plays as imitations of Euro-American drama. The rejected the canon and strove to write original, cutting-edge material. Starting in the mid-1990s, these groups grew in popularity around the country, especially in colleges and universities with large Asian student populations. What made them popular and unique was the use of outrageous self-deprecating humor. They satirized American culture and laughed at themselves to gain empowerment. Their self-deprecating humor tackled the one stereotype of Asians that had not been addressed: the stereotype of Asians as having no sense of humor.

Asians had always been the objects of laughter and ridicule as demonstrated by dramatic examples ranging from the coolies in the nineteenth century to the famed foreign exchange student Long Duck Dong in the film *Sixteen Candles* (1984). But they did not laugh at others or themselves. Unlike African American, Latino American, Jewish American, and other American cultures, Asian Americans rarely made an impression as being funny people.[18] However, when Margaret Cho emerged as one of the funniest American comedians, many Asian Americans took notice. Furthermore, her raunchy humor touched a nerve in Asian American

---

[17] Robert Hurwitt, "Hidden History of the Mission: An Enchanting *17 Reasons*," *San Francisco Chronicle*, October 30, 2002, D1.

[18] Without question, funny Asian Americans have always existed, albeit in small numbers. For instance, actor and comedian Pat Morita starred in the first Asian American sitcom, *Mr. T and Tina*, which premiered in 1976 but was canceled before the end of the first season. See www.sitcomsonline.com/mrtandtina.html. Actor Jack Soo also made Americans laugh with his portrayal of the sleep-deprived Detective Nick Yemana in the highly acclaimed television series *Barney Miller*. But no one represented the humoristic sensibility of Asian Americans on the scale and level of Lenny Bruce for Jewish Americans and Richard Pryor for African Americans. It was in the 1990s that funny Asian Americans caught the attention of Americans. For example, in the early 1990s, Steve Park appeared as a regular actor and comedian in the television show *In Living Color*, and Phil Nee won *Showtime*'s "Funniest Person in America" contest.

youth culture. Many youths saw, for the first time, an Asian American comedienne on television wildly making fun of herself, Korean culture, Asian American culture, white culture, and most famously, her mother.[19] Cho's persona had a tremendous appeal to younger Asian Americans who appreciated her honesty and the sense of humor that defied the images of Asian Americans as model minorities. The performance groups identified with Cho's sense of humor and quickly learned to spare nothing for the sake of laughter. Also, some knew about the earlier Asian American performance groups and realized that comedy had to play a more central role in Asian American theatre. Some of the earlier comedy performance groups include Cold Tofu, Not My Fault, and Intake/Outtake. Founded in 1981, Cold Tofu is an Asian American improvisation group. Not My Fault and Intake/Outtake, both, sadly, no longer in existence, performed comedy skits and were part of the Asian American Theater Company in the 1980s. Most of these groups credited the popular television show *Saturday Night Live* for comedic inspiration and staged revues that addressed current issues and events in satirical ways.

In 1989, a group of young actors (mostly college students) in the Los Angeles area formed a performance group called hereandnow, which began to find audiences by visiting as many colleges as possible with their shows. The seven founding artists of the company were frustrated by the lack of roles available for young, Asian American artists. During the 1990s the company toured universities in almost every state of the country. The performers, who created their own materials, told stories about their experiences in short skits of drama, monologue, and comedy. The company's influence on Asian American theatre was tremendous and inspired many young college students all over the country to enter the world of theatre.

In 1994 and 1995, many new groups that were both similar to and different from hereandnow began to appear around the country. Consisting

---

[19] Not everyone found her funny. She received harsh criticism from Korean Americans for degrading the culture and not respecting the elders and from Asian Americans for misrepresenting them with her "negative" image and foul language. Margaret Cho tried to change her image in the sitcom, *All American Girl*, which was based on her comedy routine but was toned down for the primetime television audience. For the show, Cho transformed from a vulgar, sexually open, and daring young comedienne to a sweet "all-American" girl whose mission was to find a nice boyfriend. As Cho would later reveal in her one-woman show, *I am All That I Want*, the show was not written by her and was dictated by producers and writers who lacked an understanding of Asian American culture. Not surprisingly, the show was canceled after one season.

of ethnically diverse members, the new groups entered the world of Asian American theatre with an "in-your-face" approach. For instance, rather than lamenting over racism in theatre and the demise of the color-blind casting policy, these actors celebrated their "Asianness" by calling their groups such names as the Slant Performance Group, 18 Mighty Mountain Warriors, Club O'Noodles, Eth-Noh-Tec Asian American Storytellers, Pork-Filled Players, and Stir Friday Night. These groups rejected the style of realistic family drama and espoused slapstick comedies, political satires, improvisations, and daring experiments. Their sensibility reflected the general American culture of the 1990s that included the national debate over political correctness and culture war and the popular culture of television, film, and stand-up comedy. Moreover, they emulated the styles of the Black Revolutionary Theater and El Teatro Campesino of the 1960s and early 1970s and more recently of the San Francisco Mime Troupe and Culture Clash, a California-based Chicano performance group. The new generation of Asian American performers were drawn to the use of satire, parody, and self-deprecating humor, which, as Harry J. Elam put it, "act as cultural correctives and social commentaries as the parodied subject is held up to ridicule, revised, and critiqued."[20]

For instance, the 18 Mighty Mountain Warriors (18MMW, San Francisco) emerged from a comedy group called Godzilla Theater (1993), which was created by actor Greg Watanabe at the Asian American Theater Company in San Francisco. Due to conflict with the Asian American Theater Company, Godzilla Theater was disbanded after eight months, and in 1994, 18MMW was formed by the remaining members of the Godzilla Theater. Quickly, 18MMW gained its independence and became one of the most successful touring Asian American theatre groups. It calls itself "kind of an Asian American *Monty Python* or *Saturday Night Live*."[21] The comparison is well deserved because, for 18MMW, no topic is safe from parody and satire. Typically, the shows consist of several comedic skits that address various aspects of the usual Asian American experience but with a major comic twist. The titles of its skits suggest the group's satiric and farcical aims: "A John Woo Family Dinner," "Feminine Evolution," "Blaine Asakawa's Self-defense Class," "World Cup 2002," and "L. A. Riot Rock Opera." From the films of John Woo to the 1992 riot

---

[20] Harry J. Elam, *Taking It to the Streets: The Social Protest Theatre of Luis Valdez and Amiri Baraka* (Ann Arbor: University of Michigan Press, 1997), 60.
[21] 18 Mighty Mountain Warriors, Personal interview (March 27, 1998). All uncited quotations by 18 Mighty Mountain Warriors are from this interview.

in LA, 18MMW takes on the challenge of subverting Asian American stereotypes, including those that had been perpetuated by earlier styles of Asian American theatre.

For the member of 18MMW, artistic freedom is more important than acceptance by the Asian American community or mainstream theatre. Harold Byun, a member of the group, notes: "I think what we do that makes it exciting is, from the activist's view point, that you can say whatever the hell you want on stage [and] not have to answer for it." For the Asian American Theater Company, this approach went against their foundational ideas that valued the literary qualities of drama. But for many younger writers, this desire to achieve literary quality meant emulating the "great white male playwrights." While Asian American playwrights have been encouraged to find models in writers such as Sean O'Casey, Eugene O'Neill, and Arthur Miller, the younger groups, such as the 18MMW found their plays unexciting.

The members of the Slant Performance Group (New York City) also found Asian American theatre an uninteresting emulation of white theatre. One of the members, Perry Yung, notes that he stopped auditioning for contemporary Asian American works because they were "Eurocentric works done by Asians in America."[22] Instead, Yung, along with Rick Ebihara and Wayland Quintero, founded the Slant Performance Group, which is "a musical satirical performance group that mocks sexual questions and derogatory stereotypes, while holding Asian men to the flames of American pop culture." The group premiered in December 1995 with *Big Dicks, Asian Men*, and has appeared at multiple venues, including the 1997 Belgrade Summer Festival in the former Yugoslavia. Their subsequent shows, *The Second Coming* and *Squeal Like a Pig, an Intergalactic Poperetta* also played to sold-out audiences around the country. The shows deconstruct images and stereotypes of Asian American men with caricatures, songs, choreographs, and their unique version of slapstick comedy. *The Second Coming*, for instance, is about a "journey of three innocent spermatozoa in their quest for life as the adventurous trio travels through different time periods in the history of Asian America, searching for an identity as they head toward the next millennium, starting with ancient Tantric Chanting monks and ending in a modern Japanese American engineer's on-line wet dreams and torture fantasies."[23]

---

[22] Slant Performance Group, Personal interview (March 28, 1998). All uncited quotations by the Slant Performance Group are from this interview.
[23] Program note for *The Second Coming*.

Figure 12. Slant Performance Group's original song parody "My Girlfriend is a Yakuza" from the show *The Second Coming*, about three monks who continually reincarnate into kooky characters in their migration journey through various periods of Asian American history. Wayland Quintero (left), Rick Ebihara (center), and Perry Yung (right).

Like other groups, the Slant Performance Group conquers stereotypes and labels by reappropriating them. "Slant is a label. We are playing against the label of 'slant,' the name itself. In the past 'slant' was derogatory but now we are changing the word around like 'queer' and 'nigger'," notes the group. Just as homosexuals and African Americans have defused their derogatory terms to express power and self-definition, Slant has taken the first steps to strip away decades-old racial connotations. The group notes that they chose "slant" because it not only has negative connotations, but also has the meaning of "a different point of view, something abnormal, etc."[24]

Both 18MMW and Slant have toured the country, performing at colleges and universities. The students actively participate in their shows as if they were at rock concerts. "Cooing and hollering and coming up for autographs. Autographing our T-shirts or CDs or piece[s] of paper," notes Wayland Quintero of Slant. The spectators at 18MMW and Slant performances feel free to shout, laugh, stand up, dance, and even sing along, especially in the case of Slant, which has released a CD of its songs. Both groups emphasize that there is a hunger for representation and recognition

[24] Terry Hong, "Men at Play," *A. Magazine: Inside Asian America* (May/June 1997), 82.

of Asian Americans on college campuses, and that the groups fulfill those needs by tapping into the younger generation's sensibility. Harold Byun of 18MMW comments on college audiences: "I think college audiences have been the most receptive [. . .] I think it's the generational thing, and the fact that younger people want to laugh. They have been raised on sitcoms and are up on the issues . . . The college campuses seek us out. They want to bring this type of work on to campus."

The questions of who wrote for Asian American theatre in the 1990s and what they wrote were complicated by who read or watched their works. As we have observed, the third wave playwrights wrote about the multiplicity of their identities and experiences for a diverse audience. Their plays, like Diana Son's *Stop Kiss*, appealed to all types of audiences because of their dramaturgical innovations and topical issues. Performance groups, on the other hand, challenged what they considered the Euro-American domination of playwriting and preferred skits, comedy, and in-your-face types of performance. They considered Asian American theatre a "model minority" theatre and lacking in critical humor. While the two groups of writers differed in a number of ways, all of them expanded the limits of what could be written for Asian American theatre. Both groups considered their racial identity as the jumping-off point, and once they jumped, they were free to land anywhere.

Merging traditions / East and West

A number of Asian American companies in the 1990s emphasized a global repertory that included works by all Asian or Asian Pacific Islander "based" artists. They incorporated the concept of Asian diaspora as their main agenda. Asian diaspora was certainly not a new topic in Asian American theatre, and, as I discuss in previous chapters, it has been commonly associated with intercultural theatre. But in the 1990s, a number of new Asian American theatre companies and artists endorsed a specific kind of theatre that promoted and celebrated a more contemporary version of intercultural and transnational theatre. For example, unlike the earlier forms of intercultural theatre that combined traditional Asian theatre forms with contemporary Western sensibilities (such as *Rashomon* by the East West Players in 1965 and community-based Chinese theatre by the Four Seas Players in the early 1970s), the new works of the 1990s utilized both traditional and modern Asian theatre and performance and attempted to broaden and sometimes conflate the definitions of Asian and Asian American theatre and performance.

Kandice Chuh and Karen Shimakawa, the editors of *Orientations: Mapping Studies in the Asian Diaspora*, articulate that the concept of "Asian diaspora" stems from a relatively new field of inquiry and "evokes multiple locations and movements."[25] The study of Asian diaspora questions, among many things, the meaning of "Asian" and "Asianness" and provides an alternative to the previous configurations and terminologies:

> The Asian diaspora as an alternative epistemological object (alternative, that is, to "Asia" and "Asian America") is itself a relation, and makes reference to a kind of conceptual ratio comparing origins and present locations. Metonymic rather than metaphoric, this comparison focuses on movement itself, on the literal circulation of peoples and cultures, and on the figurative meanings of those movements. It describes a conceptual space where attention is drawn to *how* "Asia" materializes through historically specific institutional and symbolic economies.[26]

One of the examples of how "Asia" has recently materialized in Asian American theatre comes from Theater Mu in Minneapolis.

In 1992, Theater Mu was founded by five artists, Rick Shiomi, Dong-il Lee, Martha Johnson, Diane Espaldon, and Andrew Kim, who had dreamed of an Asian American theatre company in the Midwest. Minneapolis, however, was not a typical Midwestern city: the state of Minnesota in the early 1990s saw the quadrupling of the Asian population of the previous decade and was home to the largest population of adopted Koreans in the United States. The recent immigrants from Southeast Asia, especially Cambodians, Laotians, and Hmongs, made the state and its Twin Cities one of the most diverse cultural spaces in the country. The company's name, "Mu," derives from the Korean pronunciation of the Chinese character meaning "shaman/warrior/artist who connects the heavens and earth through the tree of life."[27] The four founders brought with them a diverse artistic background: Dong-il Lee was a doctoral student from Korea and a specialist in Korean mask drama; Martha Johnson had a PhD in theatre with specialization in directing and Asian (mostly traditional Japanese) theatre; Diane Espaldon was a Korean adoptee with a marketing degree; and Andrew Kim was a Korean American living in the Twin Cities. Rick (R. A.) Shiomi was, as mentioned in Chapter 5, best known as a major second wave Asian American playwright and the author

---

[25] Kandice Chu and Karen Shimakawa, eds., *Orientations: Mapping Studies in the Asian Diaspora* (Durham: Duke University Press, 2001), 6.

[26] Ibid., 7.

[27] Theater Mu, "About Mu," www.muperformingarts.org/about.

of award-winning comedy and the detective thriller *Yellow Fever* (1984). Shiomi's experience on the West Coast as an Asian American theatre artist was highly sought after, and with the encouragement of other founding members, he signed on as the artistic director.

Initially, Shiomi envisioned "a traditional Asian American theatre company" that relied on the canon of "kitchen sink dramas and comedies."[28] But Asian American actors were scarce in the Twin Cities in the early 1990s. Moreover, the company's first production, *Mask Dance*, foreshadowed the adjustments Shiomi had to make in the following years. *Mask Drama* came out of the workshops led by Dong-il Lee, who wanted to teach adopted Koreans in the Twin City area about traditional Korean cultural practices. According to Andrew Kim, *Mask Dance* is based on "the Eight Monk Dance and the Shaman Dance from Pongsan T'alch'um style": "The Pongsan style is fast, bold, and free in spirit, emphasizing expression and energy over tight choreography. The earthy, rooted movements, set against the free flow of the *hansam* (fabric sleeves worn over the hands), the masks, and the heartbeat rhythms of the drum speak of a sublime and familiar spirit which is Korea."[29] Set in a middle-class home in a small town in Minnesota, *Mask Dance* tells stories of young adopted Koreans who struggle to find their identities. Their frustrations, sadness, and hopes, are displayed symbolically in the choreography of Korean mask dance throughout the show.

To Rick Shiomi, *Mask Dance* was a seminal work for Theater Mu because, as the company's first production, it "put a stamp of that style of somehow trying to integrate visually, artistically, a traditional Asian performance form . . . and work it into a [naturalistic] play."[30] Shiomi explains that the character Spirit in the show does not move in strictly traditional Korean style: "Her movement is influenced by [traditional Korean movement], but it's actually modern dance." Since the first production, the integration of traditional Asian performance with modern dance and a naturalistic (or Western) form of storytelling has been the signature style for Theater Mu. The seasons have included the usual canon of Asian American plays such as *Paper Angels* by Genny Lim and *Yellow*

---

[28] Oona Kersey, "Theatre Mu" (November 10 2000), www.performink.com/Archives/theatrepro files/2000/TheatreMuMinneapolis.html.

[29] Quoted in Rick Shiomi, *Mask Dance* in *Bold Words: A Century of Asian American Writing*, edited by Rajini Srikanth and Esther Y. Iwanaga (New Brunswick: Rutgers University Press, 2002), 351.

[30] Rick Shiomi. Personal interview. (May 24, 2001). Minneapolis, MN. All uncited quotations by Shiomi are from the interview.

Fever by Rick Shiomi, but what has distinguished Theater Mu from other Asian American theatre companies has been the original shows created by the local artists with their own formula of intercultural theatre.

The Asian communities in the Twin Cities, which consisted predominantly of immigrants, had a number of artists with training in traditional performance. Theater Mu took full advantage of their talents by featuring them in original productions. Josephine Lee provides a detailed study of one such production, *River of Dreams,* which was performed in 1994 at the esteemed Ordway Music Theater in St. Paul, in her article "Between Immigration and Hyphenation: The Problems of Theorizing Asian American Theater." According to Lee, the three one-acts in *River of Dreams* are "significant both ethnically and regionally; not only do they offer the perspective of immigrants from ethnic groups often excluded from discussions of Asian American theater, but they also address the growing numbers of such immigrants whose point of entry is not the East or West coast."[31] *River of Dreams* featured stories of recent Southeast Asian immigrants in Minnesota and integrated the performances of professional Southeast Asian dancers with narrative storytelling. The final piece of the show, *River of Life,* for instance, told the extraordinary story of Thonnara Hing and his sister, who were principal dancers in a touring Cambodian dance company and who, in 1990, defected during a performance at the same Ordway Music Theater. *River of Life* re-created Hing's final performance and his struggle to balance his desire for freedom with his love for the homeland. Traditional Khmer dance was combined with modern dance forms and a series of dialogues that narrated the rich history of Cambodia and Hing's personal agony over the decision to defect.

According to Peter Vaughan of *Star Tribune, River of Dreams* was "at best when the artists use the dance, music, and theater techniques of their native lands, and at its weakest when they rely on traditional scripting and dialogue-driven storytelling."[32] However, and perhaps ironically, Rick Shiomi has considered narrative storytelling a familiar way in which non-Asian audiences can access the performances. In Shiomi's view, non-Asian audiences would find Asian performances "completely alien" without the storytelling element. Unlike any other Asian American theatre company

[31] Josephine Lee, "Between Immigration and Hyphenation: The Problems of Theorizing Asian American Theater," *Journal of Dramatic Theory and Criticism* 13.1 (fall 1998), 54.
[32] Peter Vaughan, "Traditional Music, Dance Lend Strength to Plays," *Star Tribune,* October 15, 1994, 5E.

in the country, Theater Mu's audience is about 15% Asian and 85% non-Asian. And as Josephine Lee advocates, Shiomi wanted to avoid Orientalization of the performances and to refuse to "allow the dancer's body to act solely as either a sentimentalized symbol for the 'old country' or as 'decorative *divertissement*.'[33] In short, the narrative storytelling complicated the visual and aesthetic elements for audiences.

Whether Theater Mu's intercultural performances provide exotic spectacle for curious non-Asian audiences or whether, as Josephine Lee argues, they challenge the notions of homogeneous cultures – either through the incorporation of narrative storytelling or the practices of multigenerational and panethnic casting – has been a central question for the company. Rick Shiomi defends his artistic choices by contexualizing his company in Asian American theatre history. According to Shiomi, Asian American theatre since the 1960s was created to "prove that we are American":

Asian American became our term for ourselves and . . . we were going to prove that we are American. The theatrical style was basically Western, but the substance of the story was Asian American. What I have learned here [in Minneapolis] is when the population is predominantly immigrant Asian, and their cultural roots are in those traditional Asian cultures, then Asian American is an alien term. Even Asian is an alien term. I began to look at that and think that as Asian Americans, cutting yourself off from those cultural roots and those cultural forms in an attempt to prove that you are American is like cutting off your nose despite [*sic*] your face.

For Shiomi, denying Asian roots in Asian American theatre is equivalent to surrendering to non-Asian artists.

The most popular show at Theater Mu has been traditional Japanese Taiko, which the company performs regularly to enthusiastic audiences. For Shiomi, Taiko represents Theater Mu in multiple ways. First, the fact that many of the performers are of Korean descent emphasizes the pan-Asian goal of the company. Performing Taiko in the Midwest further symbolizes the honoring of Asian culture and tradition. And, most importantly, the drum beat of Taiko functions as a unifying agent that transcends language, theatrical literacy, and ethnicity. In Minneapolis, Taiko is seen less as a Japanese form and more as a cultural manifestation of Asian diaspora that demands revised definitions of race and ethnicity in America.

---

[33] J. Lee, "Between Immigration," 56.

Asian American theatre in an evolving ethnic landscape

Like Theater Mu and Rick Shiomi, many new theatre companies and artists of the 1990s deliberately attempted to move away from the Chinese and Japanese American focus in Asian American theatre and argued for a theatre that could include cultures of other ethnic groups, especially those from Southeast Asia and the Indian subcontinent. Although the first four Asian American theatre companies intended to represent all of Asian America, some ethnic groups felt excluded in both administration and production. Most of the Asian American plays done before and even during the 1990s were by, about, and for Chinese and Japanese Americans. Anyone could observe that such selections persisted because the majority of people involved in Asian American theatre were Chinese and Japanese Americans. Moreover, productions in English were widely preferred over those in Asian languages mainly for the purpose of creating solidarity and collective identity as Americans. While advantageous on some levels, the primary use of English often discouraged ethnic and cultural specificity and led to the exclusion of recent immigrants in the community.

In the 1990s, some theatre artists promoted ethnic-specific kinds of cultural nationalism that emphasized national ancestry and ethnic pride rather than the pan-Asian cultural nationalism of the 1960s and 1970s. For instance, Ma-Yi Theater Company (New York City) and Teatro Ng Tanan (San Francisco) were founded in 1989 with a focus on plays by Filipino Americans. Both companies chose names that reflected the culture of the Philippines. The name "Ma-Yi" was used by ancient Chinese traders to refer to a group of islands that is known today as the Philippines. And "Teatro Ng Tanan" means "Theater for Everyone" in Tagalog. In Minneapolis, a group of Hmong American theatre artists founded Pom Siab Hmoob Theatre in 1992, whose name means "Gazing Into the Heart of the Hmong." Some of these companies retained their ethnic specificity while others evolved into pan-Asian American theatre groups.

According to Ralph B. Peña, a co-founder of Ma-Yi Theater Company, a combination of life experiences led him to found a Filipino-specific theatre company in New York City. The first experience derived from his involvement with political theatre in the Philippines in the 1980s, during which he acted in various agitprop performances delivering anti-Marcos regime messages. He learned early on that theatre can be a powerful tool for uniting Filipinos and making social and political changes in the country. The second experience came from his years at the University of California, Los Angeles as a theatre major. Peña found the campus diverse,

Figure 13. Ching Valdes Aran, Han Ong, Mia Katigbak, and Jessica Hagedorn, stalwarts of the Ma-Yi Theater, which began as a Filipino American theatre in New York City.

but to him, the theatre department was "white": "everybody [in the theatre department] teaches you how to become neutral; to neutralize your accent, to neutralize everything under the pretext of making you a blank canvas on which you can be anything, to me that's euphemism for a white card-board."[34] Peña wanted a different sort of venue for theatrical expression, so he moved to New York City, where he soon discovered that Filipino actors rarely got cast as Filipinos: "I'd be the token nonwhite in Shakespeare or Chekhov, if the director felt adventurous. I got cast as Chinese, and I played a Korean. You never get to play your own ethnicity. Filipinos especially feel that. That got tiring."[35] When he met his former colleagues from the Philippines in New York City, he knew they had to create opportunities for themselves. They shared their frustrations as Filipino

[34] Ralph B. Peña. Personal interview (June 6, 2001). All uncited quotations by Peña are from this interview.

[35] Don Shewey, "A Troupe That Sought an Asian-American Role," *New York Times*, March 4, 2001, sec. 2, 7.

actors and agreed to form the Ma-Yi Theater Company and present their first production. Although they wanted to present a Filipino American play, they were not familiar with the genre and decided to revive a Filipino play they worked on in the Philippines together in the 1980s. However, the play, which about the Marcos regime, did not resonate with the audience, and during the run of the production, it became clear to Peña and others that the Filipino American community hungered for plays by and about themselves, not necessarily for plays from their "homeland."

Ma-Yi has since produced a number of original Filipino American plays, including the Obie-award winning play *Flipzoids* by Ralph B. Peña. Moreover, *Flipzoids* was directed by Filipino American designer Loy Arcenas, who has designed numerous award-winning productions on Broadway and Off-Broadway. With Arcenas and others on board, Ma-Yi grew into an even more established professional theatre company. Throughout the 1990s, the company has been a major artistic and literary home-base for many Filipino American actors and playwrights, including Han Ong, who received the MacArthur Foundation "genius" grant in 1997. In recent years, Ma-Yi has broadened its mission and has evolved into a pan-Asian American theatre company with special focus on developing new plays.

The Society of Heritage Performers in Los Angeles also began as an ethnic-specific theatre company that later evolved into an Asian American theatre company. Founded by Soon-Tek Oh in 1995, the Society was a revision of the Korean American Theatre Ensemble, which Oh formed in 1978. The ensemble was a bilingual company with the purpose of introducing Korean culture to second-generation Korean Americans. It usually taught and performed traditional Korean theatre such as Madang-nori (which literally means outdoor or open yard play and is similar to Western musical). But when the Los Angeles Riot occurred in 1992, Oh realized that "Korean American life in America doesn't necessarily mean Korean Americans alone; it involves other races."[36] He wanted to educate the Korean American community about the complexities of racial and ethnic dynamics in the USA. He observed that Korean Americans, from first generation immigrants to their American born children, did not attend Asian American theatre or film; rather, the most popular form of dramatic entertainment was videos of shows imported from Korea. While he understood their preference, he felt strongly that Korean Americans needed to see themselves represented on stage and screen. The Society of Heritage

[36] Soon-Tek Oh. Personal interview (August 2, 2001).

Performers was to become a theatre company for and about Korean Americans with an educational goal. In 1995 and 1996, the society produced *Have You Heard*, a large-scale full-evening show consisting of skit comedy, drama, instrumental music and dance performed by both established and amateur artists. The shows touched on the subject of multiraciality and multiethnicity by, for example, emphasizing similarities between Koreans and African Americans, whose relationship with each other was thorny after the riot. One skit, for instance, drew comparisons between the oppression experienced by Koreans in the country's history and the slavery of African Americans in US history. The purpose was to seek commonalities between the two groups and educate the audience. Although some, including the *Los Angeles Times* reviewer Jana Monji, found the comparison "insensitive" and unconvincing, it shed a sympathetic light on African Americans for the predominantly Korean American audience.[37]

In 1999, the society launched a smaller subgroup called the Lodestone Theatre Ensemble mainly because the large-scale production cost of *Have You Heard* overburdened its management. Soon-Tek Oh calls the Lodestone Theatre Ensemble "slightly emphasizing Korean American origin," but its production has been eclectic in terms of race and ethnicity. The Lodestone Theatre Ensemble began under the leadership of four artistic directors, all of whom are volunteers and were in their early thirties when they started: Bokyun Chun, Philip W. Chung, Chil Kong, and Tim Lounibos. Oh's experience in working with the East West Players and the Society of Heritage Performers told him that a group with multiple producers would have more chance of surviving and preventing the staff from burning out. Highly experimental, the Lodestone Theatre Ensemble productions have focused on workshops of new plays by up-and-coming writers in the Los Angeles area. For instance, many of their writers received training at the David Henry Hwang Writers' Institute at the East West Players. Its repertory has included *Texas* by Judy Soo Hoo and *Laughter, Joy, & Loneliness & Sex & Sex & Sex & Sex* by Philip W. Chung.

Both Ma-Yi Theater Company and Lodestone Theatre Ensemble initially began as ethnic-specific companies but have increasingly produced pan-Asian American plays and sometimes plays not about the conventional notions of the Asian American experience. And both have preferred to develop new and experimental plays. The Ma-Yi Theater Company and

37 Jana J. Monji, "*Heard*: High-Energy Look at Korean American Experience," *Los Angeles Times*, Sepember 25, 1996, F2.

the Lodestone Theatre Ensemble are only two examples of the growing number of ethnic-specific theatre companies that have enriched Asian American theatre with their diversity.

The most recent and perhaps the most significant addition to the list of such companies came from the South Asian American community. In the year 2000, at least three South Asian American theatre groups were founded: SALAAM! (South Asian League of Artists in America) and Disha Theatre in New York City; and Arthe in Washington, DC[38] As Sunaina Marr Maira describes, theatre and performance have always had a strong presence in the South Asian American community, especially in association with student groups and solo performances.[39] For instance, actor and writer Shishir Kurup created a number of solo performances, including *Assimilation* (1991) and *Exile: Ruminations of a Reluctant Martyr* (1992). Born in 1961 in Bombay, raised in Africa, and educated in the US, Kurup's solo shows have always been about his extraordinary life. In *Exile*, Kurup addresses existential questions by creating on stage a sense of imprisonment. He tells stories of his childhood and family, particularly about moments of cultural clash and confusion. For example, as he talks about a "dark-skinned" mother who's shamed into putting white powder on her face, he puts the powder on the lower half of his face. His final image is of an assimilated American who can sing a country song yet who continues to feel imprisoned like a firefly that keeps crashing into a window trying to escape, a visual image that recurs throughout the show. Other South Asian American artists to receive major productions and publications include Sunil Kuruvilla, Aasif Mandvi and Bina Sharif.[40]

To say the least, the institutionalization of South Asians as part of Asian American theatre was long overdue, especially when we consider the size and growth rate of the South Asian population in the US. Established theatre companies such as the East West Players took notice of the growing South Asian presence in American theatre. In fact, in its

---

[38] The South Asian American artists' response to the terrorist attacks on September 11, 2001 provided an indispensable voice to the larger public. For instance, in October 2001, SALAAM! organized a fundraiser to assist the undocumented hotel and restaurant workers, their families affected by the World Trade Center attack. The performances included music, dance, poetry reading, hip-hop, and comedy skits by artists of both local and international reputation.

[39] Sunaina Marr Maira, *Desis in the House: Indian American Youth Culture in New York City* (Philadelphia: Temple University Press, 2002).

[40] For a study on Bina Sharif, see Mera Moore Lafferty, "From Islamabad to New York City: Bina Sharif's Spiritual Politics," *Text & Presentation* 23 (2002), 57–69.

.

Figure 14. Bernard White, Meera Simhan and Poorna Jagannathan in the 2002 world premiere of *Queen of the Remote Control* by Sujata G. Bhatt at the East West Players.

2002–2003 season, the East West Players presented the world premiere of *Queen of the Remote Control* by Sujata G. Bhatt, a play about an upper-middle class South Asian American family in Southern California. The East West Players also produced *As Vishnu Dreams* by Shishir Kurup in 2005. A contemporary adaptation of the Hindu epic poem *The Ramayana*, the production reflected two major directions towards which the East West Players embarked during the 1990s. First, by co-producing the play with the Cornerstone Theater Company, the East West Players strengthened its efforts to work with established regional theatre companies in order to gain access to mainstream audiences. Secondly, the production was created in collaboration with the Hindu community in Los Angeles, underscoring the East West Players' commitment to involve all Asian American communities and their experiences.

Towards a new millennium

The 1990s marked the beginning of a new era for Asian American theatre in many ways. The majority of the emerging artists were younger in age than the East West Players, and their sensibility and understanding of the

Asian American experience differed quite drastically from those of the past. One of the most pertinent and underlying issues of the 1990s was who Asian Americans are and what "Asianness" or "Asian Americanness" would mean during the last decade of the twentieth century and the beginning of the twenty-first century. New artists and companies dealt with a wide-range of agendas; some departed from the traditional notions of an Asian American theatre while others embraced and continued its literary and artistic traditions. Some companies focused on ethnic specificity, others produced intercultural theatre almost exclusively, and yet others deliberately resisted any pigeonholing, as in the case of the National Asian American Theater Company (NAATCO, New York City) founded in 1989.[41]

NAATCO was founded by Richard Eng and Mia Katigbak with the purpose of producing European and American classics with all-Asian American casts. Katigbak was frustrated with the lack of opportunities she encountered as an actress in New York City.[42] She was disappointed with intercultural productions that borrowed Asian theatrical elements but often seemed contrived and gratuitous, betraying a lack of understanding of the source of the traditions. Because of her training in Western theatre, Katigbak believed that producing the classics with all Asian American casts without deliberately "Asianizing" would be a more valuable contribution to the future of American theatre. Since the beginning, the company has given rare opportunities to Asian American actors to play some of the greatest roles without having to wear "whiteface" makeup or reinterpreting the classics into pseudo-oriental settings. The range of the company's repertoire includes a production of Molière's *School of Wives* for which the company won one of the Best Plays Awards from *The Off-Off-Broadway Review* in 1995; the 1998–99 season which included William Finn's *Falsettoland* and Bertolt Brecht's *He Who Says Yes/He Who Says No* for which the company won an Obie Award; and William Shakespeare's *Othello* in 2000. In 2004, NAATCO produced Sophocles' *Antigone* with an all-Asian American cast and Mia Katigbak playing the role of the stubborn king Creon. The production provided a different kind of interpretation not only racially but also politically and artistically. In 2005, the company began a new program that featured adaptations of the classics by

[41] For a study of NAATCO, see Angela C. Pao, "Recasting race: Casting Practices and Racial Formations," *Theatre Survey* 41.2 (November 2000), 1–21.

[42] Mia Katigbak, Personal interview, September 19, 1999. All uncited quotations by Katigbak are from this interview.

Figure 15. Antigone being sentenced to imprisonment in a cave in the National Asian American Theatre Company's 2004 production of Sophocles' *Antigone*, directed by Jean Randich with original music by Robert Murphy. Eunice Wong plays Antigone with the chorus: James Shubert, Cruz Turcott, Fansto Pineda, Nicky Paraiso, Siho Ellsmore, Orville Mendoza, Elexis Camins, and Art Acuña.

Asian American playwrights. NAATCO indeed represents a new type of Asian American theatre in the new millennium.

Another indication of the growth in Asian American theatre since the 1990s has been the foundation of companies in cities other than Los Angeles, San Francisco, Seattle, and New York City. Some of the companies include: Asian American Repertory Theatre (San Diego, founded in 1995), Community Asian Theater of the Sierra (Nevada City, founded in 1994), InterACT (Sacramento, founded in 1994), Asian Stories in America (Washington, DC, founded in 1999), QBD Ink (Washington, DC, founded in 1994), Mango Tribe Productions (Chicago, founded in 2000), Due East (Chicago, founded in 2003), and the Indian-American theatre company, Shunya (Houston, founded in 2003).[43] While the overall

---

[43] For a list of Asian American theatre companies, see Roger Tang, "Directory," *Asian American Theatre Revue*, http://aatrevue.com/Directory.html.

presence of Asian American theatre has expanded nationally, New York City, since the 1990s, has been the fastest growing site. The influence of the ten-year run of *Miss Saigon* can be seen in Second Generation, a company founded in 1997 by Welly Yang with other actors who performed in *Miss Saigon*. Second Generation is most widely known for the musical *Making Tracks*, which traces an Asian American man's family history that spans six generations.

It may be too soon to provide a full evaluation of the body of work produced by the new group of artists since the 1990s. The list of new companies constantly grows, and a new generation of artists is reinventing the field of Asian American theatre. As the 1999 conference in Seattle demonstrated, the fairest assessment of the decade should involve more questions than answers, more cautious observations than conclusions. But one thing is certain: Asian American theatre has no boundaries in the new millennium.

Epilogue

On March 16, 2003, David Henry Hwang's adaptation of *Flower Drum Song* closed on Broadway after 26 previews and 172 regular performances with financial losses of $7 million. The early closing was the result of a combination of factors, including New York critics' unfavorable reviews that resisted the changes Hwang made and preferred the 1958 version by Richard Rodgers and Oscar Hammerstein. The musicians' strike that had shut down Broadway musicals in early March did not help.[1] However, Hwang's musical marked in a multitude of ways the progress Asian American theatre had made since the 1960s. Although Hwang was disappointed to see the early closing, he knew, better than anyone, the musical's significance: "The fact that for at least six months an Asian-American story was on Broadway is incredibly important to me."[2] The story, initially written by the Chinese American author C. Y. Lee, was reclaimed by Hwang, the most influential Asian American theatre artist in American mainstream theatre. Moreover, the musical featured Randall Duk Kim, who had shocked the New York theatre scene in 1972 with his performance in Frank Chin's *Chickencoop Chinaman*. Other veteran Asian American actors such as Jody Long strengthened the cast, and younger actors (many of whom were Filipino/a Americans such as Lea Salonga) had *Miss Saigon* on their resumes. Most importantly, yellowface was nowhere to be seen. Hwang's *Flower Drum Song* indeed represented what Karen Shimakawa describes as the "competing agendas" of Asian American theatre: "on the one hand . . . the goal was to put 'our' stories on

---

[1] Jesse McKinley of the *New York Times* described Hwang's *Flower Drum Song* as the "first victim" of the musicians' strike. Jesse McKinley, "Walkout Closes a Struggling Revival Early," *The New York Times*, March 10, 2003, B4.

[2] Robert Dominguez, "*Flower Drum* Beats a Retreat," *Daily News*, February 25, 2003, 42.

stage . . .; on the other hand, the objective was to combat racist casting practices."[3]

But the musical was also significant for revealing how far Asian American theatre had moved beyond the initial agendas. Many artists felt the musical had little to do with the kinds of work they were producing. Their goals were no longer overshadowed by the need to address mainstream theatre, either by reacting to racism or by requesting acceptance. In San Francisco, for instance, Teatro ng Tanan (Theater for the People) has created shows that Roberta Uno describes as "unpredictable, fresh, and completely engrossing."[4] Similar adjectives could be used to describe works by the Lodestone Theatre Ensemble (Los Angeles), Mellow Yellow (New York City), Club O'Noodles (Los Angeles), Disha Theater (New York City), and numerous other groups that have essentially rebelled against the limitations of mainstream theatre and established Asian American theatre. New forms like spoken word demand new audiences, and younger writers push the definitions of ethnic drama to the point that all labels are heading towards obscurity. It is truly the "exhilarating and precarious stage of Asian American theater in the new millennium," as Roberta Uno has put it.[5] Because Asian Americans form one of the fastest growing racial groups in the United States, Asian American theatre can be expected to evolve in wide-ranging and even contradictory directions. Perhaps when American theatre truly includes all Americans, Asian American theatre will cease to exist.

For now, however, the need for Asian American theatre is unquestioned. The first four companies continue to provide the spaces in which the first, second, and third wave artists can work together towards a common goal. For instance, in early 2001, the East West Players revived *The Year of the Dragon* and invited Frank Chin to participate in the production. It took some effort on the part of Tim Dang, the artistic director of East West Players, to convince Frank Chin to allow the revival, but once the rehearsals started, Chin worked extensively with the actors and Mako, who directed the play. Although Chin refused to enter the theatre building because it was named after David Henry Hwang, it is rumored that he did go into the theatre building to give his approval of the

[3] Karen Shimakawa, "Asians in America: Millennial Approaches to Asian Pacific America Performance," *Journal of Asian American Studies* 3.3 (October 2000): 285.

[4] Roberta Uno, "Introduction: Asian American Theater Awake at the Millenium," in *Bold Words: A Century of Asian American Writing*, edited by Rajini Srikanth and Esther Y. Iwanaga (New Brunswick: Rutgers University Press, 2001), 323.

[5] Ibid., 324.

set and lighting designs. (But we will never know for certain.) Younger artists wondered what the fuss was all about, but they nevertheless appreciated Chin's writing that had not lost its power after almost thirty years. They understood his anger because they could see how little racial politics had changed in the United States. For example, the Korean American playwright Euijoon Kim had never read Frank Chin's plays when he wrote *My Tired Broke Ass Pontificating Slapstick Funk* (which premiered at the East West Players in 2000), but his Asian American characters emulate African American speech and mannerism in surprisingly similar ways to Frank Chin's.

While many Asian American theatre artists celebrate the past decades, they are also frustrated by the lack of progress in mainstream theatre, film, and television. Every few years, studies find Asian American characters underrepresented in mainstream dramatic media, exacerbating the sense of injustice in those who have seen similar studies since the 1970s.[6] In addition, mainstream theatre companies have reevaluated the need for so-called multicultural theatre, often canceling those programs that have nurtured minority artists. In July 2005, for instance, the Center Theater Group ceased to sponsor ethnic-specific programs, including the Mark Taper Forum's Asian Theatre Workshop. Under the directorship of Chay Yew since 1993, the Asian Theatre Workshop had provided crucial opportunities to Alice Tuan, Han Ong, Naomi Iizuka, and other Asian American playwrights at early stages of their careers. Whether it was affirmative action or racial segregation in American theatre, those ethnic-specific programs that benefited Asian American artists have begun to disappear. Alice Tuan could only cross her fingers and hope for the best: "As heart-wrenching as it is to see the circle that nurtured my playwriting let go of one by one, maybe, just maybe, the lab model had to go the way of the theater curtain to make room for a paradigm that will grow, blossom and inspire the theater for this new century. May be, just maybe."[7]

Perhaps American theatre is at the cusp of a major paradigm shift, as Tuan hopes. Or, perhaps American theatre is taking back steps, and Asian American theatre artists will need to repeat their efforts. One thing is certain, however: the increase in globalization and transnationalism,

---

[6] The latest study was conducted by National Asian Pacific American Legal Consortium, which concluded that "Asians, who make up 5 percent of the US population, play 2.7 percent of regular characters in [prime-time television]." Erin Texeira, "Asian Actors on Prime-Time TV are Underrepresented, Get Little Screen Time, New Study Shows," *The Associated Press*, May 2, 2005.

[7] Alice Tuan, "A Glorious Rainbow Roll Call," *Los Angeles Times*, June 26, 2005, E1.

especially in the form of mass media and popular culture, is affecting the stipulation of Asian American identity. With the Internet and satellite television, that allow anyone to experience worldwide cultures instantaneously and simultaneously, the distinction between Asia and Asian America is fast disappearing. Mainstream American theatre may want to remain insular to such global changes, but Asian American theatre will continue to demand both inclusiveness and expansion of American theatre.

Appendix

Archival resources on Asian American theatre

Asian American Theater Company Archives: 1973–1997

The California Ethnic and Multicultural Archives (CEMA)
Special Collections Department of the University Libraries
Davidson Library
University of California, Santa Barbara
Santa Barbara, California 93106–9010
(805) 893-8563
(805) 893-3062
http://cemaweb.library.ucsb.edu/aatc_toc.html

The collection includes administrative records, grant applications, correspondence, meeting minutes, audio and videotapes, and production photographs, posters, flyers, and programs. Production scripts – the vast majority of which are not published – are also included.

David Henry Hwang Papers

Department of Special Collections
Cecil H. Green Library
Stanford University
Stanford, California 94305-6004.
(650) 725-1022
http://library.stanford.edu/depts/hasrg/ablit/amerlit/hwang.html

The David Henry Hwang Papers features both published and unpublished writings of Hwang, including essays, plays, and screenplays in both draft and final versions. Also included in the collection are notes, correspondence, interviews, grant applications, and contracts. The multiple drafts of Hwang's plays, including *M. Butterfly*, are of particular significance.

East West Players Records: 1965–1991

Arts Library Special Collections
Charles E. Young Research Library, Room 22478
University of California, Los Angeles
Los Angeles, CA 90095–1575
(310) 825–7253
http://www.oac.cdlib.org/findaid/ark:/13030/tf1489n74f

The collection consists of administrative and production materials, including correspondence, scripts, photographs, meeting minutes, records of the board of directors, newsletters, video and audio tapes, financial records, publicity materials, and grants applications.

Frank Chin Papers: 1940–2001

The California Ethnic and Multicultural Archives (CEMA)
Special Collections Department of the University Libraries
Davidson Library
University of California, Santa Barbara
Santa Barbara, California 93106–9010
(805) 893–8563
(805) 893–3062
http://cemaweb.library.ucsb.edu/chin_toc.html

Acquired from Frank Chin in 2003, the collection contains personal and professional materials, including family photos, interviews, essays, articles, novels, plays, and screenplays. Chin's extensive correspondence with Maxine Hong Kingston, James Omura, Shawn Wong, Lawson Inada, and numerous others are the highlight of the collection.

New York Public Library for the Performing Arts

The Billy Rose Theater Collection
40 Lincoln Center Plaza
New York, NY 10023-7498
(212) 870-1639
http://www.nypl.org

One of the largest archives devoted to the theatrical arts, the New York Public Library features clipping files that are collections of press releases and articles from newspapers and magazines related to a particular topic. Topics pertinent to Asian American theatre include: The Oriental Actors of America; Asian-American in the Theatre; *Pacific Overtures*; Asia Cine Vision; Basement Workshop; *Miss Saigon*; and individual artists such as Sab Shimono, Randall Duk Kim, John Lone, and Tisa Chang. The Billy Rose Theatre Collection also includes videos of the original Broadway productions of *M. Butterfly* by David Henry Hwang (with John Lithgow and B. D. Wong) and the musical *Miss Saigon* (with Jonathan Pryce and Lea Salonga). Some videos of Pan Asian Repertory Theatre's productions are also archived. Specific titles can be searched at: http://catnyp.nypl.org.

Roberta Uno Asian American Women Playwrights' Scripts Collection: 1924–1992

W.E.B. Du Bois Library
25th Floor
University of Massachusetts
Amherst, MA 01003
(413)545-2780
askanarc@library.umass.edu
http://www.library.umass.edu/spcoll/spec.html

Uno's collection includes over 200 unpublished plays written by Asian American women from 1924 to 1992. It includes works by both professional and amateur writers.

San Francisco Performing Arts Library & Museum

401 Van Ness Ave, Rm 402
San Francisco, CA 94102
(415)255-4800
info@sfpalm.org
http://www.sfpalm.org/catalog/catalog.htm

As one of only three sites in which the Actors' Equity Association allows the archiving of video recordings of theatre productions, the library has videos of some of the Asian American plays produced on the West Coast, including Philip Kan Gotanda's *The Wash* and *Wind Cries*

Mary and Velina Hasu Houston's *Kokoro*. The library holds other videos such as Lane Nishikawa's *I'm on a Mission from Buddha*. A few photos of Asian American Theater Company's productions are also in the collection.

Bibliography

Plays and performance scripts

Barroga, Jeannie. *Two Plays by Jeannie Barroga*. San Francisco: Cross Current Press, 1993.

Berson, Misha, ed. *Between Worlds: Contemporary Asian American Plays*. New York: Theatre Communications Group, 1990.

Carroll, Dennis, ed. *Kumu Kalua Plays*. Honolulu: University of Hawaii Press, 1983.

Chin, Frank. *The Chickencoop Chinaman and The Year of the Dragon*. Seattle: University of Washington Press, 1981.

Chong, Ping. *I Flew to Fiji; You Went South. Bridge: An Asian American Perspective* 5.2 (1977): 24–26.

Kind News. New Plays USA 4. New York: Theatre Communications Group, 1988.

98.6 – A Convergence in 15 Minutes. In *Yellow Light: The Flowering of Asian American Arts*. Ed. Amy Ling. Philadelphia: Temple University Press, 1999. 204–212.

The East West Quartet. New York: Theatre Communications Group, 2004.

Ellis, Roger, ed. *Multicultural Theatre II: Contemporary Hispanic, Asian, and African-American plays*. Colorado Springs: Meriwether, 1998.

Eng, Alvin, ed. *Tokens?: The NYC Asian American Experience on Stage*. Philadelphia: Temple University Press, 1999.

Gotanda, Philip Kan. *Yankee Dawg You Die*. New York: Dramatist Play Services, Inc., 1991.

Day Standing on its Head. New York: Dramatist Play Services, Inc., 1994.

Fish Head Soup and Other Plays. Seattle: University of Washington Press, 1995.

Ballad of Yachiyo. New York: Theatre Communications Group, 1997.

Hagedorn, Jessica. *Chiquita Banana*. In *Third World Women*. Ed. Toni Cade Bambara. San Francisco: Third World Communications, 1972.

Hagedorn, Jessica, Laurie Carlos, and Robbie McAuley. "Teenytown." In *Out From Under: Texts by Women Performance Artists*. Ed. Lenora Champagne. New York, NY: Theatre Communications Group, 1990. 89–117.

Hartman, Sadakichi. *Buddha, Confucius, Christ: Three Prophetic Plays*. Ed. Harry Lawton and George Knox. New York: Herder, 1971.

Houston, Velina Hasu, ed. *The Politics of Life*. Philadelphia: Temple University Press, 1993.

ed. *But Still Like Air, I'll Rise: New Asian American Plays*. Philadelphia: Temple University Press, 1997.

Hung, Shen. *The Wedded Husband*. In *The Chinese Other: 1850–1925: An Anthology of Plays*. Ed. Dave Williams. Lanham: University Press of America, Inc., 1997. 391–417.

Hwang, David Henry. *M. Butterfly*. New York: Plume, 1988.

FOB and Other Plays. New York: Plume, 1990.

Bondage. In *But Still Like Air, I'll Rise: New Asian American Plays*. Ed. Velina Hasu Houston. Philadelphia: Temple University Press, 1997. 157–177.

"Introduction." In *Asian American Drama: 9 Plays from the Multiethnic Landscape*. Ed. Brian Nelson. New York: Applause, 1997. ix-xi.

Golden Child. New York: Plume, 1999.

Iizuka, Naomi. *Polaroid Stories*. In *Humana Festival '97: the Complete Plays*. Eds. Michael Bigelow Dixon and Liz Engelman. Lyme, NH: Smith and Kraus, 1997.

Aloha, Say the Pretty Girls. In *Humana Festival '99: The Complete Plays*. Eds. Michael Bigelow Dixon and Amy Wegener. Lyme, NH: Smith and Kraus, 1999.

Skin. In *Out of the Fringe: Contemporary Latina/Latino Theatre and Performance*. Eds. Caridad Svich and Maria Teresa Marrero. New York: Theatre Communications Group, 2000.

Kneubuhl, John. *Think of a Garden and Other Plays*. Honolulu: University of Hawai'i Press, 1997.

Kwong, Dan. "Song for Grandpa" (from *Monkhood in 3 Easy Lessons*). In *Yellow Light: The Flowering of Asian American Arts*. Ed. Amy Ling. Philadelphia: Temple University Press, 1999.

From Inner Worlds to Outer Space. Ed. Robert Vorlicky. Ann Arbor: The University of Michigan Press, 2004.

lê thi diem thúy. *the bodies between us*. In *The Color of Theater: Race, Culture, and Contemporary Performance*. Eds. Roberta Uno and Lucy Mae San Pablo Buns. New York: Continuum, 2002. 323–336.

Li, Ling-ai (Gladys). *The Submission of Rose Moy*. In *Paké: Writings By Chinese in Hawaii*. Ed. Erick Chock. Honolulu: Bamboo Ridge Press, 1989.

Lim, Genny. *Bitter Cane and Paper Angels: Two Plays by Genny Lim*. Honolulu: Kalamaku Press, 1991.

Loh, Sandra Tsing. *Aliens in America*. New York: Riverhead Trade, 1997.

Lum, Charlotte. *These Unsaid Things*. In *Paké: Writings by Chinese in Hawaii*. Ed. Eric Chock. Honolulu: Bamboo Ridge Press, 1989.

Mapa, Alec. *I Remember Mapa*. In *O Solo Homo: The New Queer Performance*. Ed. Holly Hughes and David Román. New York: Grove Press, 1998.

Miyakawa, Chiori. *Yesterday's Window*. In *Take Ten: New 10-minute Plays*. Eds. Eric Lane and Nina Shengold. New York: Vintage Books, 1997.

Nelson, Brian, ed. *Asian American Drama: 9 Plays from the Multiethnic Landscape*. New York: Applause, 1997.

Okida, Dwight. *Richard Speck*. In *Yellow Light: The Flowering of Asian American Arts*. Ed. Amy Ling. Philadelphia: Temple University Press, 1999.

Perkins, Kathy A. and Roberta Uno, eds. *Contemporary Plays by Women of Color*. New York: Routledge, 1996.

Rno, Sung. *Cleveland Raining*. In *But Still Like Air, I'll Rise: New Asian American Plays*. Ed. Velina Hasu Houston. Philadelphia: Temple University Press, 1997. 228–270.
Sakamoto, Edward. *Hawai'i No Ka Oi: Tha Kamiya Family Trilogy*. Honolulu: University of Hawaii Press, 1995.
Shiomi, R. A. *Yellow Fever*. Toronto: Playwrights Canada, 1984.
Mask Dance. In *Bold Words: A Century of Asian American Writing*. Eds. Rajini Srikanth and Esther Y. Iwanaga. New Brunswick: Rutgers University Press, 2002. 351–386.
Slant Performance Group. "Diary of a Paper Son." In *Yellow Light: The Flowering of Asian American Arts*. Ed. Amy Ling. Philadelphia: Temple University Press, 1999.
"No Menus Please." In *Yellow Light: The Flowering of Asian American Arts*. Ed. Amy Ling. Philadelphia: Temple University Press, 1999.
Son, Diana. *Boy* [Act 1, Scene 2]. In *New Voices of the American Theater*. Ed. Stephen Vincent Brennan. New York: Henry Holt, 1997.
Stop Kiss. Woodstock, NY: Overlook Press, 1999.
Uno, Roberta, ed. *Unbroken Thread: An Anthology of Plays by Asian American Women*. Amherst: University of Massachusetts Press, 1993.
Uyehara, Denise. *Hello (Sex) Kitty: Mad Asian Bitch on Wheels*. In *O Solo Homo: The New Queer Performance*. Ed. Holly Hughes and David Román. New York: Grove Press, 1998.
Maps of City & Body: Shedding Light on the Performances of Denise Uyehara. New York: Kaya Press, 2003.
Williams, Dave, ed. *The Chinese Other: 1850–1925: An Anthology of Plays*. Lanham: University Press of America, Inc., 1997.
Yew, Chay. *Porcelain and A Language of Their Own: Two Plays*. New York: Grove Press, 1997.
A Language of Their Own. In *But Still Like Air, I'll Rise: New Asian American Plays*. Ed. Velina Hasu Houston. Philadelphia: Temple University Press, 1997. 451–514.
Red. Seattle, WA: Rain City Projects, 1998.

Critical and secondary sources

"About East West Players." www.eastwestplayers.org/aboutus.html.
"Acting Silly About Color." *New York Times* July 28, 1990: 20.
Aguilar-San, Juan, Karin. *The State of Asian America: Activism and Resistance in the 1990s*. Boston: South End Press, 1994.
Ahlgren, Calvin. "Dennis Dun: Questions of Assimilation Burn in *Dragon*." *San Francisco Chronicle* Aug. 15, 1992: 24.
Alejandro, Reynaldo G. "Pilipino-American Performing Arts; A Survey and Reflection." *Bridge: An Asian American Perspective* 5.2 (1977): 21–23.
Appiah, Kwame Anthony and Henry Louis Gates, Jr., eds. *Identities*. Chicago: University of Chicago Press, 1995.
Arkatov, Janice. "Narita's *Song* Looks at Roles of Asian Women." *Los Angeles Times* Aug. 28, 1987, Sec. 6: 3.
Artaud, Antonin. *The Theater and Its Double*. New York: Grove Press, Inc., 1958.
"Asian Actors Angry Over Musical Roles." *New York Times* Aug. 7, 1970: 28.

Asian American Theater Workshop. "An Overview of the Asian American Theater Workshop." (1974). The Asian American Theater Company Archive, California Ethnic and Multicultural Archives at the Special Collections Library, University of California, Santa Barbara.

"Program for The Asian American Workshop at ACT." (1973). The Asian American Theater Company Archive, California Ethnic and Multicultural Archives at the Special Collections Library, University of California, Santa Barbara.

"Vision Questions." (Oct. 30, 1975). The Asian American Theater Company Archive, California Ethnic and Multicultural Archives at the Special Collections Library, University of California, Santa Barbara.

"Letter from the Board of Directors." (Mar. 16, 1978). The Asian American Theater Company Archive, California Ethnic and Multicultural Archives at the Special Collections Library, University of California, Santa Barbara.

Atkinson, Brooks. "Newest Musical Play by Rodgers and Hammerstein set in Old Siam." *New York Times* Apr. 8, 1951: 1.

Awkward, Michael. *Negotiating Difference: Race, Gender, and the Politics of Positionality.* Chicago: University of Chicago Press, 1995.

Bacalzo, Dan. "Portraits of Self and Other: *Slut for Art* and the Photographs of Tseng Kwong Chi." *Theatre Journal* 53 (2001): 73–94.

Banes, Sally. "The World According to Chong." *Village Voice* Feb. 28, 1984: 83.

Barnes, Clive. "Stage: Identity Problem." *New York Times* June 13, 1972: 53.

"Stage: Narrow Road." *New York Times* Jan. 7, 1972: 27.

Barnes, Jessica S. and Claudette E. Bennett. "The Asian Population: 2000." *Census 2000 Brief.* Washington, DC: U S Census Bureau, February 2002.

Behr, Edward and Mark Steyn. *The Story of Miss Saigon.* London: Jonathan Cape, 1993.

Berson, Misha. "The Demon in David Henry Hwang." *American Theatre* 15.4 (1998): 14–18.

"Cultural Revolution: Frustrated with Stereotypes, They're Rewriting the Script." *Mother Jones.* 14.2 (February–March 1989): 12.

"Fighting the Religion of the Present: Western Motifs in the First Wave of Asian American Plays." In *Reading the West: New Essays on the Literature of the American West.* Ed. by Michael Kowalewski. Cambridge: Cambridge University Press, 1996. 251–272.

"Role Model on a Role: Philip Kan Gotanda's Work Grabs Mainstream Attention and Inspires Younger Artists." *Seattle Times* Oct. 10, 1996: D1.

"Naomi Iizuka: Raising the Stakes." *American Theatre* 15.7 (1998): 56–57.

Blumenthal, Eileen. "The Solo Performances of Winston Tong." *The Drama Review* 23.1 (1979): 87–94.

Blumenthal, Ralph. "Chinese Theater is on the Rise in City." *New York Times* Aug. 10, 1972: 37.

Bonney, Jo, ed. *Extreme Exposure: An Anthology of Solo Performance Texts from the Twentieth Century.* New York: Theatre Communications Group, 2000.

Boublil Alain "From Madame Chryssanthemum to Miss Saigon." www.towards-esfahan.com/pla16.html.

Breslauer, Jan. "Playwright. Amerasian. Single Mother. The Artistry of an Activist." *Los Angeles Times* July 7, 1991: 3.

"Broadway: The Girls on Grant Avenue." *Time* Dec. 2, 1958: 43–47.

Broyles-Gonzales, Yolanda. *El Teatro Campesino: Theater in the Chicano Movement.* Austin: University of Texas Press, 1994.

Brustein, Robert. "The Use and Abuse of Multiculturalism" *The New Republic* 205.12–13 (1991): 31–34.

Burnham, Linda Frye. "Getting on the Highways: Taking Responsibility for the Culture in the '90s." *Journal of Dramatic Theory and Criticism* (1990): 265–278.

Burns, Lucy Mae San Pablo. "Something Larger Than Ourselves: Interview with Nobuko Miyamoto." In *The Color of Theater: Race, Culture, and Contemporary Performance*. Eds. Roberta Uno and Lucy Mae San Pablo Burns. New York: Continuum, 2002. 195–206.

   "Community Acts: Locating Pilipino American Theater and Performance." PhD dissertation University of Massachusetts, 2004.

Byer, Jackson R. "David Henry Hwang." *The Playwright's Art: Conversations with Contemporary American Dramatists*. New Brunswick, NJ: Rutgers University Press, 1995. 123–146.

Canning, Charlotte. *Feminist Theaters in the U.S.A.: Staging Women's Experience*. New York: Routledge, 1996.

Carlson, Marvin. *Performance: A Critical Introduction*. London: Routledge, 1996.

Carrol, Noel. "A Select View of Earthlings: Ping Chong" *The Drama Review* 27.1 (Spring 1983): 72–81.

Carroll, Dennis. "Hawai'i's 'local' theatre with Hawai'i plays." *The Drama Review* 44.2 (Summer 2000): 123–152.

Chambers, Jonathan. "Staging the Dispossessed: Naomi Iizuka's Polaroid Stories." In *Theatre at the Margins: The Political, the Popular, the Personal, the Profane*. Ed. John W. Frick. Tuscaloosa, AL: University of Alabama Press, 2000.

Champagne, Lenora. "Introduction" In *Out from Under: Texts by Women Performance Artists*. Ed. Lenora Champagne. New York City: Theatre Communications Group, 1990. ix–xiv.

Chan, Anthony B. *Perpetually Cool: The Many Lives of Anna May Wong, 1905–1961*. Lanham, MD: Scarecrow, 2003.

Chan, Joanna Wan-Ying. "*The Four Seas Players: Toward an Alternative Form of Chinese Theatre; A Case Study of a Community Theatre in Chinatown, New York City.*" PhD dissertation Columbia University, 1977.

Chan, Sucheng. *Asian Americans: An Interpretive History*. New York: Twayne Publishers, 1991.

Chang, Tisa. "Program Note for *Return of the Phoenix*." 1973. Author's Personal collection.

   "Race is Crucial in Some Stage Roles." *USA Today* Aug. 17, 1990: A12.

Chang, Williamson B. C. "M. Butterfly: Passivity, Deviousness, and the Invisibility of the Asian-American Male." In *Bearing Dreams, Shaping Vision: Asian Pacific American Perspectives*. Ed. Linda A. Revilla. Pullman: Washington State University Press, 1993. 181–184.

Chaudhuri, Una. "The Future of the Hyphen: Interculturalism, Textuality, and the Difference Within." In *Interculturalism and Performance: Writings from PAJ*. Eds. Bonnie Marranca and Gautam Dasgupta. New York: PAJ Publications, 1991. 192–207.

Chen, Tina. "Betrayed into Motion: The Seduction of Narrative Desire in *M. Butterfly*." *Hitting Critical Mass: A Journal of Asian American Cultural Criticism* 1.2 (Spring 1994): 129–154.

Cheng, Meiling. "Highways, L. A.: Multiple Communities in a Heterolocus." *Theatre Journal* 53 (2001): 429–454.

Cheung, Angelica. "Playing the Asian Role." *Asia Times* Mar 14, 1997.

Cheung, King-Kok. *An Interethnic Companion to Asian American Literature*. New York: Cambridge University Press, 1997.

Cheung, Martha P. Y. and Jane C. C. Lai, eds. *An Oxford Anthology of Chinese Contemporary Drama*. New York Oxford University Press, 1997.

Chew, Ron, ed. *Reflections of Seattle's Chinese Americans: The First 100 Years*. Seattle: University of Washington Press, 1994.

Chin, Daryl. "Interculturalism, Postmodernism, Pluralism." In *Interculturalism and Performance: Writings from PAJ*. Eds. Bonnie Marranca and Gautam Dasgupta. New York: PAJ Publications, 1991. 83–95.

"Winston Tong: Three Solo Pieces." *Bridge: An Asian American Perspective* 6.2 (1978): 54–56.

Chin, Frank, Jeffery Paul Chan, Lawson Fusao Inada, Shawn Hsu Wong, eds. *Aiiieeee!: An Anthology of Asian-American Writers*. Washington, DC: Howard University Press, 1974.

eds. *The Big Aiiieeeee!: An Anthology of Chinese and Japanese American Literature*. New York: Meridian, 1991.

Chin, Frank. "Don't Pen Us Up in Chinatown." *New York Times* Oct. 8, 1972. Sec. 2: 1.

"Interview: Ronald Winters." *Amerasia Journal* 2.1 (Fall 1973): 1–19.

"Letter to Randall Duk Kim." (1973). The Asian American Theater Company Archive, California Ethnic and Multicultural Archives at the Special Collections Library, University of California, Santa Barbara.

"Prospectus." (1973). The Asian American Theater Company Archive, California Ethnic and Multicultural Archives at the Special Collections Library, University of California, Santa Barbara.

"Letter to Maxine Hong Kingston." (1976). The Asian American Theater Company Archive, California Ethnic and Multicultural Archives at the Special Collections Library, University of California, Santa Barbara.

"Letter to Michael Kirby." (1976). The Asian American Theater Company Archive, California Ethnic and Multicultural Archives at the Special Collections Library, University of California, Santa Barbara.

"Letter to the Board of Directors." (Nov. 16, 1976). The Asian American Theater Company Archive, California Ethnic and Multicultural Archives at the Special Collections Library, University of California, Santa Barbara.

"Where I'm Coming From." *Bridge: An Asian American Perspective* 4.3 (1976): 28–29.

"I'm Not Chinese. I'm a Chinaman." *City* 8.62 (Apr. 2–15, 1977): 63–65.

"This is not an Autobiography." *Genre* 18.2 (Summer 1985): 109–30.

"From the Chinaman *Year of the Dragon* to the Fake *Year of the Dragon*." *Quilt: A Multicultural Literary Journal* 5 (1986): 58–71.

"Chin on Hwang." *KONCH* (Mar 14, 2001). www.ishmaelreedpub.com/articles/chin.html.

Chin, Soo-Young, Peter X. Feng, and Josephine Lee. "Asian American Cultural Production." *Journal of Asian American Studies* 3.3 (2000): 269–282.

Ching, Frank. "Asian American Actors Fight for Jobs and Image." *New York Times* June 3, 1973: 65.

Choi, Sung Hee. "Performing the Other: Asians on the New York Stage Before 1970." PhD dissertation University of Maryland, 1999.

"Performing the Other: Asian American Actors on Broadway in the 1950s." Conference paper. American Society for Theatre Research Annual Meeting, November, 1998, Washington, DC

Chong, Ping. "Notes for *Mumblings & Digressions*: Some Thoughts on Being an Artist, Being an American, Being a Witness." MELUS 16.3 (1989–90): 58–68.

Chu, Kandice and Karen Shimakawa, eds. *Orientations: Mapping Studies in the Asian Diaspora*. Durham: Duke University Press, 2001.

Classon, Hsiu-chen Lin. "*A Different Kind of Asian American: Negotiating and Redefining Asian/American in Theater Mu*." PhD dissertation. Northwestern University, 2000.

"Looking for Peter Hyun: A Korean American Director in New York in the 1930s." Unpublished paper.

Clément, Catherine. *Opera, Or the Undoing of Women*. Trans. Betsy Wing. Minneapolis: University of Minnesota Press, 1988.

Cody, Gabrielle. "David Hwang's *M. Butterfly*: Perpetuating the Misogynist Myth." *Theater* 20.2 (Spring 1989): 24–27.

Coleman, Sandy "Theater Class Acts Out Against Stereotypes," *The Boston Globe* Mar. 5, 2002: B11.

Cooperman, Robert Russell. "Across the Boundaries of Cultural Identity: An Interview with David Henry Hwang." In *Staging Difference*. Ed. Marc Maufort. New York: Peter Lang, 1995. 365–373.

"New Theatrical Statements: Asian-Western Mergers in the Early Plays of David Henry Hwang." In *Staging Difference: Cultural Pluralism in American Theatre and Drama*. Ed. Marc Maufort. New York: Peter Lang, 1995. 201–213.

"Nisei Theater: History, Context, and Perspective (Japanese-Americans)." PhD dissertation Ohio State University, 1996.

"The Americanization of Americans: The Phenomenon of Nisei Internment Camp Theater." In *Re/Collecting Early Asian America: Essays in Cultural History*. Eds. Josephine Lee, Imogene L. Lim and Yuko Matsukawa. Philadelphia: Temple University Press, 2002. 326–339.

Corliss, Richard. "Will Broadway Miss Saigon?" *Time* Aug. 20, 1990: 75.

Cuddy, Philip Ahn. "Philip Ahn: Born in America." The Philip Ahn Admiration Society. www.philipahn.com/pacessay.html.

Davis, Robert Murray. "West meets East: A Conversation with Frank Chin." *Amerasia Journal* 24.1 (Spring 1998): 87–103.

Deeney, John J. "Of Monkeys and Butterflies: Transformations in M. H. Kingston's *Tripmaster Monkeys* and D. H. Hwang's *M. Butterfly*. MELUS 18.4 (1991): 21.

Degabriele, Maria. "From *Madame Butterfly* to *Miss Saigon*: One Hundred Years of Popular Orientalism." *Critical Arts* 10.2 (1996): 105–118.

de Jesús, Melinda L. "Jude Narita." In *Asian American Playwrights: A Bio-Bibliographical Critical Sourcebook*. Ed. Miles Xian Liu. Westport, CT: Greenwood Press, 2002. 245–250.

Dominguez, Robert. "*Flower Drum* Beats a Retreat." *Daily News* Feb 25, 2003: 42.
Elin Diamond. "Introduction." *Performance and Cultural Politics*. Ed. Elin Diamond.
    London: Routledge, 1996. 1–12.
DiGaetani, John L. *A Search for a Postmodern Theater: Interviews with Contemporary
    Playwrights*. New York: Greenwood, 1991.
Dillon, John. "Three Places in Asia: Ping Chong Delves into the East-West Collisions
    of History." *American Theatre* 13.3 (March 1996): 18–22.
Dong, Lorraine and Arthur Dong. "Chinese American Nightclubs: A Brief History."
    Introductory Pamphlet. In *Forbidden City U.S.A.* (DVD). Collector's Edition.
    Deep Focus Productions Inc., 2002.
Dong, Lorraine. "The Forbidden City Legacy and Its Chinese American Woman."
    Chinese America: History and Perspectives. San Francisco: Chinese Historical
    Society of America, 1992. 126–148.
Dreams and Promises: Northwest Asian American Theatre 20th Anniversary. Seattle, WA:
    Northwest Asian American Theater Company, 1992.
Du, Wenwei. "From *M. Butterfly* to *Madame Butterfly*: A Retrospective View of the
    Chinese Presence on Broadway." PhD dissertation Washington University, 1992.
Drukman, Steven. "Chay Yew: Interview." *American Theatre* 12 (Nov. 1995): 58–60.
East West Players. Meeting Minutes (Mar. 22, 1971). The East West Players Archive,
    Arts Library Special Collections, University of California, Los Angeles.
    Meeting Minutes (Apr. 21, 1971). The East West Players Archive, Arts Library
    Special Collections, University of California, Los Angeles.
Elam, Harry J. *Taking It to the Streets: The Social Protest Theater of Luis Valdez and
    Amiri Baraka*. Ann Arbor: The University of Michigan Press, 1997.
Elena, Tony Santa. "Life and Times of the AATC." *Bridge: An Asian American
    Perspective* 2.5 (1973): 22–24.
Elliott, Cheryle. American Conservatory Theater Press Release (May 3, 1973). The
    Asian American Theater Company Archive, California Ethnic and Multicultural
    Archives at the Special Collections Library, University of California, Santa
    Barbara.
Eng, Alvin. "'Some Place to be Somebody': La MaMa's Ellen Stewart." In *The Color of
    Theater: Race, Culture, and Contemporary Performance*. Eds. Roberta Uno and
    Lucy Mae San Pablo Buns. New York: Continuum, 2002. 134–143.
Eng, David L. "In the Shadows of a Diva: Committing Homosexuality in David
    Henry Hwang's *M. Butterfly*." *Amerasia Journal* 20.1 (1994): 93–116.
    Racial Castration: Managing Masculinity in Asian America. Durham: Duke Univer-
    sity Press, 2001.
Eng, David L. and Alice Y. Hom, eds. *Q & A: Queer in Asian America*. Philadelphia:
    Temple University Press, 1998.
Espiritu, Yen Le. *Asian Panethnicity: Bridging Institutions and Identities*. Philadelphia:
    Temple University Press, 1992.
Eustis, Oskar. "Writing for New America." *American Theatre* 11.8(1994): 30–31, 111–112.
Farmer, Martha. "East Meets West at the Asian-American Theater Workshop."
    Performing Arts Magazine (March 1980): 54–60.
Farquhar, Judith and Mary L. Doi. "Bruce Lee vs. Fu Manchu: Kung Fu Films and
    Asian American Stereotypes in America." *Bridge: An Asian American Perspective*
    6.3 (1978): 23–40.

Fergusson, Russell, Martha Gever, Trinh T. Minha-la, Cornel West, eds. *Out There: Marginalization and Contemporary Cultures.* Cambridge, MA: Massachussets Institute of Technology Press, 1990.

Fischer-Lichte, Erika. *The Show and the Gaze of Theatre: A European Perspective.* Iowa City: University of Iowa Press, 1997.

Floden, Roberta. "*Gate* Opens Hearts." *Marin Independent Journal* Apr. 9, 1994.

Foley, F. Kathleen. "Sacred Naked Nature Girls Offer a Quest for *Home.*" *Los Angeles Times* Aug. 31, 1996. Calendar sec.: F3.

Fong, Timothy P. *The Contemporary Asian American Experience: Beyond the Model Minority.* New Jersey: Prentice Hall, 1998.

Forte, Jeanie. "Women's Performance Art: Feminism and Postmodernism." *Theatre Journal* 40 (1988): 217–235.

Four Seas Players. "About Four Seas Players." www.4seas.org/about.html.

Fraser, C. Gerald. "Asian-American Actors Get Pledge From Papp." *New York Times* Feb. 22, 1979: C26.

Gates, Anita. "3 Aliens Visit Earth: Take Us to Your Culture." *New York Times* Jan. 15, 1998: E5.

Gates, Henry Louis. *The Signifying Monkey.* New York: Oxford University Press, 1988.

Geis, Deborah. *Postmodern Theatric[k]s: Monologue in Contemporary American Drama.* Ann Arbor: University of Michigan Press, 1993.

Gentile, John S. *Cast of One: One-Person Shows from the Chautauqua Platform to the Broadway Stage.* Urbana and Chicago: University of Illinois Press, 1989.

Gerard, Jeremy. "David Hwang: Riding on the Hyphen." *New York Times Magazine* 46.11 (1988): 44–45.

Ghymn, Esther Mikyung. *The Shapes and Styles of Asian American Prose Fiction.* New York: D. Lang, 1992.

Glick, Carl. *Three Times I Bow.* New York: Whittlesey House, 1943.

Gray, Spalding. "About Three Places in Rhode Island." *The Drama Review* 23 (1979): 33–34.

Gussow, Mel. "Pan-Asian Troupe Visits La Mama." *New York Times* Oct. 14, 1977. Sec. 3: 5.

"Storm of Complex Currents." *New York Times* Nov. 10, 1977. Sec. 3: 17.

"*Three Solo Pieces* by Winston Tong." *New York Times* May. 10, 1978: C22.

"Nisei *Music Lessons.*" *New York Times* May 16, 1980: C5.

"Surrealist *Bullet Headed Birds. New York Times* Nov. 25, 1981: C24.

"A Stage for All the World of Asian-Americans." *New York Times* Apr. 22, 1997: C16.

"Off- and Off-Off Broadway." In *The Cambridge History of American Theatre.* 3 vols. Eds. Don B. Wilmeth and Christopher Bigsby. London: Cambridge University Press. 2000. 196–223. Vol. 3.

Haedicke, Susan. "Suspended between Two Worlds": Interculturalism and the Rehearsal Process for Horizons Theater's Production of Velina Hasu Houston's *Tea. Theatre Topics* 4.1 (March 1994): 89–103.

Hagedorn, Jessica. "On Theater and Performance." *MELUS* 16.3 (Fall 1989): 13–15.

"Asian Women in Film: No Joy, No Luck." *Ms. Magazine* (January/February 1994) 74–79.

"Preface." *The East West Quartet.* Ping Chong. New York: Theatre Communications Group, 2004. xi–xiv.

Hall, Gina. "The Winston Tong Interview." Nov. 4, 1996. http://web.archive.org/web/20040506100043/http://www.fadmag.com/items/tong/tong.html.

Hamamoto, Darrell Y. *Monitored Peril: Asian Americans and the Politics of TV Representation.* Minneapolis: University of Minnesota Press, 1994.

Haseltine, Patricia. *East and Southeast Asian Material Culture in North America: Collections, Historical Sites, and Festivals.* New York: Greenwood Press, 1989.

Hausner, Edward "Overtures Opens Door for Orientals." *New York Times* Mar. 2, 1976: 24.

Hayakawa, Sessue. *Zen Showed Me the Way.* Ed. Croswell Bowen. Indianapolis: The Bobbs-Merrill Company, Inc., 1960.

Hayashi, Eric. "Statements by Producers." *MELUS* 16.3 (Fall 1989): 39–41.

Henry, William A. "When East and West Collide: David Henry Hwang Proves Bedfellows Make Strange Politics in *M. Butterfly*, a Surprise Stage Success in Three Continents." *Time* Aug. 14, 1989: 62–64.

"Here's Where I Belong." *Variety* Mar. 6, 1968: 72–3.

Heung, Marina. "The Family Romance of Orientalism: From *Madame Butterfly* to *Indochine*." In *Forming and Reforming Identity.* Eds. Carol Siegel and Ann Kibbey. New York: New York University Press, 1995. 223–256.

Higham, John. "Multiculturalism and Universalism: A History and Critique." *American Quarterly* 45.2 (1993): 195–219.

Hodges, Graham Russell Gao. *Anna May Wong: From Laundryman's Daughter to Hollywood Legend.* New York: Palgrave Macmillan, 2005.

Hong, Terry. "Heads Up." *A. Magazine: Inside Asian America* (March 1994): 57.

"Theatre." *Asian American Almanac.* Detroit: Gale Research, Inc., 1995. 573–593.

"Tongue Untied." *A. Magazine: Inside Asian America* (September 1995): 62.

"Men at Play." *A. Magazine: Inside Asian America* (May/June 1997): 82–83.

"Time Traveler." *A. Magazine: Inside Asian America* (April/May 1998): 78–9.

Horn, Barbara Lee. *Ellen Stewart and La Mama: A Bio-Bibliography.* Westport, CT: Greenwood Press, 1993.

Horn, Miriam. "The Mesmerizing Power of Racial Myths." *U.S. News & World Report* 104.12 (1988): 52–53.

Houn, Fred Wei-Han. "An ABC from NYC: 'Charlie' Chin, Asian-American Singer and Songwriter." *East Wind* 5.1 (Spring/Summer 1986): 4–8.

Houston, Velina Hasu. "Introduction." *The Politics of Life: Four Plays by Asian American Women.* Philadelphia: Temple University Press, 1993. 1–3.

"Uphill Fight for Asian American Plays." *Los Angeles Times* Sep. 15, 1997: 3.

Howard, Beth. "Ping Chong." *Theatre Crafts* 24 (March 1990): 26–31.

Huerta, Jorge A. *Chicano Theater: Themes and Forms.* Ypsilanti, Michigan: Bilingual Press, 1982.

Chicano Drama: Performance, Society and Myth. Cambridge: Cambridge University Press, 2001.

Hurwitt, Robert. "Hidden History of the Mission: An Enchanting *17 Reasons*." *San Francisco Chronicle* Oct. 30, 2002: D1.

"Asian American Theater Enters a Hopeful Stage." *San Francisco Chronicle* Nov. 16, 2004: D1.

Hwang, David Henry. "Are Movies Ready for Real Orientals?" *New York Times* Aug. 11, 1985. Sec. 2: 1.

"Evolving a Multicultural Tradition." *MELUS* 16.3 (Fall 1989): 16–19.

"The Myth of Immutable Cultural Identity." In *Asian American Drama: 9 Plays from the Multiethnic Landscape*. Ed. Brian Nelson. New York: Applause, 1997. vii-viii.

"Worlds Apart" *American Theatre* 17.1 (January 2000): 50–56.

Hyun, Peter. *In the New World: The Making of a Korean American*. Honolulu: University of Hawaii Press, 1995.

Ichioka, Yuji, Yasuo Sakata, Nobuya Tsuchida, and Eri Yasuhara. *A Buried Past: An Annotated Bibliography of the Japanese American Research Project*. Berkeley: University of California Press, 1974.

Ito, Robert B. "Philip Kan Gotanda." In *Words Matter: Conversations with Asian American Writers*. Ed. King-Kok Cheung. Honolulu: University of Hawai'i Press, 2000. 173–185.

Jan Mohamed, Abdul R. and David Lloyd. *The Nature and Context of Minority Discourse*. Oxford: Oxford University Press, 1990.

Kanazawa, Tooru. "Issei on Broadway." *Scene* 5.10 (February 1954): 15–17.

Kaplan, Randy Barbara. "Lane Nishikawa." In *Asian American Playwrights: A Bio-Bibliographical Critical Sourcebook*. Ed. Miles Xian Liu. Westport, CT: Greenwood Press, 2002. 251–262.

Kelly, Kevin. "*M. Butterfly, Miss Saigon* and Mr. Hwang." *Boston Globe* Sep 2, 1990: B91.

Kersey, Oona. "Theater Mu." Nov. 10, 2000. www.performink.com/Archives/theatre-profiles/2000/TheatreMuMinneapolis.html.

Kershaw, Baz. *The Politics of Performance: Radical Theatre as Cultural Intervention*. London: Routledge, 1992.

Kim, Elaine H. *Asian American Literature: An Introduction to the Writings and Their Social Context*. Philadelphia: Temple University Press, 1982.

Kim, Esther S. "David Henry Hwang." In *Asian American Playwrights: A Bio-Bibliographical Critical Sourcebook*. Ed. Miles Xian Liu. Westport, CT: Greenwood Press, 2002. 126–144.

Kondo, Dorinne. "*M. Butterfly*: Orientalism, Gender, and a Critique of Essentialist Identity." *Cultural Critique* 16 (Fall 1990): 5–29.

"The Narrative Production of 'Home,' Community, and Political Identity in Asian American Theater." In *Displacement, Diaspora, and Geographies of Identity*. Eds. Smadar Lavie and Ted Swedenburg. Durham: Duke University Press, 1996.

About Face: Performing Race in Fashion and Theater. New York: Routledge, 1997.

"Introduction." In *Asian American Drama: 9 Plays from the Multiethnic Landscape*. Ed. Brian Nelson. New York: Applause, 1997. ix-xi.

Kong, Foong Ling. "Pulling the Wings off Butterfly." *Southern Review: Literary and Interdisciplinary Essays* 27.4 (December 1994): 418–431.

Krasner, David. *Resistance, Parody, and Double Consciousness: African American Theatre, 1895–1910*. New York: St. Martin's Press, 1997.

Krieger, Lois L. "*Miss Saigon* and Missed Opportunity: Artistic Freedom, Employment Discrimination, and Casting for Cultural Identity in the Theater." *Syracuse Law Review* 43 (Summer 1992): 839–66.

Kriegsman, Alan M. "Ping Chong's Wild, Weighty *Kind Ness*." *Washington Post* May 18, 1991: G7.

Kubota, Glenn. "Internal Memo from Board of Directors." (Mar. 24, 1974). The Asian American Theater Company Archive, California Ethnic and Multicultural Archives at the Special Collections Library, University of California, Santa Barbara.

Kurahashi, Yuko. *Asian American Culture on Stage: The History of the East West Players.* New York: Garland Publishing, Inc., 1999.

Kwan, SanSan. "Dan Kwong." In *Asian American Playwrights: A Bio-Bibliographical Critical Sourcebook.* Ed. Miles Xian Liu. Westport, CT: Greenwood Press, 2002. 162–165.

Kwong, Dan. "Counterpunch: Ethnic Images, Issues and *Asian Men.*" *Los Angeles Times* Sept 11, 1995. Calendar sec.: F3.

Lafferty, Mera Moore. "From Islamabad to New York City: Bina Sharif's Spiritual Politics." *Text & Presentation* 23 (2002): 57–69.

Lee, Anthony W. "The Forbidden City." *Picturing Chinatown: Art and Orientalism in San Francisco.* Berkeley: University of California Press, 2001. 237–285.

Lee, Joanne Faung Jean. *Asian American Actors: Oral Histories from Stage, Screen, and Television.* Jefferson, NC: McFarland. 2001.

Lee, Josephine. *Performing Asian America: Race and Ethnicity on the Contemporary Stage.* Philadelphia: Temple University Press, 1997.

"Between Immigration and Hyphenation: The Problems of Theorizing Asian American Theater." *Journal of Dramatic Theory and Criticism* 13.1 (Fall 1998): 44–69.

"Speaking a Language That We Both Understand": Reconciling Feminism and Cultural Nationalism in Asian American Theatre. In *Performing America: Cultural Nationalism in American Theatre.* Ed. Jeffry D. Mason and J. Ellen Gainor. Ann Arbor: The University of Michigan Press, 1999. 139–159

"Bodies, Revolutions, and Magic: Cultural Nationalism and Racial Fetishism." *Modern Drama* 44.1 (2001): 72–90.

"Asian Americans in Progress: *College Plays 1937–1955.*" In *Re/Collecting Early Asian America: Essays in Cultural History.* Eds. Josephine Lee, Imogene L. Lim and Yuko Matsukawa. Philadelphia: Temple University Press, 2002. 307–325.

Lee, Robert G. *Orientals: Asian Americans in Popular Culture.* Philadelphia: Temple University Press, 1999.

Leong, Russell, ed. *Moving the Image: Independent Asian Pacific American Media Arts.* Los Angeles: University of California, Los Angeles, Asian American Studies Center, 1991.

Lewis, Ferdinand. "Amy Hill: A Double Agent with Personalities to Spare." *American Theatre* 11.1 (January 1994): 50–51.

Lim, Shirley Geok-Lim and Amy Ling. *Reading the Literatures of Asian America.* Philadelphia: Temple University Press, 1992.

Lin, Benjamin. "Adhesive Tape Orientals: The Use of Tape by White Actors to Portray Asians is Odious." *Bridge: An Asian American Perspective* 2.3 (February 1973): 7–10.

Ling, Jinqi. *Narrating Nationalism: Ideology and Form in Asian American Literature.* New York: Oxford University Press, 1998. 79–109.

Lipson, Karin. "Over 200 Protest Race Stereotypes in *Miss Saigon*: Firstnighters Pass by Pickets." *Newsday* Apr 12, 1991: 4.

Liu, Miles Xian, ed. *Asian American Playwrights: A Bio-Bibliographical Critical Sourcebook.* Westport, CT: Greenwood Press, 2002.

Lott, Eric. *Love & Theft: Blackface Minstrelsy and the American Working Class*. New York: Oxford University Press, 1993.

Louie, Steve and Glenn Omatsu, eds. *Asian Americans: The Movement and the Moment*. Los Angeles: University of California, Los Angeles, Asian American Studies Center Press, 2001.

Lowe, Lisa. *Immigrant Acts: On Asian American Cultural Politics*. Durham and London: Duke University Press, 1996.

Lyman, Stanford. "Strangers in the City: the Chinese in the Urban Frontier." In *Roots: An Asian American Reader*. Eds. Amy Tachiki, Eddie Wong, and Franklin Odo. Los Angeles: University of California, Los Angeles, Asian American Studies Center, 1971.

Lyons, Bonnie. "Making His Muscles Work for Himself: An Interview with David Henry Hwang." *The Literary Review* 42.2 (Winter 1999): 230–44.

Ma, Sheng-Mei. *The Deathly Embrace: Orientalism and Asian American Identity*. Minneapolis: University of Minnesota Press, 2000.

Machida, Margo, Vishakha N. Desai, and John Kuo Wei Tchen, eds. *Asia/America: Identities in Contemporary Asian American Art*. New York: Asia Society Galleries New Press, 1994.

Magwilli, Dom. "East West – A Personal View." *Bridge: Asian American Perspective* 5.2 (1977): 18–20.

Maher, Mary Z. "Randall Duk Kim: Sir, a Whole History." *Modern Hamlet and Their Soliloquies*. Iowa City: Iowa University Press, 1992. 153–174.

Maira, Sunaina Marr. *Desis in the House: Indian American Youth Culture in New York City*. Philadelphia: Temple University Press, 2002.

Mako. Meeting Minutes. (Mar 22, 1971). *The East West Players Archive, Arts Library Special Collections*, University of California, Los Angeles.

Mark, Diane. "Interview with Noboku Miyamoto." *Bridge: Asian American Perspective* 10.1 (1985): 16–25.

Marranca, Bonnie and Gautam Dasgupta. *Interculturalism and Performance: Writings from Performance Arts Journal*. New York: Performing Arts Journal, 1991.

Mason, Jeffrey D. and Ellen Gainor, eds. *Performing America: Cultural Nationalism in American Theater*. Ann Arbor: University of Michigan Press, 1999.

Matthews, Brander. "Introduction." *The Yellow Jacket: A Chinese Play Done in a Chinese Manner*. George Hazelton and Joseph Henry Benrimo. Indianapolis: The Bobbs-Merrill Company Publishers, 1913.

Maufort, Marc, ed. *Staging Difference: Cultural Pluralism in American Theatre and Drama*. New York: Peter Lang, 1995.

Mazumdar, Sucheta. "Asian American Studies and Asian Studies: Rethinking Roots." In *Asian Americans: Comparative and Global Perspectives* Eds. Shirley Hune, Hyung-Chan Kim, Stephen Sfugita, and Amy Ling. Pullman: Washington State University Press, 1991. 29–44.

McCulloh, T. H. "Grief in *Asian Men* Occurs by Occident." *Los Angeles Times* Mar. 13, 1995. Calendar sec.: F2.

McDonald, Dorothy Ritsuko. "Introduction" *The Chickencoop Chinaman and The Year of the Dragon: Two Plays by Frank Chin*. Seattle: University of Washington Press, 1981. ix-xxix.

McKinley, Jesse. "Walkout Closes a Struggling Revival Early." *The New York Times* Mar. 10, 2003: B4.

Milstein, Gilbert. "World of France Nuyen." *New York Times Magazine* Oct. 5, 1958: 12.

Minow, Martha. "From Class Actions to *Miss Saigon*: The Concept of Representation in the Law." In *Representing Women: Law, Literature, and Feminism* Ed. Susan S. Heinzelman and Zipporah Wiseman. Durham: Duke University Press, 1994. 8–43.

"*Miss Saigon* Cancelled." Advertisement. *New York Times* Aug. 9, 1990: C18.

Mitchell, David T. "Body Solitaire: The Singular Subject of Disability Autobiography." *American Quarterly* 52.2 (2000): 311–315.

Mnouchkine, Ariane. "The Theatre is Oriental." In *The Intercultural Performance Reader*. Ed. Patrice Pavis. London: Routledge, 1996.

Momii, Staci J. and Sumi Mashita. "Cold Tofu." *Tozai Times* (March 1993): 1.

Monji, Jana J. "All *Roads* Lead Home: Gary San Angel and Fellow Performance Artists Ponder Asian American Identity." *Los Angeles Times* Jul. 6, 2000. Calendar sec.: F38.

"*Heard*: High-Energy Look at Korean American Experience," *Los Angeles Times* Sep. 25, 1996: F2.

Moon, Krystyn R. *Yellowface: Creating the Chinese in American Poplar Music and Performance, 1850s–1920s*. New Brunswick, NJ: Rutgers University Press, 2005.

Moy, James S. "David Henry Hwang's *M.Butterfly* and Philip Kan Gotanda's *Yankee Dawg You Die*: Repositioning Chinese American Marginality on the American Stage." *Theatre Journal* 42.1 (March 1990): 48–56.

"The Anthropological Gaze and the Touristic Siting of Chinese America." *Modern Drama* 35.1 (1992): 81–89.

"The Death of Asia on the American Field of Representation." *Reading the Literatures of Asian America*. Ed. Shirley Geok-lin Lim and Amy Lin. Philadelphia: Temple University Press, 1992: 349–458

Marginal Sights: Staging Chinese in America. Iowa City: University of Iowa Press, 1993.

"Asian American Visibility: Touring Fierce Racial Geographies." In *Staging Difference: Cultural Pluralism in American Theatre and Drama*. Ed. Marc Maufort. New York: Peter Lang, 1995. 191–200.

Nakao, Annie. "Asian Americans Funny?" *San Francisco Examiner* Jul. 13, 1995: C.

National Archives and Records Administration. "A New Deal for the Arts." www.archives.gov/exhibit_hall/new_deal_for_the_arts/activist_arts2.html.

Neely, Kent. "Ping Chong's Theatre of Simultaneous Consciousness." *Journal of Dramatic Theory and Criticism* 6.2 (Spring 1992):121–135.

Nguyen, Viet Thanh. *Race and Resistance: Literature and Politics in Asian America*. Oxford: Oxford University Press, 2002.

Niiya, Brian, ed. *Japanese American History: An A-to-Z Reference from 1868 to the Present*. New York: Facts on File, 1993.

Northwest Asian American Theater. "Proposal." 1974.

Novick, Julius. "*The Chickencoop Chinaman*. No Cheers for the *Chinaman*." *New York Times* June 18, 1972. Sec. 2: 3.

Oh, Soon-Tek. Letter. Dec. 15, 1967. The East West Players Archive, Arts Library Special Collections, University of California, Los Angeles.

Okihiro, Gary Y. *Margins and Mainstreams: Asians in American History and Culture.* Seattle: University of Washington, 1994.
Privileging Positions: The Sites of Asian American Studies. Pullman, WA: Washington State University Press, 1995.
Oliver, Edith. "Off Broadway." *New Yorker* June 24, 1972: 46.
Omatsu, Glenn. "The *Four Prisons* and the Movements of Liberation: Asian American Activism from the 1960s to the 1970s." In *Contemporary Asian America: A Multidisciplinary Reader.* Eds. Min Zhou and James V. Gatewood. New York: New York University Press, 2000. 80–113.
Omi, Michael. "Introduction." *Fish Head Soup and Other Plays.* By Philip Kan Gotanda. Seattle: University of Washington Press, 1991. i–xxvi.
Omi, Michael and Howard Winant. *Racial Formation in the U.S.: From the 1960s to the 1990s.* New York: Routledge, 1994.
Oriental Actors of America. "Press Release." May 22, 1968. 1–2. The "Oriental Actors of America" clipping file. The Billy Rose Theatre Collection of The New York Public Library.
Osborn, William P. "A *MELUS* Interview: Wakako Yamauchi." *MELUS* 23.2 (1998): 101.
Oyama, David. "Randall 'Duk' Kim, Actor." *Bridge: An Asian American Perspective* 3.4 (1975): 29–30, 39.
"The New York Scene: Varied But Clear." *Bridge: An Asian American Perspective* 5.2 (1977): 11–17.
"Asian American Theater – On the Road to Xanadu." *Bridge: An Asian American Perspective* 5.2 (1977): 4–6.
"Asian-Americans Take Center Stage at the Public." *New York Times* Apr. 27, 1980. Sec. 2: 3.
Pacetta, Albert. "Asians for Asian Roles." *Bridge: An Asian American Perspective* 2.3 (1973): 3.
Paik, Irvin. "The East West Players: The First Ten Years are the Hardest." *Bridge: An Asian American Perspective* 5.2 (1977): 14–17.
Palumbo-Liu, David. *Asian/American: Historical Crossings of a Racial Frontier.* Stanford: Stanford University Press, 1999.
Pan Asian Repertory Theater. "Program Note for *Thunderstorm.*" 1977. Author's Personal collection.
Pang, Cecilia and Elizabeth Wong. "The *Miss Saigon* Diaries." *American Theatre* (Dec 1990): 40–43.
Pao, Angela. "Recasting Race: Casting Practices and Racial Formation." *Theatre Survey* 41.2 (Nov 2000): 1–21.
"The Eye of the Storm: Gender, Genre and Cross-Casting in *Miss Saigon.*" *Text and Performance Quarterly* 12 (1992): 21–39.
"The Critic and the Butterfly: Sociocultural Contexts and the Reception of David Henry Hwang's *M. Butterfly.*" *Amerasia Journal* 18.3 (1992): 1–16.
Pavis, Patrice, ed. *The Intercultural Performance Reader.* London: Routledge, 1996.
Perry, Shauneille. "Celebrating the Tenth Anniversary of New WORLD Theater." *MELUS* 16.3 (Autumn 1989–Autumn 1990): 5–9.
Peters, Julie Stone. "Intercultural Performance, Theatre Anthropology, and the Imperialist Critique: Identities, Inheritances, and Neo-Orthodoxies." In *Imperialism*

and Theatre: Essays on World Theatre, Drama and Performance. Ed. J. Ellen Gainor. London: Routledge, 1995. 199–213.

Phelan, Peggy. "Spalding Gray's *Swimming to Cambodia*: The Article." *Critical Texts* 5 (1988): 27–30.

"Philip Ahn Dies, Portrayed Oriental Actors on TV, Film." *Washington Post* Mar. 3, 1978: C4.

Pogrebin, Robin. "For *Miss Saigon*, Light at the End." *The New York Times* Aug. 25, 2000: E1.

Postlewait, Thomas. "Historiography and the Theatrical Event: A Primer with Twelve Cruxes." *Theatre Journal* 43 (1991): 157–178.

Postlewait, Thomas and Bruce A. McConachie, eds. *Interpreting the Theatrical Past: Essays in the Historiography of Performance.* Iowa City: University of Iowa Press, 1989.

Pottlitzer, Joanne. *Hispanic Theater in the United States and Puerto Rico.* New York: Ford Foundation, 1988.

Ramírez, Elizabeth C. *Chicanas/Latinas in American Theatre: A History of Performance.* Bloomington: Indiana University Press, 2000.

Raymond, Gerard. "Having Their Say" *Village Voice* Apr. 25, 1995: 97.

Remen, Kathryn. "The Theatre of Punishment: David Henry Hwang's *M. Butterfly* and Michel Foucault's *Discipline and Punish.*" *Modern Drama* 37.3 (1994): 391–400.

Revilla, Linda A. *Bearing Dreams, Shaping Visions: Asian Pacific American Perspectives.* Pullman, WA: Washington State University Press, 1993.

Rich, Frank. "*Miss Saigon* Arrives, From the Old School." *The New York Times* Apr. 12, 1991: C1.

"*FOB* Rites of Immigrant Passage." *The New York Times* June 10, 1980: C6.

Rodecape, Lois. "Celestial Drama in the Golden Hills: The Chinese Theatre in California, 1849–1869." *California Historical Society Quarterly* 23.2 (1944): 97–116.

Rodgers, Richard. *Musical Stage.* New York: Random House, 1975.

Román, David. "Los Angeles Intersections: Chay Yew." In *The Color of Theater: Race, Culture, and Contemporary Performance.* Eds. Roberta Uno and Lucy Mae San Pablo Burns. New York: Continuum, 2002. 237–252.

Rosa, Margarita. "Asian Actors Lost in a '73 *Miss Saigon* Case." *New York Times* Sept. 28, 1990: A26.

Ross, Lillian. "Meetings." *New Yorker* Mar. 22, 1976: 24–27.

Rothstein, Mervyn. "Equity Will Reconsider *Miss Saigon* Decision." *The New York Times* Aug. 10, 1990: C3.

"Producer Cancels *Miss Saigon*; 140 Members Challenge Equity." *The New York Times* Aug. 9, 1990: C15.

"Roy Pannell Talks to Composer and Lyricist Stephen Sondheim." *The Stage and Television Today* (London) Nov. 27, 1975: 10.

Said, Edward. *Orientalism.* New York: Pantheon Books, 1978.

Culture and Imperialism. New York: Knopf (Random House), 1993.

San, Katy. "The Asian American Repertory Theater." *Bridge: An Asian American Perspective* 2.3 (1973): 24–25.

Savran, David. *Breaking the Rules: The Wooster Group.* New York: Theatre Communications Group, 1988.

"David Hwang." *In Their Own Words: Contemporary American Playwrights.* New York: Theatre Communication Group, 1988. 117–131.

Schultz, Roger. "Non-traditional Casting Update." *The Drama Review* 35.2 (1991): 7–13.

Sell, Mike. "The Black Arts Movement: Performance, Neo-Orality, and the Destruction of the "White Thing." In *African American Performance and Theater History: A Critical Reader.* Eds. Harry J. Elam and David Krasner. Oxford: Oxford University Press, 2001. 56–80.

Seller, Maxine Schwarz, ed. *Ethnic Theatre in the United States.* London: Greenwood Press, 1983.

Sengupta, Somini. "Jessica Hagedorn: Cultivating the Art of the Melange." *Nando Times* Dec. 4, 1996. www.english.uiuc.edu/maps/poets/g_l/hagedorn/about.html.

Shales, Tom. "Unlocking Doors To Those Rooms at the Top." *The Washington Post* Aug. 21, 1977: F1.

Shank, Theodore. *Beyond Boundaries: American Alternative Theatre.* Ann Arbor: The University of Michigan Press, 2002.

Shewey, Don. "A Troupe That Sought an Asian-American Role." *The New York Times* Mar. 4, 2001. Sec. 2: 7.

"Filipino Life, Seen Through a Pop Culture Prism." *The New York Times* Mar. 4, 2001. Sec. 2: 7.

Shimakawa, Karen. "Who's to Say? Or, Making Space for Gender and Ethnicity in *M. Butterfly.*" *Theatre Journal* 45.3 (1993): 349–362.

"Swallowing the Tempest: Asian American Women on Stage." *Theatre Journal* 47.3 (1995): 367–380.

"Asians in America: Millennial Approaches to Asian Pacific American Performance." *Journal of Asian American Studies* 3.3 (2000): 283–299.

"Ghost Families in Sung Rno's *Cleveland Raining.*" *Theatre Journal* 52 (2000): 381–396.

"(Re)Viewing an Asian American Diaspora: Multiculturalism, Interculturalism, and the Northwest Asian American Theater." In *Orientations: Mapping Studies in the Asian Diaspora.* Eds. Kandice Chuh and Karen Shimakawa. Durham: Duke University Press, 2001. 41–56.

National Abjection: The Asian American Body Onstage. Durham: Duke University Press, 2002.

Shiomi, R. A. "Crossing Borders: Asian North-American Theatre" *Canadian Theater Review* 56 (1988): 16–19.

Shohat, Ella. "The Struggle Over Representation: Casting, Coalition, and the Politics of Identification." In *Late Imperial Culture.* Eds. Román de la Campa, E. Ann Kaplan, and Michael Sprinker. London: Verso, 1995. 166–178.

Siegal, Nina. "Choice and Chance." *American Theatre* 13:2 (1996): 26.

Skloot, Robert. "Breaking the Butterfly: The Politics of David Henry Hwang" *Modern Drama* 33.1 (1990): 59–66.

Sollors, Werner. *Beyond Ethnicity: Consent and Descent in American Culture.* New York: Oxford University Press, 1986.

Springer, Richard. "ACT Asian-American Workshop Continues." *East-West Journal* Sep. 26, 1974.

States, Bert O. *Great Reckonings in Little Rooms: On the Phenomenology of Theater.* Berkeley: University of California Press, 1990.

Stayton, Richard. "Never More Than a Stranger: Playwright Shishir Kurup is Constantly Grappling with Identity and Roots." *Los Angeles Times* Sept 5, 1993. Calendar sec.: 9.

Suh, Mary. "The Many Sins of *Miss Saigon.*" *Ms. Magazine* (July 1990): 63.

Sun, William H. "Sustaining the Project." *The Drama Review* 38.2 (Summer 1994): 64–71.

"Power and Problems of Performance Across Ethnic Lines: An Alternative Approach to Nontraditional Casting." *The Drama Review* 44.4 (2000): 86–95.

Susman, Warren I. *Culture as History: The Transformation of American Society in the Twentieth Century.* New York: Pantheon, 1984.

Tachiki, Amy, Eddie Wong, Franklin Odo, and Buck Wong, eds. *Roots: An Asian American Reader.* A project of the University of California, Los Angeles, Asian American Studies Center. Los Angeles: The Regents of the University of California, 1971.

Tait, Simon. "No Debut for *Miss Saigon.*" *The Times* Aug. 9, 1990: 4.

Takaki, Ronald. *Strangers from a Different Shore: A History of Asian Americans.* Rev. edn. Boston: Back Bay Books, 1998.

Takami, David. *Divided Destiny: A History of Japanese Americans in Seattle.* Seattle: University of Washington Press, 1998.

Tanaka, Jennifer. "Only Connect (interview with Diana Son)." *American Theatre* 16.6 (1999): 27.

Tang, Roger. "Directory." *Asian American Theatre Revue.* http://aatrevue.com/Directory.html.

Tchen, John Kuo Wei. *New York Before Chinatown: Orientalism and the Shaping of American Culture: 1776–1882.* Baltimore: The Johns Hopkins University Press, 1999.

Texeira, Erin. "Asian Actors on Prime-Time TV are Underrepresented, Get Little Screen Time, New Study Shows." *The Associated Press* May 2, 2005. http://modeminority.com/article1019.htmls.

Theater Mu. "About Mu." www.muperformingarts.org/about.

Thompson, Rosemarie Garland. "Staring Back: Self-Representations of Disabled Performance Artists." *American Quarterly* 52.2 (2000): 334–338.

Tong, Ben. "Asian American Theater Workshop – Alive and Well in San Francisco!" *Bridge: An Asian American Perspective* 5.2 (1977): 7–10.

"A letter to Karen Seriguchi, President of the Board of Directors." Mar 19, 1978. The Asian American Theater Company Archive, California Ethnic and Multicultural Archives at the Special Collections Library, University of California, Santa Barbara.

"True Equity Now!" Advertisement. *Variety* (August 20, 1990): 82.

Tsang, Kwan-Yuk Ann. "Pan Asian Repertory Theatre: New Cultural Needs of the Asian American." MA thesis University of Washington, 1992.

Tuan, Alice. "A Glorious Rainbow Roll Call." *Los Angeles Times* June 26, 2005: E1.

Uba, George. "Jessica Tarahata Hagedorn." In *Reference Guide to American Literature.* 3rd edn. Ed. Jim Kamp and introd. Warren French, Lewis Leary, Amy Ling,

Marco Portales, and A. LaVonne Brown Ruoff. Detroit: St James Press, 1994. 373–375.

Uno, Roberta. "Preliminaries." *MELUS* 16.3 (Autumn 1989-Autumn 1990): 1–3.

"The Way of Inclusiveness." *American Theatre* 12.1 (1995): 25.

"Introduction: Asian American Theatre Awake at the Millennium." In *Bold Words: A Century of Asian American Writing*. Eds. Rajini Srikanth and Esther Y. Iwanaga. New Brunswisk: Rutgers University Press, 2001. 323–332.

"Nobuko Miyamoto." In *Asian American Playwrights: A Bio-Bibliographical Critical Sourcebook*. Ed. Miles Xian Liu. Westport, CT: Greenwood Press, 2002. 233–238.

Uno, Roberta and Lucy Mae San Pablo Burns, eds. *The Color of Theatre: Race, Culture, and Contemporary Performance*. New York: Continuum, 2002.

Usui, Masami. "Japan's Post-War Democratization: Agrarian Reform and Women's Liberation in Velina Hasu Houston's *Asa Ga Kimashita* (Morning Has Broken)" *AALA-Journal* 5 (1998): 11–25.

Vaughan, Peter. "Traditional Music, Dance Lend Strength to Plays." *Star Tribune* Oct. 15, 1994: 5E.

Vorlicky, Robert H. "Marking Change, Marking America: Contemporary Performance and Men's Autobiographical Selves." In *Performing America: Cultural Nationalism in American Theatre*. Eds. Jeffrey D. Mason and Ellen Gainor. Ann Arbor: University of Michigan Press, 1999. 193–209.

Waggoner, Susan. *Nightclub Nights: Art, Legend, and Style, 1920–1960*. New York: Rizzoli, 2001.

Weatherby, W. J. "A March on Broadway – Protesters and Rave Reviews Greeted *Miss Saigon*." *The Guardian* (London) Apr. 13, 1991: 21.

Weaver, Jane C., ed. *Sadakichi Hartmann: Critical Modernist: Collected Art Writings*. 3 vols. Berkeley: University of California Press, 1991. Vol. 1.

Wei, William. *The Asian American Movement*. Philadelphia: Temple University Press, 1993.

Weil, Martin. "20 Held in March on Japan Embassy." *Washington Post* Nov. 18, 1969: A3.

Weiner, Bernard. "Hollywood Mirrors." *San Francisco Chronicle* Nov. 13, 1978: 47.

Werner, Jessica. "Tsai Chin: No Stranger to Change." *American Theatre* 15.4 (1998): 17.

Westfall, Suzanne R. "Ping Chong's Terra In/Cognita." In *Reading the Literature of Asian America*. Eds. Shirley Geok-lin Lim and Amy Ling. Philadelphia: Temple University Press, 1992. 359–373.

White, Robert Berry. "Back in Light." *Newsweek* (Dec. 1, 1958): 53–56.

Williams, David, ed. *Peter Brook and the Mahabharata: Critical Perspectives*. London: Routledge, 1991.

Williams, Dave. *Misreading the Chinese Character: Images of the Chinese in Euro-American Drama to 1925*. New York: Peter Lang, 2000.

Williams, Jeannie. "*Miss Saigon* Gets Raves, Protesters." *USA Today* (Apr. 12, 1991): 2D.

Williams, Mance. *Black Theatre in the 1960s and 1970s: A Historical-Critical Analysis of the Movement*. Westport, CT: Greenwood Press, 1985.

Wilmeth, Don B. and Christopher Bigsby, eds. *The Cambridge History of American Theatre*. Vol. 3. London: Cambridge University Press, 2000.

Winer, Laurie. "A Collection with Much Missing." *Los Angeles Times* Aug. 31, 1997: 42.

Winn, Steven. "The Many Faces of Asian Actor on a *Mission*." *San Francisco Chronicle* Mar. 9, 1990: E10.

"Winston Tong's Solo Show is a Mystery." *The San Francisco Chronicle* Jan. 17, 1992: D13.

Witchell, Alex. "British Star Talks of Racial Harmony and Disillusionment with Equity." *The New York Times* Aug. 11, 1990. Sec. 1: 15.

Wong, Bill. "Column: Bill Wong." *Asia Week* (Aug. 24, 1990): 9.

Yellow Journalist: Dispatches from Asian America. Philadelphia: Temple University Press, 2001.

Wong, Buck. "Toward an Asian American Theatre Form." *Bridge: An Asian American Perspective* 2.5 (1973): 41–44.

Wong, Diane Yen-Mei. "Theater's New Executive Director Brings Enthusiasm, Ideas to Job." *East/West* Nov. 28, 1984: 8.

Wong, K. Scott and Sucheng Chan, eds. *Claiming America: Constructing Chinese American Identities During the Exclusion Era*. Philadelphia: Temple University Press, 1998.

Wong, Ken. "*Avocado* Sprouts from a Sansei-tional Range of Gifts." *San Francisco Examiner* June 11, 1980: C2.

Wong, Yen Lu. "Chinese American Theatre." *The Drama Review* 20.2 (1976): 13–18.

Worthen, W. B. *Modern Drama and the Rhetoric of Theatre*. Berkeley: University of California Press, 1992.

"Staging América: The Subject of History in Chicano/a Theatre." *Theatre Journal* 49 (1997): 101–120.

Yip, Randall. "Chin Quits AATW." *The San Francisco Journal* Apr. 12, 1978: 1.

Yoffee, Lisa. "Ethnic Casting Issues Get Soapbox Treatment: Beyond *Miss Saigon* at Human Rights Hearings." *American Theatre* (February 1991): 34–35.

Yoon, Cindy. "Interview with Naomi Iizuka, Playwright of *36 Views*." *AsiaSource* Mar. 29, 2002. www.asiasource.org/arts/36views.cfm.

Yoshikawa, Yoko. "The Heat is on *Miss Saigon* Coalition." In *The State of Asian American Activism and Resistance in the 1990s*. Ed. Karin Aguilar-San Juan. Boston: South End Press, 1994. 275–294.

Yung, Judy. *Unbound Feet: A Social History of Chinese Women in San Francisco*. Berkeley: University of California Press, 1995.

Zhou, Min. *Chinatown: The Socioeconomic Potential of an Urban Enclave*. Philadelphia: Temple University Press, 1992.

Zia, Helen. *Asian American Dreams: The Emergence of an American People*. New York: Farrar, Straus, and Giroux, 2001.

Zinman, Toby. "Only Connect: An Interview with the Playwright." *American Theatre* 18.3 (2001): 28.

Personal interviews

18 Mighty Mountain Warriors. Mar. 27, 1999. Los Angeles.

Abuba, Ernest. June 12, 2001. New York City.

Arcenas, Loy. July 15, 1999. San Francisco.

Ambika, Samarthya. June 5, 2001. New York City.

Bacalzo, Dan. June 3, 2001. New York City.

Bernardo, Edu. June 18, 2001. Washington, DC.

Burrows, Suzanne. May 25, 2001. Minneapolis.

Cachapero, Emilya. June 7, 2001. New York City.

Cawaling, Manuel. May 24, 1999. Seattle.

Chan, Joanna. Mar. 22, 2002. Ossining, NY.

Chang, Tisa. June 28, 2001. Telephone interview.

Chin, Daryl. June 7, 2001. New York City.

Chin, Frank. June 22, 2000. Los Angeles.

Cold Tofu. Sep. 30, 1999. Los Angeles.

Dang, Tim. July 21, 1999. Los Angeles.

Dun, Dennis. July 21, 1999. Los Angeles.

Eng, Alvin. May 1, 2000. New York City.

Feng, Theo. June 17, 2001. Washington, DC.

Gotanda, Philip Kan. July 12, 1999. San Francisco.

Grefalda, Reme. June 15, 2001. Washington, DC.

Hagedorn, Jessica. Sep. 19, 1999. New York City.

Hayashi, Eric. June 24, 2000. Los Angeles.

Hayashi, Mark. Mar. 4, 2000. San Francisco.

Hee, Suzanne. July 20, 1999. Los Angeles.

Hill, Amy. July 19, 1999. Los Angeles.

Houston, Velina Hasu. Feb. 22, 2005. Los Angeles.

Hwang, David Henry. Mar. 16, 2000. New York City.

Hwang, Jason Kao. July 5, 2001. Telephone interview.

Iizuka, Naomi. Apr. 18, 2000. Amherst, MA.

Ing, Alvin. Mar. 15, 2002. Telephone interview.

Kan, Lilah. June 12, 2001. New York City.

Katigba, Mia. Sep. 19, 1999. New York City.

Kim, Eun Mi. Mar. 15, 2000. New York City.

Kiyohara, Bea. May 21, 1999. Seattle.

Kwong, Dan. Sep. 27, 1999. Los Angeles.

Lee, Corky. June 10, 2001. New York City.

Lee, Nathan. Mar. 3, 2000. San Francisco.

Lee, William. June 29, 2001. Telephone interview.

Mako. July 22, 1999. Los Angeles.

Manalo, Allan and Joyce. Sep. 26, 1999. San Francisco.

Margarita, Sabrina. Nov. 14, 1999. Northampton, MA.

Miyamoto, Nobuko. Aug. 6, 2001. Los Angeles.

Mura, David. May 26, 2001. Minneapolis.

Nakahara, Ron. Mar. 15, 2000. New York City.

Narasaki, Ken. May 24, 1999. Seattle

Narita, Jude. Oct. 8, 1999. Los Angeles.

Nihei, Judi. July 4, 1999. San Francisco.

Nishikawa, Lane. Mar. 4, 2000. San Francisco.

Oh, Soon-Tek. Aug. 2, 2001. Los Angeles.

Oyama, David. June 8, 2001. New York City.
  Mar. 17, 2002. New York City.

David Oyama. Apr. 7, 2003. Email correspondence.

Park, Steve. July 27, 1999. Los Angeles.

Peña, Ralph B. June 6, 2001. New York City.

Premsirat, Michael. Mar. 3, 1999. San Francisco.

Rhee, Ki-Seung. May 24, 2001. Minneapolis

Rno, Sung. Sep. 17, 1999. New York City.

Shiomi, Rick. May 22, 1999. Seattle.
  May 24, 2001. Minneapolis.

Shimono, Sab. Jan. 5, 2002. Los Angeles.

Shiraishi, Iris. May 22, 2001. Minneapolis.

Slant Performance Group. Mar. 28, 1998. Los Angles.

Son, Diana. Sep. 29, 1999. Los Angeles.

Steinberg, Eric. Sep. 28, 1999. Los Angeles.

Tang, Roger. May 24, 1999. Seattle.

Tokuda, Marilyn. Sep. 30, 1999. Los Angeles.

Trang, Jora. Mar. 4, 2000. San Francisco.

Tuan, Alice. July 27, 1999. Los Angeles.

Uno, Roberta. June 27, 2000. Amherst, MA.

Uyehara, Denise. Oct. 7, 1999. Los Angeles.

Weir, Jennifer. May 25, 2001. Minneapolis.

Woo, Alex. Apr. 5, 2002. Telephone interview.

Wu, Pamela. July 13, 1999. San Francisco.

Yang, Welly. Sep. 17, 1999. New York City.

Yu, Ryun. Jan. 27, 2000. Boston.

Index